"Building long-term relationships with customers [illegible] Dr. Crandall gives us a list of fresh imaginative ways to build tho[illegible] today. This book offers real things every company can do r[illegible]out making a big investment—to get the greatest impact fr[illegible]magination."
— Martha Rogers, *The One to O[illegible]*

"A whole book of real-life, how-to examples that give you lots of inspiration to get started. The emphasis is on relationship building—where it should be. You can't miss by buying, reading, and implementing the ideas in this book."
— Dr. Tony Alessandra, *The Platinum Rule* and *Charisma*

"Rick helped me to see where my customers come from and to cultivate those resources. For someone leery of sales pitches, Rick shows many ways of developing business without compromising your values."
— Frederick Liebes, general contractor, Frederick Liebes Construction

"Rick Crandall's ideas *work*! This practical, humorous book is filled with innovative recommendations which will make your marketing effort more effective and definitely more fun. The book has broad appeal because its easy-to-implement suggestions can be tailored to fit many professions, personalities, and marketing temperaments."
— Roney Wiseman, CPA, Stempek Associates

"Rick's book reads like many of us think—a concept followed with a specific example. His ideas stimulate my own creative thinking, and his chapter-end reminders gently encourage putting new ideas into action."
— Debbie Watson, MFCC, psychotherapist

"This book is a delight! It overflows with interesting and useful ideas to improve the marketing of all types of services. Why didn't somebody think of this before?"
— Dr. Ron Goldsmith, Department of Marketing, Florida State University

"Rick Crandall's enthusiasm is both exciting and very contagious."
— Alice Stanford, design consultant, Design Focus

"Crandall has done a lot of digging to find this 'gold mine' of gems that can increase your sales power."
— Gerry Michaelson, *Winning the Marketing Wars*

"If Rick Crandall's book were just the great commanding list of practical and common-sense strategies suggested by its title, it would be enough to make your business more productive. His book, however, offers way more: By showing how marketing is about building relationships, Dr. Crandall not only takes out the daunting from marketing but makes it fun."
— Maria M. Benet, writing consultant

"Don't let this book out of your sight—it's jam-packed with hundreds of practical, ready-to-use ideas you can put to work right away. Your only problem will be deciding which idea to try first!"
—Christian P. Heide, editor, *Sales and Marketing Management Report*

"Creative, realistic, and very easy to understand. A must read. It will validate all your current marketing efforts, and then give you more effective marketing ideas for further success."
—Ernest M. Bergman, CFP

"An amazing collection of easy-to-apply ideas, any one of which would pay for the book tenfold."
—Maureen Broderick, Broderick and Associates

"In clear, easy-to-apply examples, Dr. Crandall's book surpasses anything I've seen on the subject of selling your services. And I've been at it for over 40 years."
—Alan Cundall, creative director emeritus, Hayes Orlie Cundall Inc.

"If you think you don't have the knack for marketing, this book will give you an about face. These ideas are great!"
—Myra Delzeit, massage therapist

"This book is about as close as I've come across to having a monopoly on great ideas. My advice: Buy it and read it before your competitors do. Your bank account will be glad you did."
—Benjamin DuBois, president, Customer Intelligence, Inc.

"This is a fantastic book—a real idea generator. If you can't find at least three ideas in every chapter that you should be doing, you're not paying attention."
—Christian Frederiksen, Frederiksen & Co., CPAs

"Extremely helpful . . . covers a lot of territory in a creative fashion."
—Peggy Huff, artist

"Well-written, informative, and practical advice on marketing your services."
—Craig Hughes, attorney

"A must-read for the small business entrepreneur . . . full of great ideas for small budgets. Get it and go out and market while having fun!"
—Michael J. Ladd, shipping consultant, UniShippers Association

"A smorgasbord of provocative marketing tips for our firm's practice development agenda."
—James P. Petray, Lautze & Lautze Accountancy Corp.

"This book will more than pay for itself, even if you just skim one chapter. A suggestion for readers: There simply are too many ideas to read at one time; go through it in small portions with a highlighter so you won't miss anything."
—Art Sobczak, editor and publisher, *Telephone Selling Report*

1001 WAYS TO MARKET YOUR SERVICES

Even If You Hate to Sell

RICK CRANDALL, PH.D.

CB

CONTEMPORARY BOOKS

Library of Congress Cataloging-in-Publication Data

Crandall, Rick.
    1001 ways to market your services : even if you hate to sell / Rick
Crandall.
        p.   cm.
    Includes index.
    ISBN 0-8092-3158-1
    1. Service industries—Marketing.   I. Title.
HD9980.5.C7   1998
658.8—dc21   97-41744
                                               CIP

Cover design by Scott Rattray
Interior design by Select Press
Illustrations by Monika Chovanec

Published by Contemporary Books
An imprint of NTC/Contemporary Publishing Group, Inc.
4255 West Touhy Avenue, Lincolnwood (Chicago), Illinois 60646-1975 U.S.A.
Printed in the United States of America
International Standard Book Number: 0-8092-3158-1

18   17   16   15   14   13   12   11   10   9   8   7   6   5   4   3   2   1

Contents

Introduction

T his is the only book that lets you pick from more than 1,001 real examples of successful marketing. The more you know about marketing and the more imaginative you are, the more you'll be able to adapt. Single ideas have produced millions of dollars for some companies. Why not see what they can produce for you?

If you're in a hurry, flip to any chapter, and you'll see ideas that you can use. I believe in practical value, not theory. For a further brief discussion on the themes of this book—and instructions on how to contact me—see the Afterword. (For a general "Bible" of marketing that covers the topic from A to Z, you may like my book *Marketing Your Services: For People Who Hate to Sell.*)

Marketing is defined as *anything* you do to get or keep a customer. For people who think they hate marketing, the good news is that customer service is the best marketing. And among the "anythings" in this book, I guarantee you'll find many ideas you'll like! (And I guarantee your results or your money back—see page 365.)

In order to sort out the 1,001+ ideas for your use, check or highlight those you like as you read. This is proven to help your memory and your action. Don't be overwhelmed or distracted by the large number of examples. This book should be a feast. Take what you need, and come back for more anytime. To help you take action, each chapter ends with some quick reminders, ideas, and nags—your Action Agenda.

Good hunting!

1

Who Are You? And Whom Should You Accept?

"People suffer from the same disease as products. They try to be all things to all people."
—Al Ries and Jack Trout,
Positioning: The Battle for Your Mind

You may be surprised to know that the most important thing you can do about your marketing is not choosing what methods you use but rather defining *who you are*. Before you can attract and serve others, you must make it clear to them—and yourself—what you offer them.

Even in a world of intense competition, who you are is more important to your clients and customers than *how you do what you do*. Who you are is often even more important than *what you do*, since it determines how you actually help people.

For services, people must "buy" you before they will consider buying what you offer. Credibility and trust are crucial. Your "bedside manner" can be more important than your technical skills. And people will judge your "manners" more quickly.

TECHNICAL WAYS OF DESCRIBING WHO YOU ARE

The marketing field has many technical terms that concern who you are and who you serve. These include "positioning," "niche markets or marketing," "targeting or target markets," "segmentation or market segments," and "USP" (unique sales proposition).

The best definition of positioning is how you are seen, *in the minds of prospects and customers*, compared with their alternatives. Delivering services is a relationship, however small in some cases. Clients/consumers must have relationships with you in their minds, or they will not buy your services. If you accept the importance of relationships, it's up to you to establish and maintain them with your market, and one-to-one with each customer.

> ### Positioning
> Positioning can involve who you are and what you do. But it can also be defined by how you do it, where you do it, or for whom. Remember that your biggest competition in the customer's mind is probably inertia: most people end up doing nothing!

THEY SELECT YOU AND YOU SELECT THEM

The first part of this chapter gives you examples of how service businesses have established positions in different ways, with different markets. But relationships are a two-way street. Not everyone will want to consider a relationship with you. And *you should not try to do business with everyone*. So, the second part of the chapter will show you examples of how to find, or select, the right customers.

+ + +

Clean Contractors . . .

To position yourself, you have to know your competition. One contractor asked his competitors' customers what they liked and disliked about competitors' jobs. He found that the contractors' images were often of dirty workers, old trucks parked in front of houses, and messes left behind. So, he issued uniforms to his workers, had them park in back or out of sight, and gave them vacuums to clean up after themselves. Business boomed.

A More Playful Image . . .

The law firm of Bartlit, Beck rented an office with a central space big enough for a basketball court. So, they put one in! When clients visit, they can't take their eyes off the basketball setup and eventually end up playing. This puts their relationship on a different basis, humanizes the firm, and can't be forgotten.

Positioning Against Big Competitors . . .

Price is a tough way to compete, but some services can do it. A Florida accountant goes right after his main competition with this headline in his mass mailing: "Why go to H&R Block when you can have a savvy tax accountant prepare your taxes for the same price?" He guarantees to meet the Block price if you make an appointment by February 15. I'd change the headline to "Why go to H&R Block when you can have a *real* tax accountant for the same price?" A little shorter, and emphasizing that H&R Block workers aren't accountants. His headline produced 791 new clients from a list of 100,000 over-$40,000 income earners. By focusing on higher-income earners, he was able to point out that they needed more advice. If you're competing with a bigger, more well-known player, you look stronger advertising straight at them.

Positioning with <u>and</u> Against the Big Guys . . .

An ad in the *Business Journal* said, essentially: Foot, Cone and Belding is the biggest and one of the best ad agencies in California. Now you can get the same creative ad, but without the big overhead. We are a group of ex-FCB creative people who have formed our own firm, etc.

This approach allows them to play on their credentials with the big firm's name. They appeal to the types of clients who want to save money but are willing to pay for big-time service.

Be Approachable

If you're part of a big company or a status profession, you may tend to intimidate people. Humanize yourself to put people at ease. Tell a lawyer joke if you're an attorney, for instance.

Positioning and Publicity Through Speed...

When you're outspoken, you make good copy. Robert Macdonald of LifeUSA insurance company has offended much of the industry by insulting their slow procedures, while building a $273 million business. And he gets lots of publicity! They pay agents within 24 hours. They issue customer policies within 48 hours. And they answer questions from agents within 48 minutes! When you pick a simple rule such as speed or customer service to build your company around, you can achieve great things and get attention.

Be an Advocate...

If your clients have an "enemy," you can position yourself well by attacking it. For instance, one accountant became a popular radio show guest on taxes because he aggressively went after the IRS, and he was an ex–IRS agent! A similarly toned yellow pages ad carries the headline "Sorry Uncle Sam." It then goes on to explain that the company protects clients from the demands—over demands—of the IRS. It also offers a free consultation. They report that the ad worked well. But what it misses is some sort of guarantee that if there is ever a dispute, or you're audited, they will go to bat for you free, take care of it, and so forth. That's the kind of attitude clients want!

Competitor Bashing...

Competitors make it almost too easy for Glendale Federal to get attention by bashing big, impersonal banks. And it works, because it's cute, and true! They've opened 6,000 new checking accounts a month from their all-media campaign. And they get lots of publicity for their attack ads such as: "I just got a letter from my bank. I knew it was from my bank because they spelled my name wrong!" On voice mail: "For a summary of the new ways we'll be jerking you around, press 1. . . ." Wells Fargo claimed harassment when GF

> **Offend Someone**
>
> If you're not offending someone, such as the IRS if you're an accountant, or competitors, you may not be taking a strong position.

employees passed out aspirin in its parking lot! More publicity for Glendale!

Extra Niche Services . . .

To help out, one accountant started to offer a bill-paying service for senior citizens. This takes a chore off some, and is necessary for others. More important, it positions him as unique and service oriented. It ties him together closely with clients so he gets lots more referrals from this group—two to three per month. It also makes it easier for him to do their taxes later.

Farming a Neighborhood . . .

Farming is a realty term that means "specializing in a specific neighborhood." You usually send a newsletter on home prices to local owners and others and generally are considered *the* expert in that area. Use this idea to become an expert in a niche. You might be the only professional in your area to "farm" certain trade group meetings. Some real estate agents cooperate with other providers to better serve their areas: for instance, getting a chimney sweep to offer a special to the neighborhood they farm. Or a window washer, a roofer, a painter . . . ?

> **Joint Marketing**
>
> Combine your efforts with others to take care of your similar clients. Jay Levinson calls it *fusion marketing*. It can "explode" your business!
>
>

Leading-Edge Technology . . .

Printers, and many other service providers, sometimes try to get the jump on competition by having capacities that others don't have. PrintSource was the first U.S. installation of a digital machine that allows custom printing. Being a test user can give you an edge—but it can also cost you a lot of time as the bugs are worked out of a new machine. Doctors have the same benefits/problems with new high tech.

Get Your Foot in the Door . . .

Norm Pilgrim sends repeated mailings out locally. They pick a low-cost service to advertise which gets people in the door. They show the low rate and ask, "Are you paying too much for _____ ?" They've grown from 34 clients to 1,250 in five years. Once people are in the door, they find other services to sell to customers. They do no other prospecting.

Become a Cause . . .

Bob Juniper is a good example of representing a cause to improve your visibility and marketing. His body shop was expected to get in bed with insurers that controlled payments. Instead, he chose to attack the whole system. Radio ads and billboards were his biggest media, but the message was the key. One ad asserted, "Quality collision-repair standards are being systematically destroyed by insurance direct repair programs." Bob says that insurance companies encourage consumers to go to certain shops where they have negotiated lower rates for lower-quality work! He's positioned himself as the consumer advocate by yelling that individuals can go to any shop they want, distributing educational literature, and so forth. Since the heavy marketing, annual revenues are up from $1.2 million to $6.1 million. Some people hate him, but other shops now pay for the right to use his proven ads in their markets!

Auto Body for Women . . .

Wahkins Paint & Collision decided to focus on women as clients. The owner, Terry Roarke, started by talking to every woman who came into the shop. This resulted in teal awnings, softer lighting, plants, and women's magazines in the waiting room. Bathrooms were toned up and decorated with art. Employees went to seminars on listening, and a new manager was appointed who was particularly patient and gracious.

Denying Your Heritage . . .

The Corporate Image Store says they are *not* a PR firm. But that's what they do, just in an unusual way. You pay

---

Being Easy to Buy For

If you are strongly identified with an industry or a hobby (positioning), it's easier for people to remember you. You should buy others presents related to their personal interests. The bonus is that they'll do the same for you.

only for actual results with the media. They use a two-page fax to explain their approach and list specific prices for results. Positioning yourself as "not like a lawyer", etc. highlights your differences.

Evangelical Marketing . . .

If you really believe in the value of what you're selling, like Ted Tencza, at Dialogic (which sells computer telephony), then you're out there helping everyone, promoting the entire industry, and faxing out free information to anyone who asks. That's why he gets mentioned in the most relevant trade magazine, which says, "We love him." They also put his articles on their website. Become an evangelist for your area and reap the rewards too. (See Guy Kawasaki's book—listed in the References section—for more on evangelical marketing.)

Toy Publicity . . .

Top gun Leslie Fastiff has the reputation of doing almost anything it takes to win a case for his clients but also of having the charm to get along with opposing teamster lawyers. Trucking firms have been major clients. A page-one business story featured him in front of a collection of model trucks representing every major firm he had represented. It's an eye-catcher in itself and impressive in the numbers represented.

If your niche-oriented practice is strongly associated with a particular industry, when people come into your office, they should see things that signal that industry to them.

Niche Research

Find out the trade publications of your customers in *Standard Rate and Data* at the library. Even easier, ask customers for old copies of magazines they get—many publications have coupons for free subscriptions.

Leading-Edge Positioning . . .

Sorrento Mesa Printing has lots of clients in technology and the sciences. They position themselves as the preferred consultant by reading high-tech publications and keeping up on cutting-edge issues. They say, "Our customers want more than a good price. They want some-one they can turn to for advice, a sustaining educational resource rather than a vendor."

Go with What Customers Know . . .

Bellcore wasn't as well known as their best-known software switch feature "ISCP." So, they developed a logo that featured the ISCP initials for all of their software. This raised the profile of their other services and products and opened sales doors for them.

Environmental Marketing . . .

Many printing companies such as Ink Works and Alonzo have specialized in soy-based inks and recycled paper for years before it became popular. This business practice gives them an environmental niche appeal that has helped them to be successful. Associating with a cause will tend to draw people to you, whether it's cosponsoring events or speaking out for something in which you believe.

Positioning Success . . .

CompuTrainers sells E-mail systems. Their competition varies from the much bigger Lotus to freebies on-line. Through careful positioning, CompuTrainers grew from zero to $1 million in one year. Their best customers are suggested by their positioning statement: Somebody who has already tried basic E-mail and wants more, but doesn't want to spend the money and time customizing Lotus Notes. If you don't want to sell on price at the bottom, and aren't big enough to sell at the top, this is a logical position for you.

Selling on High Price . . .

High price is one way of suggesting that you are the highest quality. It works for the Big 6s and McKenzies of the world. One such consulting firm considers it great advertising to publicize the fact that they won't take on reengineering or consulting clients for less than million-dollar jobs. This positioning can also work for smaller service providers. You can operate under a slogan of "We're the most expensive and darn well worth it." Some people like to buy the highest price, either for status, or because it reassures them about quality. If you charge more, you'll attract the types of clients who don't quibble about price, and you'll be able to afford to offer little extras that your competitors can't.

> ### "Productize"
> Develop units of your services that you can sell like a product. This makes your services more tangible so customers know exactly what they're getting.
>
> SERVICE PLAN A
> Yearly Consulting
> WE DO X then Y is GUARANTEED

Specialize, Specialize, Specialize . . .

In realty, you've heard of the value of location, location, location. Niche specialization works wonders too. Jim Richardson specializes in selling real estate to biotech companies. He realized that they were a huge, growing business segment in his area. Further research showed that they had different stages of development that required different amounts of space. By specializing, he knows individual company requirements and has cornered that niche.

Products Enhance Services . . .

Here's an extreme example of "productizing" your services. The Seattle office of a Danish computer consulting company, Computer Resources International AS, was almost defunct. They had some proprietary software coding that helped them achieve their consulting goals and also helped their clients develop their own software. The new president, George Schaffner, began to use the software as the entering wedge to compete with bigger companies with better reputations such as EDS and Andersen Consulting. The software was unique and proprietary. They were able to sell that, then customize it and consult on how to use it, rather than the other way around.

Necessity was the mother of invention. Since they didn't have a budget, they were forced to bootstrap. To create the product, they forced their consultants to do the programming necessary to turn the code into a product. They also used their own product to create the software, thus giving them a closer view of what users faced. Schaffner also changed the positioning of the one-million-dollar product to "insurance" rather than a programming tool, because it could keep projects from failing.

> SUSPECTS: People or companies you suspect should need your services because of the business they're in, or similar reasons.
>
> PROSPECTS: People or companies who recognize their needs for your services and have the money to pay for them.

DO *THEY* DESERVE TO WORK WITH YOU?

The last section made the point that who you are—positioning—is very important. You can't market and build relationships effectively unless prospects and customers understand what you do. And more important in today's world, many of them want to know *what you stand for* as well. In their eagerness to obtain business, too many companies don't ask that same question of their prospects and customers.

Many prospects are not qualified to do business with you. They don't recognize a need and have the budget, authority, time, or attention to hire you. Just as others judge you before they enter into a relationship with you, you should judge them. Don't waste your time with unqualified prospects. Even further, grade your customers by what they offer you. Then fire those who aren't worth a relationship!

Qualify Giveaways . . .

Business Matters always gave prospects a free 30-day period to evaluate their software. But some people who took the software weren't qualified prospects. Worse, because they had no real commitment, many didn't get around to evaluating the software. Now Business Matters requires a credit card or purchase order up front. It's still a 100 percent money-back guarantee, and they won't process the payment for a month. The sales conversion rate has jumped from 50 percent to 70 percent. Giving away seminars, newsletters, or other

samples of your service can be a good strategy. But make sure you have serious prospects. And get a commitment if possible.

Be Selective . . .

Printing Resources originally took any business that walked through the door or responded to their mass newsletter mailings. Then they realized that by being more discriminating about whom they mailed to, they saved money and got larger, better customers. They analyzed their database to find that 20 companies comprised 40 percent of their business. They used these 20 as profiles of idea prospects to go for and cut down the frequency of their mailings to small-volume customers.

Give Customers Exclusives . . .

One firm works with only one customer from a given industry. This way, they can partner fully without any conflicts of interest. Because they can have only one of each type of customer, they research and choose their prospects carefully. It makes for more careful selection, and prospects are flattered when they're told.

Help Them Assess Their Own Needs . . .

Capella Networking integrates computer systems and sells computer services and products: about $14 million a year worth. They recently started offering modeling services of people's computer networks. They found that this additional service was a high-end tool that helped presale communication and showed clients the benefits they get from the other products and services they bought.

When Not to Hire Us

Create a checklist of reasons people shouldn't hire you. It gets attention, and helps attract and qualify the right prospects.

A business consultant or accountant might offer an entrepreneurial self-assessment test as a low-cost product. It would pinpoint needs and build credibility about the provider's expertise with entrepreneurs.

Providing Consultants for Clients . . .

The Master Group sells computer training and software. But many of the company's clients and prospects weren't sophisticated enough to know when to buy its services. So, Master added an outside consultant who helps customers with paperwork, budgets, and the like. He shows prospects how to benefit from the cost savings Master can provide. With the new approach, Master's closing rate has gone from 50 percent to 90 percent. Hiring a consultant to help your clients is a way to build serious goodwill, as well as help them appreciate you more.

Reach Out to Buyers . . .

Robin Rhodes actively recruits the right types of buyers for houses he has listed. For instance, if he has a house listed on the water, buyers can come from the immediate area, from among boat owners, from people who are renting on the water, from country club members, and from members' referrals.

Rather than sitting back and waiting for people to find you, who can you go find?

Tests Help Prospects Qualify Themselves. . .

Many people like tests because they can learn something about themselves. The Practice Builder Association, which helps professionals build their businesses, has a one-page, seven-item quiz about your marketing to attract interest. It uses true/false statements like the following:

1. There have been negative changes in my client mix the last six months.
2. Competition is costing me clients.
3. I have no formal marketing plan.
4. Bigger companies on one side and software solutions on the other are costing me business.
5. My business growth rate is going nowhere.

Fire Weak Customers

If certain customers are more trouble than they're worth, get rid of them. It will leave you more resources to thrill your better customers.

6. I'm thinking of adding new staff.
7. I'm thinking of adding new locations.

If you answer "partially true" or "very true" to three or more questions they suggest that you need their help with a marketing plan immediately!

The questions you want to generate should help people qualify themselves. Base them on who needs your service, and help them start to sell themselves.

Better-Quality Prospects . . .

The Comprehensive Health Education Foundation was spending too much time with low-potential prospects. Revenues had declined 30 percent for three years. They created a scoring system for their prospect database. It uses 12 criteria, such as past spending, budget size, distance, and quality of rapport. Since reps started concentrating on the top 20 percent of prospects, the sales decline has reversed.

Could you score your prospects? What variables would you use?

Buying Leads . . .

Many services (such as Dun & Bradstreet) will sell you the names of companies by standard SIC codes (type of industry). You can also buy directories of companies. Other services specialize in selling actual leads. These would be "suspects" who fit fairly specific profiles. For instance, Computer Intelligence in California (619/450-1667) is considered "the best in the business" by Vanguard Technology. Vanguard specifies that they want a Fortune 1,000 company running a certain kind of network with at least 200 users, and they even get the name of the company's IS manager in most cases. Vanguard buys leads for about $2.60 per name and figures their hit rate is about 1 in 30. This makes the leads a bargain for the large-ticket systems that Vanguard sells.

> TARGET MARKETING: Aiming your marketing at a specific group so that you can present a stronger, more personalized case for your services.

Find Your Audience . . .

Most people don't even know what paintball is, let alone have tried it. (It's a game in which players shoot balls of paint at each other with air guns.) So, the best place to advertise paintball fields is in paintball stores. The next best way is to offer deep-discounted tickets in person where you can explain it to people as you sell them a packet of tickets. It works for Mare Island Paintball. If you offer more traditional entertainment such as theater or music, you'll find your audience at other entertainment venues, as well as at stores like Blockbuster and The Wherehouse. In general, marketers will find their prospects in about the same places their customers are. That's a big reason why word of mouth works.

Make Room for Bigger Customers . . .

Dayprint Printing decided to go after bigger, more profitable work. They didn't want to compete with the franchise copy shops. By clearing the board of some small work, they had more time to spend on the clients that generated 75 percent of their volume. They had been missing a lot of untapped dollars from them.

Data Mining . . .

Data mining is a term for pulling valuable information out of your database. National City Bank mails and telemarkets to segments of its two-million-household customer base selected on as many as 30 different criteria to personalize the offer. Recently the bank was selling 18 different products. Targeted mailings are more cost-effective, letting National City do even more marketing.

Selecting the Right Prospects . . .

Renting the right lists to solicit can make a *huge* difference in your results, whether by mail or phone. In one case, I found a 20-to-1 difference in the responses of professional speakers versus consultants, who otherwise looked similar. When you find a rental mailing list that pays off for you, eventually it will wear out. But Roy Schwedelson points out that by selecting only the zip codes of those who buy from you, you can use only the parts of the list that will do better for you. You can also delete certain zips that seldom buy. You can use more complicated ways to select names as well if you know who your customers are.

Roy also points out that some brokers will do selections free as a service to help you rent more names from them. Good idea. Can you help your prospects be more selective, which makes them more successful and eventually lets them buy more from you? Long-term relationship versus short-term profits!

· · · ACTION AGENDA · · ·

"A journey of 1,000 miles begins with the
first step."

—Chinese proverb

This chapter gets you rolling with 36 items. And there are multiple ideas to apply in some of them. But these ideas will work for you only if you work on them. The sooner you start after you have an idea, the more momentum you'll have. Go back to the items you've marked as relevant and choose one you can get started with today.

Here are a few general ideas that may help you focus on action.

First, who are you?

➜ Define your core competencies. What are you best at?

➜ How do you want customers and prospects to see you compared with their alternatives (your position)?

➜ What is the one thing you have that makes you better than your competition?

If you're not sure about the answers to any of these questions, call customers, or otherwise talk to your marketplace, and ask them. Then decide how you can communicate your strongest position to your customers and prospects.

Second, who are your ideal customers?

➜ What is the lifetime value of a customer to you?

➜ Who are the 20 percent of your customers who account for 80 percent of your profits?

➜ What percent of your best customers' business do you have in your area?

If you're not sure of these answers, analyze your records, talk with customers, and so forth. Develop a profile of your ideal customer. Now develop a list of specific new clients you'd like to have. Start gathering information on them and then begin to build a relationship with them.

Third, who *shouldn't* be your customer?

➜ Make a list of your worst customers and fire them. This will make room for more work from your best customers and new better ones.

➜ Encourage your sales staff to spend more time with fewer customers.

➜ Decide how you can qualify prospects and customers better. Try frankly telling them what you're looking for in a customer, as well as what you have to offer them.

Now schedule a specific time to work on any of the above for half an hour in the next day.

2

Integrated Marketing

> "If Putnam was to have a new look, we had
> to . . . project a consistency and rationale for
> what we were doing in all our markets."
> —Lawrence J. Lasser, CEO, Putnam Investments

There will always be new buzzwords in marketing. *Integrated marketing* is a new term for commonsense ideas: Make sure one hand knows what the other is doing, learn all about your customers, and design your marketing efforts to give consistent messages.

Most of the chapters in this book cover specific methods, or tactics, of marketing such as advertising, publicity, or sales. Integrated marketing focuses on coordinating your efforts. You may notice that many items could have been placed in different chapters. This is because most marketing involves more than one thing. Plus, one activity tends to lead to another. Getting publicity creates new networking contacts who become partners in marketing efforts. An advertisement produces sales calls, which generate referrals. Great customer service leads to publicity, and so forth. The harder you work on any part of your marketing, the "luckier" you'll be with others.

Integrated marketing can have an effect even bigger than the sum of all the single methods. Here's an easy way to think about your marketing: picture the ideal prospects you want to reach. Then coordinate your different marketing efforts to reach them in different ways but to appeal to them in a consistent way.

+++

Expensive Integrated Marketing . . .

Integrated marketing is one reason Putnam Investments manages $150 *billion* in assets. Putnam includes their office environment as part of their marketing. Not only does it project an image to customers, but it also projects an image to Putnam's own employees, who, in turn, reflect it to customers in their pride and enthusiasm. Design firm Carbone Smolan also showed Putnam how design and content must interrelate consistently. Their literature for mutual funds has to stand out from the clutter of competitors, relate across different services and products, and provide strong sales tools for their "dealers."

Look the Part

Pay attention to your image with clients and prospects. *You* are a big part of your marketing, so you need to look successful.

Simple Integrated Marketing . . .

A simple example of integrated marketing is Viva Knight, a script consultant. He advertises in a magazine all year long. It pulls adequately. He also rents the mailing list for the same magazine and sends out a flyer. This pulls even better because readers are familiar with him. In a full, integrated marketing effort, you would use even more methods. For instance, a detective could write articles for publicity in the same magazine in which she advertised and speak at a conference sponsored by the publication.

A Marketing/Speaking/Sales Plan . . .

It took James Carter more than a year to get his first client; then they started to come regularly. His business plan followed five steps:

1. Read the weekly business events calendars in the local papers.
2. Look up the sponsors and industries of the events at the local library.
3. Imagine a conversation with the director of each group.
4. Call each group and volunteer to speak for free. (He got 100 talks during this period.)
5. Follow up with personal visits and phone sales calls to the contacts made by speaking.

Selling Your Child . . .

Most architects don't like to market. But David Davis had a "product" he believed in—his high school–age son. They researched buyers (schools), pursued key contacts through phone and mail, played one offer against the other, and negotiated deals. They generated more than $85,000 in scholarships at the school they wanted. Their key contacts at each school were members of scholarship committees and music department heads (young Davis's field). They kept in touch weekly by E-mail.

Are you pursuing your key contacts as single-mindedly?

Generating Big Leads . . .

Both the MetLife and Geico insurance companies have committed to generating 10,000 leads a week for their agents through direct mail, advertising, tele-marketing, and the Internet. By focusing their campaigns on a big number of leads, they motivate their people to charge ahead with databases and proven marketing.

Your big number could be anything from 1 a week to 10,000—but having a goal helps.

A Low-Cost Integrated Marketing Plan

Choose from activities like these to integrate your marketing inexpensively:

- Speaking to groups
- Writing letters to industry publications
- On-line discussion groups
- Networking at groups
- Postcards to keep in touch
- Follow-up phone calls

Attention to Details Pays . . .

Ralph Francis has his own small intellectual property practice with two associates. He has a master's degree in engineering, which makes his engineering clients comfortable. He got his second-largest client from volunteer work he did in juvenile court. He's the only lawyer to attend local meetings of the national materials science society. He hires a proofreader for his briefs (not billed to clients) so they'll be perfect. He writes articles for publications that clients read. These little things add up to building a successful practice.

Annual Reports . . .

If you're a public company, you're big enough to afford serious marketing. But many companies ignore their annual reports as marketing tools. You don't have to be supercreative like the companies that do their reports in comic book form, but don't overlook the chance to express a clear personality for your shareholders and employees who can be your most loyal customers and referrers.

Promoting Your Services to Managed Care . . .

Qualifying their services as preferred providers with health maintenance organizations (HMOs) is crucial for the survival of many therapists. Some of these efforts will need a discipline-wide effort from social workers, psychologists, MFCCs, and others. The Virginia Psychology Association's effort used a four-prong approach. It included a market study of major employers and their attitudes toward outpatient therapy; personal visits by members to each business; a newsletter; and a media campaign. A Michigan group started with a series of seminars for both benefits developers and state legislators.

Combine Methods . . .

A common use of two methods is the phone and the mail. You can call to say you're sending material, which

will get the material more attention. But I think it's more efficient to mail and then call. That's what Mellon Bank did to introduce its new charge card. You save the costs of calling those who respond to the mailing. And the others are more receptive to your call.

Coordinated Attack . . .

The Green Route, an African destination management firm, got major attention for a mailing. They used it to invite people to their booth at a trade show. They also got major PR in *Meetings and Conventions* magazine. The mailings were artistic, used recycled paper, and featured animal themes. They also featured a "mysterious formula" revealed across several mailings as an effective gimmick.

Check Your Graphics

Big companies have "style guides" about how their logo and "look" can be used on trucks, websites, and so forth to ensure consistency in their images. What are your rules?

Keep Jabbing . . .

BayBanks used advertising to set the mood and then followed up with direct mail for a new computer banking service. They advertised with billboards, newspaper, radio, and TV. They demonstrated the product in stalls near automatic teller machines (ATMs) and in their branches. Then they wrapped up with mailings to their best prospects. Each piece stressed the same theme and personality. An integrated campaign like this can give you a cumulative effect.

Lay Out the Details . . .

Two consultants specialize in helping banks sell. One of their clients, Bank One, says that a benefit of their program is that it details everything for everyone. When you get back to the office after a training session, you know just what you have to do. Everyone in the bank, from tellers on up, has specific tasks.

Combining clear steps, support and vision from top management, and challenging goals leads to success for many clients. Are you giving clients all the details that can help them benefit from your work?

Create a Product . . .

To make your intangible services more tangible, "productize" them. Create simple, inexpensive products. Or give them away to make your intangible products more concrete. For instance, Lisa Smith, a writer and marketer, has produced a number of booklets such as *Better Business Writing for Better Business* and *Solve Testy Punctuation Problems*. She prices these from about $7 to $10. Every time she produces one she is able to do publicity, send them out to local media, sell them to clients, promote them in newsletters, and so forth. Her clients and fans can also give her testimonials about the booklets that she can use to sell her services. Huge consulting firms like McKenzie produce white papers and their own glossy magazines to document some of their cases. For the small carpet cleaner or plumber who doesn't like to write, it might be one page of 10 ways to protect your rugs, or handle your plumbing problems. Products like these also make good handouts for seminars.

Service Creates Products . . .

If you are a computer consultant, you often do custom programming for clients which can then be turned into a generic product. For instance, Client Server Factory made a deal for Gupta Corp. to sell the add-on product that they developed for Gupta software. It was very profitable for a few years and led to future deals with Gupta.

Creating Service Products

How can you "productize" your services? How about a lawyer who develops a database of contract clauses and sells them as a software product, or gives them away to clients? Or any consultant who writes a manual, newsletter, or book based on problems solved for clients?

Does this apply to nonprofessional services? How about Bill, the gardener who developed a source for free, bagged horse manure? He both gives it away and sells it, delivered, for what his customers pay at the local gardening store. Or the testing lab or commercial laundry that develops custom processes for new materials and then sells them nationally? Or beauticians or barbers who could turn the stories they tell clients to keep them entertained while working on them into an audiotape for them to listen to in their cars and give to friends as a present?

Focus on Profitable Work . . .

Costney Brothers Heating & Air Conditioning kept themselves and their 20 employees plenty busy, but they weren't making any money. Now they've more than doubled volume to almost $3 million. They advertise on buses, cable TV, and billboards. They use radio, direct mail, and newspapers—almost any media they find. (They now spend about 8 percent of revenues on marketing.) The brothers' success started when they began focusing on management and marketing, instead of doing direct work. After analyzing their business, they dropped unprofitable new home installations and began to specialize in repair and replacement work. Then they expanded their market area.

> **Award-Winning Marketing**
>
> Costney Brothers Heating & Air Conditioning has won awards for its marketing. But there's no magic, just testing every advertising media the company can find, good focus, tracking results, and a service orientation.

Visible Publicity . . .

McCormick & Schmicks opened a new seafood restaurant in Corte Madera, California, in a weak location. But it could be seen from the freeway, so they put a huge inflatable crab on the roof. This got attention, including from the authorities, who said they had to take it down. This got them a front-page picture in the local paper. Then they followed up in their ads by asking, "Where's Jake?" (the crab) and suggesting various reasons why he was gone.

Selling Prevention . . .

Here's a good example of targeted, integrated marketing for a worthy cause. The Breast Examination Center of Harlem used ads, brochures, and other media featuring actress Whoopi Goldberg promoting free checkups. They also got radio public service announcements, publicity, and hand distribution of flyers. Their mass distribution brought in more people than all past campaigns.

Charity Cookbook Marketing . . .

A group dental practice in Minnesota decided to raise money for a charity by selling a cookbook. They gathered recipes from their own staff, patients, food editors in the local newspapers, the charity the money was for, and government officials, including the president of the United States. It gave them great publicity as they solicited recipes, and they got on local television and in the newspaper. They sold the cookbook to pay for production and raise money for the charity.

A cookbook, or a book of short items, is a good project because anyone can contribute. It could be jokes, stories like *Chicken Soup for the Soul*, most memorable experiences, and so on. Just have a strong, local tie-in and a charity, and you're all set. Also a great project for a Lions Club, Rotary, or similar service group.

Turning Around an Image—and Reality . . .

A large health insurance company wasn't doing well penetrating a particular geographic market. They used focus groups to discover two problems prospects had with them: (1) they were seen as huge, remote, and unconcerned with the human factor, and (2) medical assistants who had to contact them about patient benefits hated dealing with their impersonal procedures. To attack these two issues, they streamlined their procedures for handling consumer inquiries. Then they did a mailing to every assistant in the region with pictures of the reps who would handle their questions. Medical staff got pens and file cards with the names of their reps and were encouraged to ask questions. Public advertising featured reps stating their commitment to providing great service. After years of stagnation, sales soared.

Big Integrated Marketing . . .

Lufthansa Cargo wanted to become number one in the U.S. air cargo market. They worked hard to build a database of prospects. They advertised with radio, TV, and print. Sweepstakes (plus

> ### Image versus Reality
> Integrated marketing will more powerfully let people know you're there. But if the reality of your service doesn't match your image, good marketing will make you fail faster,
>
> because people will try you faster, be disappointed, and pass the word.

premiums) and employee incentives motivated individual prospects and employees. The sales force followed up leads. Dollar increases from the campaign varied from 57 percent to 264 percent in different regions. They became number one in tons shipped.

Guerrilla Marketing . . .

Alta Technical Services works to get exposure almost free. When Joe Yesulaitis started, he bartered computer consulting services for space in someone else's office and the part-time use of the office secretary. This gave Alta a bigger image than they could otherwise afford to start building a client base. They used postcard mailings because they're cheap and effective. They avoided expensive brochures. They got exposure on-line. They grew.

Charity PR . . .

The Raun Hairdressers and Day Spa bartered services for public relations help. Then they gave away massages at high-profile charity functions and did on-site massages on local radio call-in shows during which they awarded gift certificates to callers. Radio led to television. They went from too poor and having to barter, to success and a big marketing budget.

IBM Audio Promotes Web Services . . .

IBM wanted to strengthen their position in Web services. Despite their well-known name, they weren't a name on the Web in late 1996. They recruited smaller partners to do much of the specific work. Then through advertising, PR, and direct mail, they offered a free audiotape: "Secrets of Building a World-Class Web Site." With the tape came a letter promoting the potential of the Web and encouraging an 800-number call for those ready to act.

Audiotapes are a very popular item for people who spend time in their cars today. They are inexpensive to produce, get attention, and are saved.

· · · *ACTION AGENDA* · · ·

"I can give you a six-word formula for success:
Think things through—then follow through."
—Eddie Rickenbacker

Of the 23 items in this chapter, decide what you can borrow from the ones you checked. Also consider the following:

→ Look at your business card, stationery, brochures, and other marketing material. Do they all have the same color scheme, typefaces, and "family" look?

→ If you market in different ways, is your message consistent? Compare your sales scripts, telemarketing scripts, ads, direct mail, newsletters, PR, Web page, literature, and so forth. Improve their consistency, plus see if one of them has more successful positioning statements or other elements that the others can use.

→ Write one paragraph, on half a page, listing at least three marketing tools that you would use that will work together to reinforce your message.

Schedule a half hour today or tomorrow to write your half-page plan and decide when you can get started on simple integrated marketing.

3

Personal Contacts Bring Business

> "All our relationships take on the spirit of team-ing, partnering, synergistic cooperation and interdependency."
>
> —Stephen Covey

*M*arketing is about building relationships. And the best way to build relationships is through personal contact.

Most people *want* to know the people they do business with. And they want to be treated as special people. That takes a personal touch. When you meet people, they expect you to tell them what you do. And it's also normal to briefly explore if you could help each other. When you don't do this, people may assume you are unfriendly, or don't want to work with them.

If people don't have an immediate need, but may offer future business, they expect you to demonstrate your interest and sincerity by staying in touch and remembering them when they have a need later. If working with you is a big commit-ment—of money, time, and so on—they will also want to get comfortable with you as a person, before they commit.

This all means that personal contact is very important in your marketing. You may or may not want to call it selling. Many service providers avoid anything to do with that "four-letter word," s-e-l-l. However, the differences among personal contacts, selling, and networking blur quickly when you soft sell. Later chapters cover networking and sales techniques. See what you can find in this one that will help you build relationships.

It all starts with your attitudes.

+++

Plant Seeds . . .

Selling is like farming, says Glenn Jagodzinske. Every day you plant seeds by making prospecting calls. You cultivate your crop by keeping in touch with clients on their birthdays, with a newsletter, by offering a seminar, and so forth. And you harvest every day by having sales appointments that grow from your planting. Farming isn't glamorous, but it's a relationship-building model for long-term success.

Sell the Relationship First . . .

You have to sell *yourself* in most service businesses before people want to do business with you. Find out what they care about in life. It could be their family, their kids' successes, their hobbies, or their pets. Financial planner Douglas Cartwright says, "Make the emotional connection, and the financial one will follow—guaranteed."

Long Sales Cycles . . .

Julie Allecta is a partner specializing in investment management law in San Francisco. She first decided to try to win a Seattle broker/dealer firm as a client in the fall of 1992. She dropped in when she was in town, corresponded, and so on. It took until June 1996 before she got the first business. And she expects it may be three more years before any big work comes her way. This is professional relationship building.

Relationships Take Time

It takes time before people will entrust million-dollar work to you. Instead of just hoping that big work falls into your lap, build a list of specific clients you want and start your research on each one. Then show that you're patient about building a relationship.

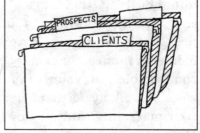

Great Sales Line . . .

An IBM salesman had moved the appointment along. All that was needed was a signature on the order. The president of the company said, "I just can't place an order like this with a perfect stranger." The salesman leaned forward and said, "First of all, I have to admit I'm not perfect. You'll find that out. And I'm not a stranger. I'm just a friend you haven't gotten to know very well yet. This order will help you find that out too."

The part about not being perfect is a cute line. The part about being a friend you don't know well yet appeals to customers who want to build relationships. If you essentially tell people that the first business you do together is not a big deal—it's just a way of getting to know each other—this can be reassuring. If you're in it for the long run, not the short profit, you'll take care of them over time.

Overcoming Your Cold-Calling Fears . . .

Cold calling scares all of us sometime. Ram Yellen deals with his fears by asking himself these questions:

- What's the worst thing that can happen if I make this call or proposal, or ask for a referral? (They can say no, no, a thousand times no!—or is that from a Victorian soap opera?)
- What's the best thing that could happen? (You could make a new, lifelong friend.)
- What would I do if I knew that this person needed my services tomorrow?
- Pin up a picture of someone successful in your business and ask yourself what he or she would do in this situation. [If it's a competitor, you can do it just to show them up!]
- Acknowledge the fear and do it anyway.

Fear of Rejection

A rejection can't be personal unless people really know you. By being persistent, you're showing a sincere interest in building a relationship for mutual benefit. If they reject you, it's their loss.

Give Yourself Permission to Fail . . .

Having permission to do terribly can release you from the fear of failure. Many smart people give themselves "practice" or a quota of rejections to meet. And in the process, they get a lot of good leads. Brian Jeffrey managed a pager sales force. He told them to go to an outlying area and cold call, but to expect to accomplish nothing. Of course, when they made the calls, they got results from an area they would have ignored. And the practice built their confidence for "real" calls.

Be a Part of Their Business . . .

Robert Haus of the Practice Builder Association says business consultants, accountants, and others who counsel businesses should think of themselves not as advisers, but rather as if they were part of the business they are helping. Your advice will be more frank and to the point. One client said, "It was a bit of a surprise. The words were really direct. I knew he cared, and I knew he was right."

Create Comfortable Relationships . . .

Psychological research says that giving people unconditional acceptance is the most powerful thing you can do to make them feel safe and comfortable with you. A salesperson reports that one customer said that their interactions were like sitting in a living room with a best friend. The rep now makes that feeling the goal in every customer interaction.

Commodities with Personality . . .

Barbara Sigman of Advanced Systems Group deals with a number of leasing companies for her customers. She says, "There is more similarity than difference between leasing companies, so much of it comes down to personality. Who's the most helpful; and who are you most comfortable working with?" In other words, service and relationships sell. If you're competing with other people very

---

Don't Be Average

"Anybody who is any good is different from anybody else."
—Supreme Court Justice
Felix Frankfurter

much like you, you'd better have a personality that prospects like!

Invited Sales Calls Are the Future . . .

One Penton Research study shows that 52.6 percent of sales calls are requested by decision makers. An Arthur Andersen study of one field estimates that 78 percent of purchases will be initiated by customers by the year 2000. These studies mean two things. First, when they ask you in, a nonpressure selling approach is even more appropriate. (See Chapter 4.) Second, you need to be visible to prospects so they'll think of you when they're ready to act. Maintain contact through newsletters and other low-key ways to keep in touch.

Follow Up Nonsales . . .

Persistence pays. Jeffrey Mandell had lost a contract for a corporate medical plan in both bids over eight years. But he kept in touch with the prospect, mainly on the tennis court. The third time, he won it.

Remember, you take rejection more personally than the people dishing it out. Be a masochist and succeed! (But don't go to whips on your bedroom wall!)

Build in Permission to Follow Up . . .

After consultant and author Jeff Berner has a good phone conversation with a prospect, he asks permission to call the prospect back later to follow through. This accomplishes two things. It puts the responsibility on his shoulders to keep the contact going, and it plants the seed in the other person's mind that they'll have ongoing communication. Since you usually don't do business until after multiple contacts, having an effective follow-through system is crucial.

Prospects Test You

Prospects often measure your sincerity by how persistent you are. If you're easily discouraged, you must not care much about them, they reason. Or if they make you invest more to get them, they think you'll invest more to keep them happy too.

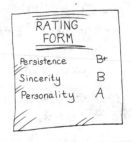

RATING FORM

Persistence   B+
Sincerity   B
Personality   A

Closing Is Expected . . .

Worried about being too pushy about closing a sale? David Zehren of First Chicago Bank points out that prospects expect you to try to do business with them. They can get annoyed if you *don't* try to finish the deal!

Guaranteed Publicity Performance . . .

Marsha Friedman, of Event Management Services, gets people publicity. In particular, she specializes in getting authors on talk radio and TV. One unusual sales feature is that she gets paid only for publicity you actually receive. Once you identify yourself as a prospect, she also keeps in touch. Every few months, she'll drop a note about a new program, or a chance to meet at a book event.

Many prospects will hesitate if they don't know you. By following up regularly, you build their comfort level.

> **Customers Come Second**
>
> The Rosenbluth Travel Agency puts employees first because they think that helps employees put customers first. The owner has even written a book called *The Customer Comes Second and Other Secrets of Exceptional Service.*

How You're Rated . . .

Your employees are your best salespeople. Do you treat them that way? Here's a sample of research results on items that improve the favorability rating of your company:
- I know someone who works or worked there. (+30 percent)
- I use (or used) their products/services. (+12 percent)
- I've often seen their names on buildings or vehicles. (+7 percent)
- I've heard or read news about them. (+5 percent)
- I've seen their advertising. (+2 percent)

Your employees are your best salespeople. Do you treat them that way? Promote yourself to employees first, with booklets and newsletters, and your vision.

Train Your Staff to Promote You . . .

Your clerical, delivery, and line staff can have high credibility when they recommend your services because they are not the direct providers. One accountant, for instance, trains his staff to say—when asked what they do—"I work for the best accounting firm in town." That's a strong testimonial, and believable as well. When your employees are treated well, they'll be proud to speak up for you.

Prospecting First Class . . .

Ray Leone, a consultant and speaker, would like to see more exclusive frequent-flyer clubs and first-class sections on airplanes. That's because he attributes $1.25 million in business to contacts he's made in those places over four years. He likes to work with top management who fly first-class. He interests them in leadership training and other services with questions that raise their discomfort level about their companies' lack of "more than management" training. One hundred percent ask him to send information, and about 20 percent end up buying.

Say "For You" . . .

Jim Meisenheimer, a sales pro, took a tip from a restaurant that asked servers to use the words "for you" when interacting with patrons. He has asked salespeople to practice working it in. Why bother? The servers reported tips up 20 percent. A "you" emphasis always works better than a "me" emphasis. I try to do it in this book . . . for you!

Selling for Your Associates . . .

If you're a rainmaker, you are great at generating business. But if you can't refer work to others within the practice, it will never grow. A rainmaker realized that he had to keep his associates busy, so after he found out prospects' key problems, he started selling the appropriate associate from the beginning. This

---

Building Associates Helps You

Developing work for associates in your firm helps keep your schedule more flexible so that you can go after even bigger clients.

way, instead of the prospects being disappointed because they couldn't work with him, they felt they were getting the right specialist on the case. Result: 19 percent increase in business by associates within the firm.

Wrestling for Sales . . .

Here's a dangerous example of "personal contact" to close a big deal with the military. The general was an enthusiast of wrestling. It turned out to be a passion of one of the salesmen too. The general offered to take him on. To the horror of everyone in the room, the two stripped down to their shorts and had it out. The match was called even, and the general signed the order then and there.

If you show passion for something, you run the risk of offending other people. At the same time, your prospect knows you're sincere.

A Card to Play With . . .

Touch-it Paper in Ogden, Utah (801/394-4300), makes cards on colored, heat-sensitive paper. When you touch them, they change color. People like to play with them, so they keep them, show them around, and remember them.

Business Card Plus Discounts . . .

Here is a novel business card. It's laminated, with the person's picture on it. On the back are 15 small advertisements for discounts from local merchants. Target Publishing (800/722-6951) has a patent on this particular card. They now put 18 ads on the back and say the cards are used by lots of insurance agents, body shops, doctors, and dentists. Because of the discounts, people tend to keep them in their wallets, where they are a reminder for you and for referrals.

Tips for Better Cards

- Choose a color that copies and faxes well. (Most blues, browns, and oranges are poor choices.)
- Choose an easy-to-read typeface.
- Give everyone in your company a card.

Waterproof Card . . .

Dusty Leer, of Sausalito Underwater Search, rents scuba divers out for projects. His card is printed on plastic. This is a novelty, which gets attention, and is also practical. Many times when he comes out of the water, people ask him for his card. He can keep these in his wet suit and surprise people by having them handy. The same card would be useful for window washers, boat captains, or ski instructors—anyone who works in wet environments. Other cards that would get attention and link themselves to your occupation include brass for a metal worker, one cut into a tooth shape for a dentist, a bowling pin for a bowling center, and so on.

Different Business Cards . . .

There are many ways to have an unusual business card. Advisors Marketing Group can get you one like a baseball card (619/721-3737). Polaroid can do holograms for you (800/237-5519), and Totally Chocolate (800/255-5506) or Sweet Impressions (800/323-8037) can do edible cards.

Keep Cards Everywhere

What can represent you personally more than your business card? There's no excuse for not having business cards with you at all times. Keep redundant supplies in your car, coat, and purse or wallet.

· · · ACTION AGENDA · · ·

"You miss 100 percent of the shots you never take."

—Wayne Gretzky, hockey great

This chapter gave you 24 examples of how to build personal contacts. Glance back and pick out one or more you marked to take action on.

Other actions to consider:

→ Create a list of people or companies you'd like to work with. Start a file on each and start building contacts by sending them a newsletter or other material.

➜ Schedule a leisure activity you've "been meaning to do" that will put you in contact with people you have things in common with.

➜ Decide on a card that will be memorable for people you give it to.

➜ Give your employees cards, and enlist them to be enthusiastic referral sources.

4

Santa Claus Selling

"A purchase is not a decision to have an 'affair,' but a decision to get married. This requires a new orientation and strategy for the would-be seller."
—Tom Peters

Your interests and your clients' interests should not be at odds. Yet, old-fashioned sales training makes you adversaries. That's why sales has a "hard-sell," pushy image. And that's why most service providers don't like to sell.

It turns out that aggressive sales techniques don't work well, especially for building long-term relationships. If you work *with* your prospects and clients to solve their problems, you can feel better about the sales process. When you've built rapport, prospects will want to work with you.

The term I've created for this philosophy is "Santa Claus Selling." I named it after Kris Kringle in the movie *Miracle on 34th Street*. One of the reasons they originally think he might be crazy is that he starts recommending that people go to other stores. The store manager tries to give Kris a list of toys to push that they're overstocked on, which he throws away. If you remember the scene, a mother whispers to him not to tell her "Johnny" that he can have a certain truck because she can't find it anywhere. Instead, Kris says he *can* have it. When the mother bawls him out, he says, "Ma'am, as Santa I keep a close eye on the toy market." Then, rather than push the Macy's equivalent, he pulls out his black book and tells her which other store carries it, and mentions that it's at a very good price too.

She's flabbergasted and goes to the manager. She says she never was much of a Macy's shopper, but if their new policy is to put the customer first, she'll be back and tell all her friends. Macy's receives hundreds of congratulatory letters on its new "policy." Later Macy's and Gimbel's compete to outdo each other in supporting customers, rather than in unloading what they have in inventory. Not a novel idea to put the customer first! But few really do it.

One way to demonstrate a true customer-first attitude to prospects is to always mention some things you *can't* help them with, and give them good referrals. If you behave like a true consultant—with only the customer's or prospect's interests at heart—why wouldn't they always come to you first? You've done their homework for them. This gives you much more credibility when you say what you *can* do for them. You become a resource—a partner—rather than a vendor.

A number of other people have put forward related concepts using terms such as "relationship marketing," "consultative selling," and "SPIN selling." These are referenced at the end of the book and illustrated by some of the cases in this chapter.

+ + +

Training in Listening . . .

Facilities Management, a $10 million contractor, worried that their sales force was selling more than customers needed. They created a training program based on Stephen Covey's rule to "Seek first to understand, then to be understood" to improve listening skills. They credit the training with getting a recent $3.5 million contract because their people asked better questions and were able to tailor the proposal to exactly what the client wanted.

How to Be a Better Listener

- Don't interrupt.
- Don't be thinking what you're going to say.
- Ask questions of clarification.
- Listen for unspoken implications.
- Repeat back to show, and clarify, that you understand.

"He who knows nothing else knows enough if he knows when to be silent!"

—Japanese proverb

Don't Sell—Help People Buy . . .

Lawyers Title Insurance instituted a new sales approach. They take their representatives through the sales process, looking at it as a *buying process*. The focus on helping people buy means you have to understand buyers' concerns and needs and communicate how you can help them. It also happens to be nonmanipulative, nonpressure, consultative selling. Sounds obvious. Why don't more people do it?

Consultative Selling . . .

Mack Hanan, originator of the term *Consultative Selling*™, defines it essentially as adding to your customer's bottom line with your services or products. As a computer consultant, Amadaeus Consulting Group takes that approach. Amadaeus helps its customers make more money by using computers to improve the output of their own customers (in this case sales of stocks and bonds).

Free Consulting Sells . . .

An insurance agent who works with construction companies approaches them as a free safety engineer. By going on-site and helping them adjust procedures, he can lower insurance costs, thus proving his value before he signs up the client. Who could you demonstrate your value to with free consulting?

Meet Customers' Goals . . .

Edwin Bobrow realized that by being a consultant to his customers he could be more useful. He took this now standard approach one step further. He developed

Creating Customers Is the Purpose of a Business
by Peter F. Drucker

There is only one valid definition of business purpose: to create a customer.

It is the customer who determines what a business is. It is the customer alone whose willingness to pay for a good or for a service converts economic resources into wealth, things into goods. What the business thinks it produces is not of first importance—especially not to the future of the business and to its success. . . . What the customer thinks he or she is buying, what he or she considers value, is decisive—it determines what a business is, what it produces, and whether it will prosper. And what the customer buys and considers value is never a product. It is always utility—that is, what a product or service does for him or her. And what is value for the customer is . . . anything but obvious.

Marketing is the distinguishing, unique function of the business. A business is set apart from all other human organizations by the fact that it *markets* a product or a service. . . . Any organization that fulfills itself through marketing a product or a service is a business. Any organization in which marketing is either absent or incidental is not a business and should never be managed as if it were one.

yearly goals and strategies *for* each customer. He kept his eye on customers' long-term goals, which helped them achieve what they wanted, thus making customers happy to work with him.

Teach Them to Do It Themselves . . .

Acting as a consultant means teaching clients how to do things themselves so they won't be trapped with you. Born Information Services helps clients install big computer packages. On one large job, they trained five of the client staff, for six months, in how to run the new system. They say, "There's a lot of teaching people how to fish."

> **The Secret to Success**
>
> "You can get anything you want, if you *first* help other people get what they want."
>
> —Zig Ziglar, speaker and author

Educate Your Customers . . .

When Insty-Prints began accepting customers' artwork on computer disk, they ran a series of six programs to educate customers on how to do it. The next month was their most successful sales month of the year. First Impressions Imaging offered a similar seminar and a plant tour. The event enhanced their image as a state-of-the-art service provider. Their monthly newsletter continues the image-building year-round.

Be a Resource . . .

If you really know your niche, you're a resource for people you meet. Like Maje Waldo who supports his art director clients by knowing their issues and taking a partnership approach. This creates repeat business because people want to work with him.

Bring in the Big Boys Yourself . . .

By putting your clients' interests first, you can often protect your own position as well. For instance, a small accountant auditing a firm that wanted to go public got a Big 6 partner early. That way, he could keep doing much of the work and help the client have "status" audited figures for later. (It also encouraged referrals from the big firm.) Any client going public will eventually be advised to go the Big 6 route. If you don't help them do it, you'll lose them.

Coaching Guarantees Improvement . . .

Personal coaching is a relatively new form of consulting with individuals on a more personal basis to help them advance their skills or careers. Marshall Goldsmith is one of the few personal coaches who offer a money-back guar-

> 360° FEEDBACK: Collecting input from everyone around you—bosses, subordinates, peers, suppliers, and customers.

antee. Especially when you're selling something that looks intangible or "soft," a guarantee can be very reassuring. Your problem is figuring out how to measure results. Because it is so subjective, his proof of results is to have clients give out brief questionnaires to colleagues and customers in a 360° feedback manner, scoring them from plus-three to minus-three, on whether the client is more effective, less effective, or unchanged for target behaviors that were coached. It's not unusual for 100 percent of the raters to see improvement.

Help Customers Buy More . . .

Contrad International, export services, had a buyer in Japan who couldn't buy in bulk because of high warehouse costs there. Contrad offered a warehouse service in lower-cost locales. The customer got a better price, even paying for warehouse space. Contrad got bigger orders and positioned itself as a partner with its buyer.

How can you help your customers use your services better? A gardener could buy plants and the like in bulk for groups of clients, a nonprofit could set up a buying club, a transportation company could aggregate shipments, and so on.

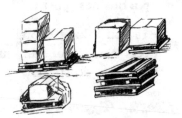

Help Customers Not Buy . . .

Sometimes clients call Micro Advisors because they hear about some new "wizzimagig" that sounds great. Micro uses this as a free consulting opportunity to determine what clients are trying to get done. When the new item doesn't look good, Micro says so and doesn't make the sale. This positions the company as the objective expert source, with clients' interests above its own.

SPIN Selling Details . . .

A consultant always had trouble understanding Implication questions in the SPIN™ Selling model. Then when a prospect who he *knew* should buy turned him down, it got clearer. Every reason why the client was wrong was an implication that the consultant hadn't asked about. He redid it right and got the business.

Questions Sell Better Than Presentations . . .

Inc. magazine would be a big client for any graphics firm selling format redesigns. George Gendron, editor, says that the first designer did a two-hour presentation of capabilities, complete with impressive slides. The second one spent two hours asking about what the magazine was trying to accomplish, its readership, and so forth. The designer's only comment about himself was, "What would you like to know about us?" Guess who got the job? Gendron said, in the second case "you feel like you're signing up a business partner."

> **Selling with Questions**
>
> *Spin Selling™* focuses on questions, not hard sell. The four kinds of questions (Situation, Problem, Implication, Need-Payoff) are complicated.
>
> - *Situation* questions should come early and clarify the facts about the situation.
> - *Problem* questions invite prospects to tell you their needs by probing for dissatisfactions.
> - *Implication* questions show prospects that their problem is bigger than they thought.
> - *Need-Payoff* questions help prospects tell you the benefits in solving their problems.

Are you asking enough questions to know what prospects need? Do your questions show your abilities by educating prospects?

Antiselling Closings . . .

Rich McQuinn gives the closing check back to clients and says he can't take their money until he's sure they know just what they're buying. When they give him back his key sales points, it cements the sale. And it also trains your clients to explain you to referrals!

Relationship Selling . . .

Andrew Lanyi has nearly a thousand clients with $150 million in assets. But he doesn't consider himself a great salesperson. He built his business based on a personal method of picking stocks. He sells a philosophy to people. He puts customers' interests ahead of his own sales in the short term, which makes for long-term referral business and repeat business. He tries to be nicer and friendlier to the customer "than anyone has since Mom." He even wrote his own book, *Confessions of a Stock Broker*, with many of his humorous lines that he uses to build rapport with customers.

Sell Solutions, Not Tools . . .

Cadence Design Systems started out by selling software. Then the company found it was more powerful to sell design services. What customers really wanted to do was accomplish a job, such as designing an expensive chip. When Cadence can tell prospects that it will add several hundred million dollars to their bottom line, guaranteed, clients are happy to share a few million dollars with Cadence. This is easier for Cadence than selling its $200,000 design tool (which is how it does the work).

Find Out What Prospects Need

"Seek first to understand, or diagnose, before you prescribe, is a correct principle manifest in many areas of life."

—Stephen Covey

PROBLEM ANALYSIS FORM

1. How important is it to the prospect?

2. Do they show these symptoms?

3. What do the employees on the front lines report?

Analyze Their Needs . . .

Lighthouse Technology illustrates the value of good questions in the sales process. The company tells prospects that if it understands their business better, it can offer a custom service. Different customers want to be safe versus daring. They also have different short- and long-term needs, budgets, and so on. If you don't ask, you won't know.

Diagnose Before Prescribing . . .

Like any good "doctor," a consultant needs to understand the client's true situation before selling services. CAD Solutions, a $55 million computer consulting firm, won one big defense contractor's business because of its thorough study of the prospects' engineering *process*, before it suggested solutions. CAD's goal was to understand what each department did and how they did it to better take user needs and preferences into account.

Unselling Your Own Sale . . .

When someone has agreed to do business with you, you're usually so relieved that you stop there. But some people don't mean yes the way you think, and other people change their minds. One professional tells clients, "Now that you've decided to work with me, what, if anything, could happen to change your mind?" Or be more aggressive and say, "Psychologists find that after a decision to buy is made, people often have second thoughts, called 'buyer's remorse.' Are you sure you are ready to work with me? Is there anything else you need to consider?" It sounds scary, but it's better to learn about problems immediately so you can handle them.

Sell at Multiple Levels . . .

If you're a consultant selling to one level of the organization, expand the people you talk to. Then multiple levels in the organization can support working with you. For instance, one computer consultant sells training for CAD (computer-aided design) not just as a drawing tool but also as a communications tool. Says Enninger-Mulch Associates, "That message rings true with the executives."

Selling an "Investment" . . .

Motek Information Systems is one computer specialist that uses the old sales idea that its services are not an expense but rather an investment. If you can demonstrate that your clients will get a 20 to 40 percent productivity boost, plus a return on their investment (ROI) in one or two years, then why shouldn't they buy your services? Many new software systems, properly installed, can achieve just that, as Motek does.

· · · *ACTION AGENDA* · · ·

"*Rule 1:* Practice only one new behavior
at a time.
Rule 2: Try the new behavior at least
three times.
Rule 3: Go for quantity before quality.
(Don't worry about how you do at first.)
Rule 4: Practice in safe situations."
—Neil Rackham, *SPIN Selling*

There are 22 examples of selling to benefit your customers in this chapter. Which could you practice now? How about:

→ Work on improving your listening skills.
→ Do a flowchart of the buying process for your prospects. If you're not sure, ask them.
→ Be able to express the value of your services in return on investment terms (ROI).
→ Learn the differences among Situation, Problem, Implication, and Need-Payoff questions.
→ Decide how you can showcase your expertise with free consulting for prospects.
→ Develop a list of strong people you can use as referrals for your clients.

5

Seminar Selling

"If you are an expert, you don't need to be a
Winston Churchill [caliber speaker]. The audience
wants your knowledge, so they forgive your presentation flaws."

—Lily Walters, *Secrets of Successful Speakers*

S eminars give you a way to provide a "sample" of your
expertise. Like selling, they are usually in-person.

Even more than in selling one-to-one, you can structure
the situation to your advantage as you present information, ask
questions, and gauge reactions. You can lecture, have multimedia aids, involve the audience, and control the environment.
Seminars are used effectively by service providers of all sizes.
Here are a few examples.

+++

Encourage Fast Seminar Registration . . .

Leahy Document & Information Management sent a
seminar invitation to 600 selected companies in its database. Seventy-five accepted. The seminar was free if they
faxed their registration, but four paid $75 at the door.
The seminar produced lots of prospects for a new document storage solution.

Follow Up Your Seminars . . .

The Hundley Group, a computer consulting firm, says that 75 percent of the sales generated by its seminars occur as much as six months *after* the seminar. The remaining 25 percent take even longer!

Free Prospecting Seminars . . .

Here's an ad for a joint seminar by a real estate agent and mortgage broker. They emphasize "free." The ad says they show you "how to shop for a home, qualify for a loan, close escrow, first time buyer programs, and more." Seminars are also good for free publicity listings.

Prospects Pay to Hear You . . .

I used to do a seminar for new home buyers, sponsored by a local college, for which people paid $25. If I'd been a real estate agent, I would have had 50 paying prospects a night! It was called "How to buy your first home in 90 days." You're welcome to use the title. People who attended also got a 50-page handout of forms and materials.

Seminars Reach the Affluent

"Seminar selling continues to be one of the best strategies to reach an affluent client base like the corporate and executive market."

—Paul Karasic, *Managers* magazine

New Home Seminars . . .

Another profession that has benefitted from seminars for people who plan to buy a home is accounting. (These services come in largely after the home is purchased.) One accountant cosponsors monthly seminars with a loan broker. He ends up with about 10 clients from this source in an average month.

Many Possible Seminars for Prospecting . . .

Here are a few seminars that got free publicity in just one issue of one paper:

- A home buyers seminar with speakers from Bank of America, a realtor, a home inspection service, and a title company.

- An estate planning seminar by a lawyer, cosponsored by the American Heart Association. This one cost $20.
- An on-line conference on legal issues with many lawyers presenting.

Offer In-Company Seminars . . .

A financial planning consultant got Cray Research to hire him to give a talk for employees on how to pay for a college education. The class was such a hit that many employees signed up to pay for financial planning specifically tailored to their situations. If you can't get a large company to pay you to come in and give a seminar as a benefit to its employees, it may be worth it for you to do a brief lunchtime seminar for free. This is a win-win-win. Employees get an informative talk, the company offers a benefit to employees, and you get new prospects.

In-Company Seminar Tour . . .

Ernst & Young, the big accounting firm, got Merck to host a traveling seminar on financial planning at its different locations around the country. Ernst & Young gets the business, Merck helps employees, and employees get a free seminar. Win-win-win again.

Select Good Communicators . . .

Microtraining Plus requires new salespeople and trainers to be able to speak to prospects. To screen for what they need, they require a one-hour presentation to their staff as part of hiring. They make it on a topic *other* than computers. They're looking for presentation skills, not technical knowledge. (They hear some informative talks and learn about people's interests.)

> ### Speaking Body Language
>
> "Good public speakers walk with their shoulders back, their heads high, and use a lot of hand and arm gestures. It's pretty hard to feel inadequate if you walk and act like you know what you're doing."
>
> —Ken Blanchard, author of *The One Minute Manager*

If marketing will be part of your employees' assignments, you need to demonstrate this to new hires from the beginning.

Sell Seminars with Questions . . .

Acordia Insurance sent out a nice invitation to a free employment liability seminar. They cooperated with an expert speaker from a consulting firm, giving them both a benefit. A novel feature is that they printed five important client concerns on their flyer, such as "Our interview questions may be well-intentioned, but are they legal?" Anyone who couldn't answer them might be worried enough to come to the free seminar.

Prospecting Seminars Can Include Customers . . .

Mike Van Horn runs support groups for small businesses. He markets with paid seminars "How to grow your business without driving yourself crazy." This gives people a sample of his expertise and style. He also encourages current group members to come so they can meet prospects and subtly help sell them.

Nonprofit Seminar Mailings . . .

Some seminars on topics such as successful money-management are franchised. They have a nice, preprinted brochure, then you imprint your name on them, and the name of a nonprofit sponsor such as a local recreation department or YMCA. Nonprofit postage is really low (about one-fourth of first class). By getting nonprofit sponsorship you can then afford to mail to many more people in your community—which exposes you as the expert, even if the seminar itself is not particularly profitable. A "franchise" flyer also has the benefit of having been tested in other places successfully before you use it.

Upscale Financial Seminars . . .

An estate and financial planning group uses a direct mail letter to invite people to seminars on how to beat the IRS so the government will not get the majority

Include Live Testimonials

Influence Technology says that having a satisfied customer *talk* at its seminars can be very valuable to reassure prospects. Computer Smith, Inc., says to make sure the customer can speak to the point. They suggest having the customer do a three- or four-minute overview of how he or she uses your services and then answer questions.

of your estate. They offer a free guide, "How to Take Control of Your Estate," and even an estate planning videotape. They use upscale paper and an upscale approach to appeal to people with estates well over the $600,000 range where estate taxes start kicking in.

A Professional Sell

Seminars are particularly good for professional services. They help build up your expertise and give prospects a low-risk sample of working with you.

Business Opportunity Seminar . . .

A free business opportunity seminar in the middle of nowhere at 8:30 Saturday morning attracted more than 100 people. (And some even paid $10.) The ad in the paper was headlined "FREE WORKSHOP, How to Start and Run a Home Business." They made big promises and offered a free report and tape. Many people there bought something. They sold by making the offer big and good only at the seminar.

Partnering in Your Seminars . . .

Here's a double seminar, offered by two ophthalmologists who provide laser eye surgery. They've saved money by teaming up to take one ad, offering both seminars, in different counties. The biggest word in their headline is "Free," which is a good start, but then they don't tell you very quickly and clearly what's free. An advantage they have is that by setting the sessions up in their offices, they can handle small turnouts and still get good results.

Supportive Marketing . . .

Restland Cemetery and Funeral Home used to advertise a lot on radio and television, which worked. They also had billboards. Then they set up a seminar to help grieving families, and invited related charities to come and gain exposure. They drew more than 1,000 people to the first one! There was no sales pressure at the seminar, just help. Response in building their image was tremendous. Since the success of their new, community-oriented programs, they've dropped their advertising agency and channeled most of their advertising dollars into public relations and community events.

Technical Seminars . . .

Attorneys in the construction industry have to combine the skills of an engineer with law in order to figure out how a project should have been built under ideal circumstances. That's why T. Douglas Folk was able to do a seminar on CAD risk management in combination with Jeffrey Gerrick of Professional Underwriters. They were sponsored by the Arizona Consulting Engineers Association, helping all three.

Fax Seminar Marketing . . .

NetLan, Inc., uses seminars to target prospects in the computer industry. They find that faxing invitations works well in getting attendance. For local distribution, broadcast fax is almost free. Here's a broadcast fax invitation from another company for two seminars on customer service. It has a fake-personalization. Someone has put the name of the recipient in a note which reads, "I think you really should get some of your people in this, Jeff." It also has endorsements as well as a lot of cosponsors such as chambers of commerce. Merrin Information Services sells to computer software companies. They include testimonials from satisfied customers in their seminar invitation. That's good. The thing they fall down on is not saying one word about their credentials or the person who is teaching the seminar.

Niche Market Seminars . . .

One accountant offers free monthly breakfast seminars for senior citizens at a local restaurant. He covers financial issues in 90 minutes and works the room to say hello to everyone. He uses seniors as greeters and to give testimonials. He also offers free follow-up appointments

---

Market Two Programs at Once

You can often promote two seminars for the cost of one, in the same fax, mailing, or ads. Try combining beginning and advanced seminars. Or one for owners and one for employees. It highlights more of your expertise, while closely targeting each group.

and calls those who don't make appointments. He gets about five new clients per 50-person seminar. Because he got deals on the breakfast and using a postcard mailing, plus free distribution at the restaurant and other sites, a seminar costs him only $250.

Better Greeting Service . . .

It's not uncommon for people to have trouble finding your meeting room. The Ana Hotel in San Francisco stations a person at the front door to direct people who look lost to a seminar that's going on there at the time. This is a little extra service that most hotels don't do.

Which Words Sell? . . .

One firm sells safety training seminars around the country for the industrial boiler industry. Research showed that when the words "teach" and "learn" were used, they were a turnoff. This audience responded better to "hands-on training." Little changes in headlines and sales scripts can make big differences. Ask your audience and experiment.

"Dead" Seminars . . .

No one wants to see ads for caskets. So, Johnson Creative developed educational seminars with ads featuring the funeral directors in office settings. The service-oriented approach built their image and business.

> **Better Speech Humor**
>
> Don't start off your talk with a joke. It looks contrived. Better, plan some "spontaneous" light-hearted comments you can make about yourself, the setting, or the topic.

Finding Speaking Opportunities . . .

One associate at a small law firm got a list of conferences coming into the local convention facility. He contacted them and was able to quickly get on a panel of an engineers group as a last-minute fill-in.

Fun Pay for Seminar Questions . . .

Ross Murphy likes seminars for selling. He also likes to have good questions, so he gives a group of silly awards at his seminars. I've seen presenters toss these to people on the spot when they asked a question or made a contribution. "Dr. Murphy's Happiness Pills" are a package of M&Ms. "A two-week gambling package" is a deck of cards. "A beauty treatment" is a bar of Ivory soap. The silliness also tends to loosen people up and make the seminar seem friendlier.

Get "Name" Guests . . .

Big-name guest speakers don't have to be famous. They can be from name companies. For instance, someone from FedEx can speak at a small business seminar on how to save money on shipping costs. A banker from a big bank can speak on financial controls for your business. Each guest speaker you invite can be a plus on the invitation.

High-Status, Low-Cost Locations . . .

If you're a consultant who helps people implement software, such as an accountant or a trainer, you can offer seminars around the country at the offices of your partners who produce the software—like Novell or Microsoft. SBT Software Company does. Doing so saves them money on seminar sites and gives them the name cachet of their larger partners.

Seminar Cosponsors

Guest speakers, your suppliers, and others can also enhance your credibility and turn out more people for your seminars. Look for respected people or companies with their own followings and mailing lists.

Partnering for Impact . . .

If you're a smaller business, joint venturing with a biggie can help your image and credibility, while you bring the larger firm leads, flexibility, speed, and so forth. Computer consultants Centron DPL used 40 seminars around the country to build its image. One reason the seminars worked is a partnership with IBM. IBM provided travel costs for speakers, expenses, and help with promotion. All told, Centron got about $300,000 worth of support. And the IBM name helped draw more people to the seminars and establish Centron as a big player to prospects.

Mission Impossible Invitation . . .

Here's a cute invitation to a free seminar about market-ing on-line. The cover says, "Who says marketing is Mission Impossible?" Inside are the locations and times plus the names of the sponsors, and a folded note under the words "Here is your mission." The note explains the benefits in more detail and gets reader involvement. (It also gives the sponsors more space to tell their story.)

Produce "Keeper" Handouts . . .

Whenever you give a talk, make sure that your handouts are "keepers." If you want to keep a handout literally in front of them, include interesting quotes done in fancy calligraphy on separate sheets of papers with your name at the top or bottom. Often people will post these in their offices if they find them inspirational or interesting. It works for Jean Nave, owner of Motivational Dynamics.

Regular Seminars . . .

One professional has a *regular* public seminar every month at the same time. This approach saves a lot of organizational work and provides a free service to clients. The information also goes on her answering machine message with the topic of the month. When prospects want to see her in action, they can drop in.

Seminar Charity Cosponsors . . .

You should seek out nonprofit cosponsors for seminars you use to attract prospects. But why would a group of 25 charities sponsor a free seminar with six expert speak-ers on financial and estate planning? Because people can give assets to charity for a tax deduction, still control-ling the asset while they live. This is a win-win-win mar-keting event (charities, presenters, prospects). The 25 agencies can notify their supporters. Plus, it qualifies for calendar and other free media coverage. Try it; you'll like it!

Seminar Generates $500,000 . . .

Flexible Personnel offered two sessions of a free all-day seminar attended by about 500 clients and prospects. They covered labor law, the ADA, and the like. Further contact came from questions later. The last seminar generated 45 new orders totaling $500,000, including one from a prospect the company had been after for three years.

Speaking as a Profit Center?

Speakers can be paid thousands of dollars. However, at colleges, fees are often limited to a few hundred dollars unless you draw big crowds. And even low-paid slots are very competitive.

Speaking for Others . . .

Speaking at junior colleges, YMCAs, park districts, etc., can get you a lot of visibility. Some private firms such as Learning Annex or Learning Exchange also plaster the town with course catalogs. For instance, some of the junior colleges mail to every household in their districts. Many people have gotten calls simply by being listed as a speaker, in addition to the leads that come from people who pay to hear you.

Seminars Take Time . . .

Hopkins and Sutter is a big law firm in Chicago. They developed several regular seminars to which they could invite different types of clients and prospects. They often had presenters from outside the firm, such as the state bank commissioner on banking issues. Prospects knew they were getting top information and contacts. In one case, bits of work started coming from a seminar within a year. In another, it took three years before the firm got to even bid on new work for a prospect. But they never would have had access to this top executive without the seminar.

Too Many Seminars a Headache? . . .

Bayer Aspirin owns Agfa which sells high-quality color systems for printers. Agfa set up a schedule of free seminars around the country, knowing that people are deluged with seminar offers. One of their headlines was "This is not your typical free seminar." Then they explained why this half-day seminar was particularly valuable for meeting professional needs. The seminars themselves included product demonstrations from vendors, who probably also paid a share of the costs.

· · · *ACTION AGENDA* · · ·

"The definition of insanity is doing the same thing over and over and expecting a new result."

—Albert Einstein

There were 35 items in this chapter. If you've never tried seminars, why not plan one? An easy way to get started is to involve a friend who has similar clients. At the least, you can hold a small seminar in one of your offices and introduce each other's services to your clients.

Here are some other new things you can try.

→ Call your local colleges, YMCAs, and park districts and ask for their schedule of noncredit courses.

→ Make a list of bigger companies that might want to cosponsor your seminars. Remember that they may also allow you to present to their employees as a sample.

→ Develop a handout with 10 tips in your area. You can use it for talks or publicity.

→ Make a list of organizations where you could practice speaking, such as Toastmasters, Rotary, and other business groups. Decide how to contact them.

→ Ask your clients what topics they'd like to know more about.

→ Go to a few seminars and make notes about things you like and dislike.

→ Find some inexpensive giveaways as prizes for those who attend.

6

Trade Shows and Event Marketing

"It costs 62 percent less to close a lead generated
from a show than one originated in the field."
—Center for Exhibit Industry Research

Trade shows are a way to see lots of prospects at once.
They are more common for products but can be valuable
sales tools for services as well. Unfortunately, most companies
that use trade shows waste about half their time and money!

The first key to trade show success is to promote to your
audience *ahead of time*. Give people a reason to look for you.
The second rule for success is to train your booth staff well.
They are not there to collect cards or greet people. They are
there to build relationships. You're not there to give away pens.
You're there to develop specific leads, as well as show the flag,
do research, service customers, and so on.

Event marketing means creating or sponsoring events that
will be of interest for themselves. Then through your identification with the event, you derive publicity, goodwill, and leads. In
recent years, more and more events are created and sponsored
by businesses. Whether sports or charity fund-raisers, there's
something for everyone.

+++

Trade Show Comarketing . . .

The Comdex computer show is big, even in the spring. But they still co-located with the Consumer Electronics Association show in Atlanta. Some shows share marketing costs. But the big benefit is more people willing to come to two shows, and the extra booth traffic which makes exhibitors happier to buy booths.

Selling to Other Exhibitors . . .

One moving and storage company exhibited at a trade show on corporate relocation. They gave out free moving boxes after the show was over in return for business cards. They got lots of goodwill and some leads that turned into business.

Big-Time Conferences . . .

The independent power industry is one of many that have a "can't-miss" conference every year. It is sponsored by a major publication and is so important that their competitors even attend and give them plugs. The real business gets done in the hallways and bars of New Orleans. An international law firm sponsors a party after the riverboat cruise.

If the "right" conference looks expensive, but you want to work nationally, you need to go.

Sponsor a Conference

If you really want to be identified with a particular field, consider sponsoring a local conference. You might even make a profit while building your image.

Better Booth Giveaways . . .

If you've been to many trade shows, you've seen free pens or candy to attract people to booths. Try something more distinctive. At home shows, many people collect refrigerator magnets. The most unusual general giveaway I've seen is fingernail clippers. Murphy's Law says you'll get hangnails on trips when you don't take clippers. The Prudential insurance company has been giving away novel potato chip bag closures at local chamber of commerce shows. It's like a *very* wide clothespin. Brewer and Lord Insurance says that a hardwood walking stick that doubled as a yardstick was the "rage of the show" where they gave them out. Advertising specialties are in your yellow pages.

Your Own Customer Expo . . .

The Just Cruising travel agency sponsors an annual trade show. It features only cruise ship providers. They put a 16-page newspaper supplement in their local paper featuring the show and the major lines. They get advertising dollars from most of the lines. They attributed $1.3 million in bookings to the show and now plan two a year.

Publicity Stunts . . .

Bank of Marin hired a student to walk around the aisles in a cardboard ATM at a local chamber of commerce show. It attracted lots of attention to their booth. And it added to the festive nature of the event. Anytime you're willing to make a fool of yourself, the media will almost always bite. In this case, the bank got to hire someone to do it, and still made the local paper in color.

To Succeed at Shows

Shows take an outgoing personality. You and your staff need to actively greet people walking by to engage them. Good signs saying what you do, comfortable shoes, and a giveaway of 10 tips with your name on it also help.

Business Opportunity Prospecting . . .

Franchise and new business expos often sell odd franchises to people who don't know any better. Smart buyers get professional advice early. So, one accountant/consultant took a booth at a two-day show and got 10 clients and lots of leads. More important, he found two franchisers who were willing to send his brochures out with their material—quite an endorsement.

High-Status Flea Markets? . . .

Most lawyers want to maintain an upscale image. But for family and small business prospects, your status image is associated with high prices and puts people off. I know of two lawyers who took booths at local flea markets! The one I've talked to set up a booth with a cute sign, "Ask the Lawyer, $5." He made a few dollars and had a pleasant day in the sun. But he also got several long-term clients.

For instance, one was too cheap to pay the $5 but hung around and chatted. (The prospect was an older man, not a kid killing time.) They had lunch later. Eventually, this contact alone led to handling a couple of small matters, then a larger probate. Meanwhile, it also led to a contact with the man's son and more fees, plus referrals and invitations to speak. And so on, and so on!

If flea markets are too low-class for you, try county fairs, craft fairs, community events, and the like. This can work for any service. For instance, a young chiropractor distributes information at fairs and has a chair to give brief back checkups. He reports that he gets about one person an hour who will pay $29.95 on the spot for an office appointment worth "hundreds." And more than 90 percent make repeat appointments once they've sampled the service! Flea markets aren't as good as other fairs for him.

Neighborhood Street Fairs . . .

Some urban neighborhoods or towns have yearly street fairs where you can take a booth. One accountant got two or three new clients from his booth, which didn't impress him. The next time, he decided to do it right. He blew up big testimonial letters from clients, had a huge drawing box for accounting service prizes, and offered a 20 percent discount for anyone making an appointment on the spot. He also hired students to walk around the fair handing out his drawing entry forms and flyers. He followed up all the entries with a letter afterwards and a consolation prize of a discount on services. Total result: 100+ new tax clients!

Look for Novel Sales Leads . . .

One company that exhibits a lot looks for unusual prospects. For instance, women at the huge Comdex computer show are in the minority. They're often better prospects than men, but they get ignored more. Same for men at a nursing trade show.

Local Festivals . . .

Corte Madera, California, has a town festival every year, on the grass in the sunshine. It offers entertainment, food, and craft booths. Local businesses also take booths, many running games and donating the proceeds. At a recent one, Dean Witter stock brokers, Frank Howard Allen Realty, and American Savings were among those representing services. Lots of leads can develop if you handle these right.

Marketing by Train . . .

If politicians can do it, why not companies? The AutoDesk distributor in Italy created an exciting "whistle-stop" event. They rented a private train and went north to south through the country. They invited customers and prospects to join them at various stops. And some rode along with them, enjoying the best in food and wine. Technical demos were available. The event was a big success in getting attention and building relationships with clients. In this country, many private train cars, most historically interesting, are available for rent. They can be attached to regular trains for your own private party car.

Novel Event Sponsorships . . .

When the Iterod dogsled race was fairly unknown, one sponsor got front-page coverage in *Time* magazine because they sponsored a woman in the race who did well. Get on board an event early, and you'll have a chance to become a major sponsor with top visibility at a moderate price.

> **Publicity from Events**
>
> "You can get more free publicity from a great event than by winning the Nobel prize! (After all, the media have more fun.)"
>
> —An anonymous editor

Olympic-Quality Marketing . . .

NationsBank generated $9 million in new loans from their sponsorship of the Olympics. They used a number of promotions to highlight their sponsorship, including free tickets for buying tickets with their sponsored charge cards, and a joint sweepstakes with other sponsors. They got further mileage out of their sponsorship by also rewarding their employees for Olympic-quality service for three years leading up to the event.

Selling to Other Event Sponsors . . .

Sensormatic is well known for antishoplifting tags in retailing. They decided to become the first Olympic security firm sponsor, in order to showcase their other services and network with big corporate sponsors. They estimate that they received 134 million mentions before, during, and after the games. More important, within a few months after the Atlanta games, they'd tracked $30 million in business, largely from other cosponsors. They expect that to increase to $100 million over three years.

Open House Sales . . .

Good Copy Printing Center produced a number of ideas for their winning open house when they moved. They made it a theme for which staff wore recognizable outfits. They added balloons and rotating banners outside before the event for several days and after. (This will give you extra attention in general.) After the open house, business went up 20 percent in the new location where they were less known.

Give people T-shirts or some other appropriate item that reminds them of your event. Get them involved with games, trivia, contests, drawings. Make the event so interesting that they can't stay away.

Promoting Events . . .

Leonard Weingarten offers these tips he's used to promote many charity and other events:

- Find a printer to be one cosponsor. This gets all your printing done free.
- Remember to go for mentions in the company newsletters of your

Event Publicity Sources

When going for event publicity, try everywhere in the same media. Try specific columnists. You might make the society, business, news, or sports pages with the right tie-in. And don't give up. The media might respond to your fifth idea better than your first.

sponsors. This reaches their employees who are a big audience. Plus, being informed makes employees feel like part of the event. When others ask them about the event, they should have an answer.

- Be persistent. When marketing an after-exhibit a year following the L.A. Olympics, Leonard thought the tie-in to the stadium looked possible. Baseball had been a demonstration sport at L.A. and the Dodgers were in the play-offs. Why not go for an announcement on the stadium "Diamond Vision" board? The corporate PR guy said no way, so Leonard went directly to the man in charge of the board. He said fine, and they got three big announcements.

Celebrate Any Anniversary . . .

Carpenter Reserve Printing in Cleveland used Cleveland's 200th anniversary to create a series of posters highlighting their prominent local clients. It gave their clients a plug. It showed that Carpenter had high-visibility clients. And it allowed them to demonstrate some of their graphic capabilities. Several of the clients they featured purchased thousands of the flyers for their own use or even paid to have them inserted in different publications.

> **Charities Motivate Employees Too**
>
> Westamerica Bank gets lots of volunteer work from its employees to make its charity event work. And collecting auction items for the event gives staff a reason besides business to call on customers and prospects.

Local Team Sponsorships . . .

Who better to sponsor children's teams than people who serve kids such as pediatric doctors and dentists? Darrell Quirici is one of many who sponsor Little League teams. For a few hundred dollars, all the parents know your name, plus you're seen as public spirited.

Major Charity Golf . . .

EvaluMed sells services to doctors and insurance companies. They created a Monday golf tournament at a local country club. (Monday was less costly, but everyone who was invited came.) Donations were requested for a diabetes charity. They carefully matched foursomes to balance skills and to put one of their people with key prospects. Then they all had dinner together. The daylong event really built relationships, and the phone rang off the hook with new leads.

Local versus National Events

Being the lead sponsor at a local event can be worth as much in business to you as being an Olympics-type event sponsor where you can be lost because of the size of the event.

Bring Your Own Snow . . .

Every winter, Marine World Africa U.S.A. brings in a mountain of snow. It's a great attraction for families who can't drive to get to real snow, and it uses some of the dead space in the parking lot during the slow season. If you're an entertainment destination, bringing in occasional, new attractions can only help to bring back that repeat business.

Controversial Event . . .

Having silly events seems to fit many bar atmospheres. And the best ones seem to create some controversy, like midget tossing. In New Zealand, a bar in a bowling alley had bowling with frozen chickens. The local SPCA was not amused, but it couldn't hurt the chickens! A nice touch would have been to donate the chickens to a food bank.

Sailing Event Marketing . . .

CitiBank sponsored a sailing "regatta." They got lots of publicity as the name sponsor. They got to invite clients and prospects to big event parties and to a cruise on the sponsor boat. And they gathered $9 million in new deposits immediately.

Help Your Cosponsors . . .

Hinckley and Schmitt cosponsors a lot of events with government agencies. At the first meeting, they ask sponsors what they want to achieve. Usually, it's increased attendance at their events, or increased visibility with donors. Hinckley then uses some of their resources to make sure that their partners' goals are met.

Tie Promotions to Holidays . . .

There are calendars full of events you can tie your message to. Major holidays are Christmas, Thanksgiving, and New Year's, but you can also take advantage of lots of minor days. For accountants, an example is using May as Artimus Woodword Month, because Artimus was the first director of the Internal Revenue Service (only a tax accountant would care)! It's a good promotion right after April 15 tax season. For instance, one accountant sent out balloons with the words "Artimus, go away" on them. He also offered a free consultation and a free tax planner. This produced 16 new business clients the first year, and 23 the second year.

> ### Ask for the Best
>
> Ask for the involvement of the biggest names you can imagine in your charity events. Some of them just might say yes!

Hospital Event Marketing . . .

The Lakeside Hospital Fund-Raising Foundation has had major events featuring U.S. vice presidents, surgeon generals, past presidents, presidents' wives, and so on. The hospital is the smallest in town with only 72 beds. They work hard to get the big names who make the events financial successes.

Publicity Stunt Supports Town . . .

UFOs lead to UFDs (unidentified flying dollars)! New Mexico is a poor state. And the city of Roswell is poorer. But there are reports of a 1947 alien crash there (plugged in the movie *Independence Day*). To take advantage of the interest, the town has a summer festival that brings almost 100,000 tourists. Visitors can spend their money at three UFO museums and at most of the stores in town. Roswell promoters figure it's worth $5 million a year in a town of 50,000. Insiders claim it's a big hoax. But people want entertainment.

Restaurant Fashion . . .

Many restaurants use fashion shows to fill seats. At one working class bar, it's a lingerie lunch show. There are companies that specialize in putting these together for you.

At upscale "joints," it's fashion from Paris. Hold your event as a fund-raiser with the Junior League (whose members model at such events) or any charity for extra impact.

Restaurant Gimmick . . .

One restaurant had a huge scale. They charged children by what they weighed. And the kids loved it. You also might be able to use this gimmick as a novel trade show attraction.

Running for Charity—and Publicity . . .

A CPA in Seattle loves running, so he sponsors a yearly marathon for charity. It has become a big event in town with lots of media splash. Anyone could sponsor a 10K, a bicycle race, a soapbox derby, and so on.

Theme Marketing . . .

Ed Debevic's restaurant, in Chicago, opened an Elvis Presley theme dining room on the anniversary of the King's birthday. As a grand kickoff, they hired 61 Elvis impersonators, because it would have been Elvis's 61st birthday. Once they got going, they wouldn't stop. They competed for hours doing impromptu performances throughout the restaurant and outside. Business doubled during the promotion, so it looks as if it's going to be a yearly event.

> **For Better Media Interviews**
>
> - Prepare your own questions and answers. Often interviewers won't be prepared, so give them some sample questions.
> - Work in plugs for your event or services by using phrases like "We solved an interesting problem for one of my clients in that area . . ."
> - Relax and enjoy yourself. If you can communicate your enthusiasm and pleasure in your topic, both the interviewer and your audience will respond.

Upscale Dinner Invitations . . .

Group 121 Interactive got a huge, 52 percent response to an expensive mailing attracting top high-tech execs to a dinner and presentation about their Web services. They overnighted gold-wrapped invitations and commemorative plates to 80 CEOs and top management. By arranging for John Sculley (ex-Apple CEO) and Ed McCracken (Silicon Graphic CEO) as speakers, and making it an exclusive event, they got the big attendance to build relationships at the top. Expensive, but worth it!

Mission Marketing . . .

The term *mission marketing* has been used to mean supporting a cause closely linked to your core organizational philosophy. The "Strokes Against Strokes" campaign by the PGA with stroke victims has a nice ring. You may be most likely to find a cause that really fits your organization by looking at the personal experiences of your employees rather than at your mission statement.

Sponsorships Create Identity—and Identification . . .

When consumers perceive that everybody is the same—like banks—then they'll buy products or services such as checks or credit cards on the basis of shared identity, also called *affinity marketing*. First USA is building its image and credit card business through sports sponsorships. The bank is already the official card of USA Soccer, the Men's and Women's National teams, and Youth Soccer. They are constantly on the lookout for new sports tie-ins.

> **Affinity Marketing**
>
> You don't have to issue your own branded charge card to use affinity marketing. Getting another service provider who is a referral source to send out a special letter about you to his or her clients can be even more powerful.
>
> Dear _____
> your friend,
> _____,
> Suggested
> I contact
> you...

Open-House Demonstrations . . .

An open house can be a good way to build relationships with customers and prospects. Unique Printers used a Halloween theme at one open house and demonstrated new equipment at the same time. Rather than just sending invitations, they worked the phones to get more people to attend. They demonstrated the speed of a new press by having a caricature artist draw clients' faces, then produced a caricature mask on the new press for each person. They created a second mask by taking digital photos of people and outputting them on the same press. They also had speakers giving brief presentations about the press's unique capacities.

Partnering with Your Clients . . .

Barbara Stennes, a consultant and trainer for larger companies, decided to do a major seminar. She invited Dr. Edward DeBono to give a major lecture on creativity in her hometown, but his fees were far more than she could guarantee. She called on one of her major clients and asked if they would support bringing him into town. They agreed to partner with her by committing to sending 200 people for training, which paid half DeBono's fee. Once she had this commitment, she was able to get another large company to send employees. Her clients got world-class training, and both she and they got major publicity as well.

Special Memorial Event . . .

Restland Funeral Home finds that the holiday season is particularly difficult for people who have lost a loved one. In response, they've created their own festival of lights as an annual holiday program. They group 10 or 15 Christmas trees with lights and provide special ornaments to each family with the name of the deceased family member. They have a choir and a ceremony in which the families hang the ornaments on a tree in remembrance. It builds great relationships with the community.

> ### Basketball Lessons
>
> If you wonder if your event will get any attention, think of the case of an expansion sports franchise, such as the Orlando Magic basketball team. They were guaranteed to lose for a while. So, what the successful ones do is make the event entertaining, independent of the team. You can too. Make sure everyone who comes gets door prizes and extra surprises they'll talk about.

Restaurant Speakers . . .

The White Dog Cafe in Philadelphia attracts business with speakers. They get big names too, like Anita Roddick, CEO of The Body Shop. White Dog's owner got even more publicity by winning an award for building a sense of community through the talks.

Demonstration Events . . .

ComputerSmith consultants present a variety of computer tips and technologies at regular events several times a month. These are more cost-effective than single customer demos and also allow customers to see technologies they might not have been exposed to. The events attract an average of 100 prospects each time and produce about 35 percent of the company's leads.

Partnering for Charity . . .

A hospital in Fresno wanted to create business in a new area in which they weren't known. They partnered with a local TV station, the American Cancer Society, and the city for a campaign against breast cancer. They created an educational packet, raised money for the Cancer Society, got the TV station lots of news, and got the city good PR. Without partnering, they couldn't have afforded the daily TV coverage and other exposure.

Help Events Happen . . .

For the Fourth of July, the city of Sausalito decided to stage its fireworks display from a barge in the bay right off the Margaritaville Restaurant. It was worth thousands in business.

You can help your business by working on the "festival" committees in your town to encourage events that bring people to celebrate at your restaurant or other facility.

Advertising on Boats . . .

John Sweeney created a class of sailboats (11 meter) that have sponsors' ads on their sails. The sailor has costs covered, the advertiser gets novel exposure, and the coordinator gets paid for finding the sponsors. They also get Sports Channel coverage, publicity, and so on. Now they're playing with huge barges that carry floating billboards around. The city fathers hate them!

Beach Party . . .

The Paragon Bar has a once-a-year beach party for the Labor Day weekend. They bring in tons of sand and get their suppliers to have specials for the event. It blows out the doors and generates lots of word of mouth, so no advertising is necessary. No one "cool" wants to miss it.

Cause-Related Marketing . . .

American Ophthalmic partners with the local Meals on Wheels. Their public service efforts include giving away free eye screenings and raising money. Along with elementary school visits, these activities generate about 25 percent of their paying business—$5 million +!

··· *ACTION AGENDA* ···

"You can do anything you want—but not everything you want."

—Anonymous

Pick one or two ideas from the 44 items in this chapter to do. For instance:

→ Is there a trade show where you could exhibit? Whether it's a local chamber or a national showcase, get the details. If you're not sure of the value, share a booth the first time to cut costs.

→ What sort of giveaway would people keep and remember? A ruler for a contractor? Vinyl restorer for a car detailer? Travel scissors for a barber? Correction fluid for a secretarial service? A 10-pin key chain for a bowling center? A calculator for a research consultant? Or mouse pads for a computer consultant?

→ Is there a local festival, fair, or flea market at which you could take a booth?

→ Can you have a party or open house at your office?

→ Is there a charity event in which you could play a big role? Could you start one with friends or clients?

7

Promotions

"Promotion is an activity and/or material that acts as a
direct inducement, offering added value or incentive
to resellers, salespersons, or consumers."
—From *Dictionary of Marketing*

The term *promotion* may be the most misused in the marketing field. When it's used as one of the "Four Ps," it means most of marketing. When it is used in retailing, it means special offers to customers. When used with trade shows, it means something done to draw people to your booth or event. I use it here in the latter sense—as special activities designed to create immediate action. Many promotional activities are coordinated with trade shows, event marketing, and seminars.

Also included in this section is the use of specialty advertising items, also mentioned in the last chapter. These are giveaways with your name on them. They can help capture attention when used right. This overlap of types of marketing further illustrates how your marketing activities are interrelated and need to be coordinated. See what you think.

+++

Marketing the Train . . .

Amtrak Trains had a very successful summer promotion. Anyone who bought a ticket for $35 or more could get two coupons for free movie passes. Amtrak also sponsored trivia questions and played commercials on theater lobby TVs to advertise the deal. In two months, 27,000 customers picked up the free passes.

> **The Textbook "Four Ps" of Marketing**
> - Place (where)
> - Price (how much)
> - Product (what)
> - Promotion (marketing)

Direct Mail Success . . .

The R. W. Neilsen Printing Company mailed a series of seven letters to 1,100 firms that were potential users of printing services. Each letter had details of one of its services and an entry blank that recipients faxed back for a drawing offering prizes of printing services worth from $250 to $1,000. Over the seven-month period of seven mailings, Neilsen received 743 responses from 330 firms. Giving away prizes was a win for the company because they were all credits toward future printing jobs.

Get Others to Sponsor You . . .

Karen Shulman charges $10 for a sitting-up, fully clothed neck and shoulder massage at your place of work. She's gotten employers such as Libbey-Owens-Ford to pick up half the cost as a perk for stressed-out workers who use computers. Analogously, companies can sponsor a lunchtime talk by a flower designer, therapist, lawyer, or the like.

Who might promote your services at lower-cost "bulk" prices to their workers?

Attention-Getting CD Shapes . . .

It "turns out" that compact discs don't have to be round to "turn around." DiscArt produces CDs in almost any shape with pictures printed on them. The company has done them like a U.S. map, a rock star, and a soft drink can. They can get attention for you with recipients (914/426-2590).

Marketing Utah . . .

Utah got major attention with tiles modeled after 50-million-year-old fossils found in the state. Site consultants asking for information about Utah during the campaign got a 3½″ × 5″ tile with a fossil model in it. The $6,500 campaign generated 30 percent of the inquiries the state received the month after mailing and won an award. If your customers see lots of solicitations, you need to be different.

> ### Police as Promoters?
>
> Towns from Skowhegan, Maine, to Tiburon, California, have gotten publicity by having police pull people over and give them local gift certificates or commendations for safe driving. And nobody got a heart attack!

Show Your Capabilities . . .

If your name is "mud" and you do quality color printing, your promotions better be colors other than brown! Mudra is a multicolor printer. To call attention to their color capacities, and gain community goodwill, they produced a booklet featuring local artists. They believe it has called attention to their quality and generated part of their 22–37 percent annual growth rates. (They could also get attention with a sense of humor by playing with their name a bit in their marketing.)

Selling Tourism . . .

Canada got the list of a meeting planners magazine and mailed a box to subscribers. (Boxes always get opened.) It said, "What does it take to lure your top executives away?" Then it played with the "lure" theme by promoting fishing and beauty. It added a bribe for the planner by offering a free boxed fly set for responding to a questionnaire showing interest, and entry into a drawing for a free vacation. It was attention-getting and it worked.

You can use a box. You can offer a gift to "underlings" when they can move you ahead. You can also use a drawing or game as many web-sites do.

Phone Card Promos . . .

Prepaid phone cards are a popular promotional item. For instance, HBO sent out 10,000 cards with five free minutes of calling to cable operators and distributors who they were trying to get to carry their movie service. White Hall Laboratories inserted free phone cards in its home pregnancy test kits. Of course, phone service companies, such as GTS, are also big users of these cards as promotional items, since they provide samples of the company's service.

> **Phone Card Sources**
>
> Companies that create custom phone cards include: Phone Card Express (305/981-5214), The Phone Works (800/777-2255), GTS (800/929-4301), and World Call 2000 (800/261-0159).
>
> PHONE CARD
> ———————»»»
> 6330 510834 613

Promoting Listening . . .

Patterson Printing's promotion was headlined "How can good listeners help you?" It went on to say that Patterson enjoyed listening because it wants to help you meet your goals with increased efficiency and reduced costs. The whole piece was twice the size of a business (#10) envelope. Half could be torn off and mailed back. It's a novel approach that gets attention. Many people feel that no one listens anymore. It would probably work even better for many other services—like yours?

Golf Ball Advertising . . .

If your clients love golf and you give them balls imprinted with your name or theirs, the printed information tends to get scuffed off. Now there is a custom ball that allows you to put a color picture under a special protective cover so that it lasts as long as the balls (Pick Point Sports, 603/569-1533).

Novel Giveaway . . .

If you're a dermatologist or tanning salon, here's a novel giveaway for you. It's called Sun Aware UV Intensity Meter. It's a credit-card-sized promotional product that can be imprinted with your name and information. It has a stripe on it that is exposed to direct sunlight for 20 seconds and then registers the level of sunscreen needed. This is the kind of item that people might keep in their wallets for a long time if they are concerned about sun-damaged skin. It could also be used by a plastic surgeon or makeup artist. (It's made by Teraco and should be available from many advertising specialty firms.)

Promoting Your Town . . .

So much building is going on in Myrtle Beach, South Carolina, that the locals have dubbed the construction crane their state bird! Their key to standing out from other tourist destinations was combining the promotional budgets of multiple hotels and golf courses to market a "golf holiday." This gave them a major presence in golf publications with their ads. Joint marketing can give you more pull too.

> ### Common Giveaway Program
>
> The old basic Welcome Wagon programs can still work. They give away your coupons to new residents. It works well for one house-cleaning service.

Sports Card Promotion . . .

Hollis Digital Imaging created a series of local high school sports cards to promote its capabilities. The company finds sponsors to underwrite half the cost and gets booster clubs to pay the remaining half. They get a free promotional opportunity, plus help the local sports teams.

Giving Frequent-Flyer Miles . . .

Some people are crazy about frequent-flyer miles. They'll do almost anything to get more. You can buy them from the airlines for about two cents a mile in bulk. Then you can award them to customers, no matter what your business. Or you can use them to reward staff for referrals. Charles Schwab discount brokerage is one company to offer frequent-flyer miles, through Delta. Likewise, North American Mortgage is giving 1,000 frequent-flyer miles for every $10,000 borrowed. Miles are given when the loan is taken, not later as it's repaid. This got big publicity.

Attractive Security . . .

Alpha & Omega Services supplies mounted security guards to shopping malls. The Mountie-looking guards and showy horses are a marketing attraction at the malls, plus surprisingly effective against escaping thieves, muggers, and carjackers. Alpha grossed $1.35 million recently, which isn't hay!

Chocolate Phones . . .

Giveaways need to be valuable or creative to get attention. BellSouth Mobility got customers' attention and national wire service PR by giving away chocolate cell phones for Christmas to big customers.

Restaurant Attention-Getters . . .

Here are some novel marketing gimmicks that restaurants use to get attention and attract customers:

- Turtle races
- Toga party (*Animal House*) theme night
- Pajama party theme night (Annette Funicello won't attend, but you could play the movie!)
- Bar nights in which local distributors subsidize the costs for one drink using their brand, give out prizes, and so forth

If you follow the trade magazines, you've heard of many others. The secret is to do them! Any service with a sense of humor could use these ideas for an open house, anniversary party, or charity fund-raiser.

There Was a Free Lunch . . .

Taco Bell introduced its new light food items with a massive giveaway. One radio station liked the general idea so much that the station subsequently cooperated with Dunkin' Donuts to give listeners a free cup of coffee during morning drive time. This helped sell advertising.

If you're a big firm in your city or nationally, and want to create a big splash, a giveaway in coordination with a company like Taco Bell or Dunkin' Donuts will definitely get attention.

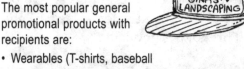

Most Popular Giveaways

The most popular general promotional products with recipients are:

- Wearables (T-shirts, baseball caps, sunglasses, etc.)   19.7 percent
- Writing instruments   13.4 percent
- Glassware and mugs   10.8 percent
- Desk and office accessories   9.2 percent
- Calendars   8.7 percent
- Sporting goods/leisure products   7.2 percent

If you tie it into a charity event, such as Heritage Month or the celebration of the hundredth anniversary of your town, it will do even better.

Service Samples . . .

Sampling is normally thought possible only with products. But anytime you present a seminar, write an article, or give advice, you're showing what you can do. Contractors can offer free home inspections; lawyers free contract analyses; and so forth. Printers are perfectly positioned to sample. WIGT Printing gives out six-month calendars twice a year. They use art from staff or clients and make it a beautiful production. The twice-annual issuance is a good touch too: it's that much more contact. Anyone could send six-month calendars.

Create Your Own Line . . .

Years ago, the producers of the blockbuster movie *Cleopatra* hired slow, arthritic ticket takers for the opening, in order to cause big lines. Lines made people more eager to get in, made the crowds seem bigger, and increased general anticipation. You may have noticed the same effect at a trade show where the table that has people around it attracts more people, who want to see what's going on. It's standard psychology. If people see your name a lot, they'll want to work with you more because you're successful.

Bank Keeps the Kids Happy . . .

About the simplest promotional item that Westamerica and other banks use is stickers for children. They keep the kids quiet for the minute you need, and remind the parent of the bank. Low cost, good impact for the young family demographic.

> **Free Sample Services**
>
> One way to expose yourself is to give out free samples. Four dentists gave free oral cancer screenings promoted by the American Cancer Society. What could you do as part of a local event?
>
>

> DEMOGRAPHICS: Observable variables such as age, race, sex, and income that may make a difference in how or why people buy.
>
> PSYCHOGRAPHICS: Psychological variables that make a difference in how or why people buy. These can include risk taking, status orientation, self-esteem, and many others.

Agents Learn and Win . . .

Puerto Rico wanted to build business during the slower summer season. It targeted travel agents with a sweepstakes that required them to answer crossword puzzles that educated them about Puerto Rico. It also offered special summer travel packages. Everyone won something for entering. The sweepstakes generated 21,000 entries. Hotel registration was up 13.1 percent, and tours up from 17 to 35 percent.

Cash for Cash . . .

What better way for banks to promote ATM usage than to have random extra money distributed for customers who withdraw cash from the machines? Colonial Bank used the giveaways with new ATMs installed in Wal-Mart and Sam's Club stores. When you give away money, the word spreads. Even better would be to add a stamp to make the bills you give away collector's items.

Donating Services . . .

RWA, a telemarketing firm, builds their company on giving back to their communities. It's something that their thousand employees can get behind. They donate telemarketing services for worthy causes. Contributing helps build team spirit and job satisfaction. They even use part of the program for on-the-job training. You also get publicity, as they did in their trade magazine. They judge projects to donate to by asking: (1) How does it benefit the community?, (2) Is the money going to a really worthwhile cause?, and (3) Does the activity show RWA as a socially enlightened and involved citizen?

For greatest effect, be sure to involve your workers in the choice of causes so that they really feel that it's theirs.

Fun "Education"

A brew pub is offering a "Master of Beer Appreciation" Certificate. Customers have to have their "transcripts" stamped by sampling four new brews a month. Eventually you get your "degree" and a T-shirt declaring your mastery. At last a chance to get a meaningful degree!

Money Giveaway . . .

Cleo's Duplication Service buys sheets of 16 two-dollar bills or 32 one-dollar bills from the Bureau of Engraving in Washington, D.C. (They cost the face value plus $10.) The company gives them away as promotional gifts or rewards to good customers. They are novel and in great demand. They'd be perfect for a bank or for any other businesses that say they make a difference to their customers' bottom lines.

Movie Charity Promotion . . .

The UCI theater chain in England wanted to improve the slow months of February and March. They produced two short films with famous personalities. They added these to first-run comedy films during the promotion and asked customers to pay about 15 cents extra (10 pence) for the "triple feature." They called it a comic relief fund-raiser for a big charity event and donated the proceeds. The promotion produced an extra 90,000 customers and was a huge success.

> ### Theme Promotions
>
> Making a visit to your office a surprise sets you apart from the competition. For instance, a children's dentist could have monthly country themes in the office featuring decorations and quizzes with prizes. A gardener could have employees dress like different cultures each month to attract attention and publicity. (They could give employees prizes related to the country and could also sell customers plants from each region.)

Music Marketing . . .

Acumen, Inc., produced a Christmas music CD for charity. Musicians donated their time and talents, so costs were minimal. The cover featured Acumen's logo and plugs for the sponsors. Sales of the disc raised money for the charity, and Acumen's visibility.

Offer Variety, Entertainment, and Education . . .

If you're an Italian restaurant, you should know there's more to Italian food than spaghetti! Il Fornaio is a chain of nice Italian restaurants. It developed a "passport" program to introduce regional Italian food to customers. Every month, the restaurants featured the bread, food, and wine of a different region of Italy. For instance, from the little-known Molise region, vegetables and cheese were emphasized, with little meat. People like to learn painlessly. This "educational" approach attracts serious diners rather than coupon users who come only when you offer discount programs.

Coupon Promotion . . .

Palm Beach promotes itself as a destination to meeting planners and companies with a $500 free coupon book giving discounts from area merchants and restaurants. You could put together discount offers from neighboring businesses and all give them out as gifts to clients.

Promotion Bites Big Banana . . .

Here's a retailer's great recovery from a mistake that you may be able to adapt to a service promotion. An electronics store in Seattle advertised that stereos would be only 250 bananas that weekend. They used *bananas* as slang for *dollars*, like *clams*, and so forth, but some people took them literally and brought in crates of bananas. Rather than be accused of false advertising, they bit the banana and gave away the stereos. But they also hired a person in a gorilla costume for the parking lot, called the media in, and donated the bananas to the local zoo. They got a ton of publicity, and my informant remembered it for years to tell me the story.

If you wanted to support the zoo as a charity, it wouldn't cost you much to sell your services on a special weekend priced in bananas, or other edibles the zoo wanted. (For instance, cavities filled for bananas this weekend.) Just make it your weekend "hobby," and you'll probably attract a lot of attention and some new clients.

Attention-Getter or Bribe?

When you give something that has value to a prospect, if it is novel or very personalized, most see it as acceptable. However, some companies have official policies about the value of a gift employees can accept. Look for items that don't exceed these cost limits.

Screen Saver Advertising . . .

CompuServe is among many companies that have used promotional screen savers as giveaways. They find it a great way to keep their name in front of computer-savvy prospects. They gave them out both on-line and on promotional disks with other material. Many vendors can do the programming for you. If budget is a concern, the trick is to find a vendor who will use a less expensive template rather than customize everything. (4Point Software, at 800/618-3278, is one possibility.)

Telephone Company "Bribes" . . .

Cellnet is England's second-largest cellular carrier. The company used a campaign of prizes, merchandise incentives, and a new-car sweepstakes to encourage dealers and salespeople to sell. New customer hookups increased 84 percent during the promotion. Employees, dealers, and prospects all like a chance at something extra.

Give Them Nothing to Lose . . .

One insurance agency offered to buy small contractors "the biggest steak dinner in town" if the agency couldn't save them money on their business insurance. This challenge made the telephone ring off the hook.

Use Special Discounts . . .

You can often get your customers big discounts from other vendors, free to you, just for letting the vendors obtain exposure. Or you can buy discount certificates for pennies on the dollar that make your customers feel they've gotten a great deal. For instance, Sanwa Bank gave out two free plane tickets to Hawaii in its California branches to every new checking account. The trick was, customers had to buy at least a week in one of the participating hotels. This puts enough money in the package that airfare is essentially free to the bank. Customers could probably get a similar deal themselves through discounters, but the program still packed a punch.

··· ACTION AGENDA ···

"To succeed, jump as quickly at opportunities as you do at conclusions."
—Ben Franklin

Of the 34 examples in this chapter, pick one or two that suggest ideas you could jump quickly at. Here are a few possibilities:

→ A promotion often involves other companies. Make a list of other firms with which you could do a joint effort. Contact them with an idea from this chapter, and see what other ideas they have.

→ Consider a drawing or sweepstakes for a prize of your services. Add prizes from others for a bigger promotion. What about offering frequent-flyer miles?

→ What about sending a custom phone card to customers you haven't heard from in a long time and asking them to "phone home"?

→ How could you use a unique giveaway item analogous to the fossil, golf ball, or sun measurement examples?

→ Can you offer free "screenings" to assess prospects' situations as a fund-raiser for a charity?

→ What providers can you promote to who will in turn promote your services to their customers?

8

Using the Phone to Build Relationships—and Sell

"Speech is conveniently located midway between thought and action, where it often substitutes for both."
—John Andrew Holmes

"Telemarketing is a growing $48.9 billion consumer market and $56.3 billion business-to-business market."
—Direct Marketing Association

Do you enjoy talking to customers or prospects who call you on the phone? Most people do. But how fast is your phone response in returning calls? What about when you have to call out? For many people, calling a stranger is torture.

The telephone varies from a very personal tool for keeping in touch and serving clients, to a mass telemarketing tool for "cold calling." If you're willing to use the phone, you should find some ideas here of interest.

+++

Telephone Persistence . . .

Following up and keeping in touch means personal telemarketing. One consultant made 50 phone calls to one company working his way through five departments to the ultimate decision maker. He got the job. And one of the reasons was the buy-in from the five departments as he progressed. His deep contacts should also help for future work.

Service by Phone . . .

A number of smaller consulting operations have set up consulting by telephone, where you often never meet your consultant. With a good computer database (e.g., helpdesk program) to back them up, you can get by with lower-paid staff. Many professional firms could offer a special lower phone rate this way.

Bunch Your Calls

When you're making calls, group them by type so that your mind is in one groove. For instance, sales calls, get-acquainted calls, returning calls.

8am Sales calls
☑ Sally Jones
☑ Bill Chen
☐
☐
1pm Return calls
☐
☐
4pm Networking calls
☐
☐

Quick Phone Responses . . .

Snell and Wilmer is the largest law firm in Arizona. In order to quantify its idea of high-quality service, one of its practice groups promised to return client telephone calls within two hours. This is a standard that almost anyone could use. It doesn't mean you have to have the answer within two hours, but it means you at least get back to the caller. If your "lawyer" is in court, have an assistant get back, find out what the problem is, and set up a phone appointment.

Free Phones for Customers . . .

Express Press has a phone in the lobby especially for customers. It is clearly marked for their use. A nice courtesy, often ignored!

Pager Marketing . . .

Old-fashioned pagers are cheaper than cellular phones, and less intrusive. Mortgage Length equips all of its employees with them. They can't afford to miss a call when they are competing with big banks and finance companies. It's a simple technology, but it makes Mortgage Length's people more available than competitors'.

Personal Phone Service . . .

When customers want to reach you with a problem, any delay can annoy them. Magline had international customers who called at off-hours. To handle it, they now give out home phone numbers of technical, sales, and service people. Customers don't call much, but just knowing they can makes them feel wanted and lets them hold off on most calls.

You should give your home phone number to good customers. And you might consider putting it or your pager number on your office message for emergencies.

Can Your Phone Spell? . . .

Having a phone number that spells out something related to your business can make you look big-time. It can also make it easier for people to remember your number if you advertise on the radio. Most of the great words are already taken. But here's a free website that will figure out what your current numbers spell for you: www.pbvoicemail.com/Fun.

> **Time Your Return Calls**
>
> Tell your staff when you'll return calls (or put it on your answering machine). Grouping your calls at one time saves you time, and callers prefer to know when you'll call back.

Your Local Phone Presence . . .

With toll-free 800 phone numbers common today, call forwarding is a largely forgotten service, but it recently fooled me. I called a temporary services agency that had a local phone number and address in the yellow pages. To my surprise, the call was forwarded to the agency's real office 30 minutes away, which I never would have called, even if it were a free call.

Local numbers give you a stronger local presence in different areas. We used local numbers for an upholstery service years ago when we advertised in different areas but had only one office. People probably like the thought that they can run over to your office and yell at you conveniently if anything goes wrong!

Breaking Through Voice Mail . . .

When you're frustrated about voice mail and nobody returning your calls, Steve Shirley says try a dash of humor. He varies the message he leaves until people return it. For instance, he might say, "I'm so desperate that if I don't hear from you soon, I might leave town and join the circus, or start wearing Hawaiian shirts to the office." Shirley says, "Almost anything silly will do the trick." His calls get returned, and these buyers tend to return future calls as well.

Cold Calling Pays . . .

Dan Hirsch started his telecommunications business making 20 cold calls a week. Now when business gets slow, he makes 100 phone calls in a couple of days and has plenty to do. Your calls don't even have to be cold to start. Practice on past clients, and you'll find new work while you reinforce your relationships.

The Value of Nonbuying Callers . . .

One old saying in sales is that even your rejections are worth money to you because it takes a specific number of rejections to reach each sale which is worth x dollars. One practitioner used this math to impress the people handling the phones who may not have been as courteous as they could be. By knowing how many callers it took to get one case, he was able to calculate a figure of $35 per caller. When he presented this figure to his staff and explained it, they began to realize the value of each call and handled them a little bit better. Soon, the conversion rate for callers went up, and so the value of each inquiry became $44! Keeping this value plotted on a graph, posted, and mentioned in every staff meeting kept employees on their toes, and more positive to callers.

Handling Return Calls . . .

When you leave a message for people and they return your call, there are few things more embarrassing than forgetting why you had called in the first place. Even if you had left a detailed message, they may not have gotten the whole text and may not repeat it to you. And when you've made several calls and one party calls back days later, it can be really hard to remember. Art Sobczak (*Telephone Selling Report*) says to keep a list of people you've called by your phone, or in a good database. Then, whenever they call back, you can get up to speed and make your presentation quickly.

Getting Past Screeners

Don't try to fool gatekeepers. Either enlist their help to get your information in front of the boss or call when they're not there, such as before work, at lunchtime, or after work.

Cold-Calling Big Companies . . .

LogicData hires telemarketers to cold-call major industrial customers who might use the company's manufacturing software setups. They start with a list selected by SIC codes (which tells them what general business prospects are in). Callers ask for top management rather than the computer people (IS), who they feel have their own agendas. LogicData account managers are trained to ask lots of questions to understand the business problems of prospects. Since the company's software integrates information from different departments, telemarketers try to talk with each department head for input and to build consensus. For instance, they continued to build relationships during one $100,000 sale. Now they are selling the client more training and technology as the company's business doubles.

Service Centers Can Sell . . .

MaxWest Services handles 500,000 inbound customer calls a month for MaxWest Bank. The company's 300 customer service reps also generate 55 percent of the bank's consumer credit applications. "It's crazy to tell customers to go to a branch, give them another number to call, or make them hang on the line while they are transferred, when you can help them right there," says a MaxWest rep. The bank sees sales as helping service, not contradicting it. MaxWest uses close monitoring and training, "mystery customers," and lots of other programs to both check on and reward good customer service reps who also sell. Reps can earn up to 80 percent of their standard pay based on both customer satisfaction and sales.

Your approach will differ depending upon your circumstances, but letting people know about services they are not using that might be appropriate for their situation can be positive service, not pushy selling.

MYSTERY CUSTOMERS: People who are paid to call or visit like customers and rate the service they receive, often on a rating form you choose.

A Telemarketing System . . .

HB Insurance in Canada set up a fancy computer system to help phone reps sell insurance. For inbound calls, the computer displays the caller's phone number and then checks to see if the owner of the number has a file with the company. That provides personal handling information on the reps' screens. HB reps can handle the types of calls they prefer—new sales, current clients, and so forth. Callers are prioritized as they wait: VIPs get faster service. The system can tape calls for training purposes. The next model will also make coffee!

Hiring Telemarketing . . .

If you hate the idea of cold calling, you can hire to have it done. Outsiders won't be so sensitive about rejection, since it's not their egos on the line. Research shows that unemployed actors (which is 95 percent of them most of the time!) make great telemarketers. They do well getting into the "role."

More on Hired Telemarketers . . .

One professional used local business school students to make prospecting calls for her. For minimum wage, plus bonuses for appointments and eventual sales, she got lots of takers. Not everyone can handle calling, however. Training should focus on behavior. Have the staff practice a call on you and on prospects. If they can't hack it, move them out quickly. One consultant used women with young children who worked from their homes. A pay scale of $10 an hour for setting appointments worked great for him and them. Even when they set only three appointments a week working half-time, the numbers worked out well. (His average job was worth $1,000, so even closing only a third cost him just $200 per job, not counting repeat business.)

New Cellular 800 Numbers . . .

The Seattle branch of Great Expectations, a video dating service, used a new 800 *cellular* number in its radio ads. For the first time, radio generated enough responses for the service: people listening in automobiles could call immediately when they heard the ad. They associate their cars with dating? That idea won't take a "backseat!"

Shorter Cellular 800 Numbers . . .

Hilton Hotels, Budget Rent-a-Car, and FTD Flowers are service providers using the new cellular 800 numbers. The new technology also opens up *extra* 800 numbers because they don't need to be 10 digits. For instance, Great Expectations used 800DATE.

Service on Hold . . .

Union Electric has to put lots of customers on hold. Its system starts with a voice-responsive automatic message that can give answers or switch callers elsewhere. For customers who have to wait for a "live" response, the system selects from 200+ messages on hold that might best fit the customer profile or the choices they selected from the automated attendant. Customers get better treatment, and Union sells more services. Upgrades will let people sign up for new services and get account information automatically.

> ### Selling by Answering Machine
> Margie Seyfer adds descriptions of new training topics to her voice mail greeting. Callers are invited to request more information. In one case five companies calling about other topics requested details on a new program in a week. She knew she had a winner. What could you offer?
>
>
> OUR NEW SERVICE THIS MONTH IS . . .

Longer Sales Message Optional . . .

It's good to have a sales message on your answering machine. But it can annoy people. Jim Otto sells voice mail, so he should use it well. His message says, "If you have a minute, I have an exciting idea to share. Just press 1 to hear it before you leave your message. If you're in a hurry, stay on the line."

"500" Phone Numbers . . .

You've heard of "800" numbers, "888" numbers (newer toll-free), and "900" numbers. And by now, you may have heard of "500" numbers. These are "attached" to you and can be switched to follow you to any phone number or car phone where you're located. In addition, you can keep the number forever. You can screen certain calls, and so on. The convenience for your clients is tremendous.

A Phone-Answering Benchmark . . .

Magline's delivery service was rated terribly. Their phone system was slowing them down. The solution? Most calls were orders. These didn't have to be handled by sales reps, but instead could be switched to lower-level order takers. They also invited orders to come in via fax machine. Now 60 percent come in this way, freeing up more time. They set a standard that reps would pick up the phone by the second ring and return all customer calls within one hour. Their service department is now rated the best in the business.

Telephone Hello . . .

Here's a novel way to touch base with people when it's their birthday. If you call them on a Touch-Tone phone and punch in 4-4-5-4-9-8, the tones form the first six notes of "Happy Birthday to You." It takes practice to get the right rhythm hitting the numbers. For someone with a sense of humor, it can be a fun way to keep in touch.

Call Tracking . . .

Bell South was the first phone company to offer a service it calls AdWatch. When you advertise, you can insert different phone numbers. AdWatch then tracks how many calls come to each phone number while routing them to your real phone number. This can also be used like call forwarding to have a presence in different local calling areas.

Cold-Calling Disney . . .

Most people hate calling people they don't know and who didn't invite the call—cold calling. Don Ritzman is a filmmaker. He cold-called the Disney studios to try to get their cooperation on a Native American theme movie to follow up *Pocahontas*. It took a year and a half to do the deal with Disney and the Discovery Channel, but it worked. Although it always helps to have an initial entry contact or a referral, you can make deals from cold calls. If you get out there, things happen.

Beepers Provide Service . . .

Many service providers with waiting rooms could take a lesson from occasional restaurants that give patrons beepers while they wait for their tables. How about doctors' or dentists' offices with a wait letting people wander around the local neighborhood before they're beeped for their appointment on a just-in-time basis?

Hiring for Service . . .

Here's a hiring tip for you from Southwest Airlines. It's been said many times that it's easier to hire friendly people and train them to do the service job than vice versa. Southwest Airlines has each job candidate make a brief presentation to a roomful of other candidates. Applicants think they're being evaluated on their presentation skills. But they're really being observed to see how supportive and attentive an audience they are. If you act caring in that setting, they figure you'll take good care of airline passengers.

When to Call

The best hours to call prospects are early in the day. Depending on your business, calling between 8 and 10 A.M. usually helps you reach people before they are involved in other activities. It also gets your day off to a good start when you've made connections early.

Better Phone Answering . . .

One company renamed itself Check Network just to slow its people down when they answered the phone. A name like Joe's Auto can be slurred into "Jozotto"—making callers wonder where they are for a second. Remember that your first impression on the phone can be very important. Work with your people to answer in a friendly, professional way that makes people glad they called. For instance, when I recently called IBM, the woman answering gave her full name and also asked if voice mail would be acceptable before she patched me through to another number.

Better Voice Mail Messages . . .

By creating several phone answering messages, one professional customized her announcements for evenings, weekends, and special events. She also rotates messages several times a month for variety.

Cold Calling Through Directories . . .

Joe Girard, a famous salesman, offers this tip. If you are cold calling through directories that other people use too, start from the back, not the front. You will have less competition. I have done this myself, and when calling people who were late in the alphabet I even mentioned that I started calling from the back. Often they got a chuckle out of it, since they are used to being last in the alphabet in school and everywhere else. They appreciated the fact that they were first even though it was a cold call.

Telephone Scripts

When cold-calling people, always introduce yourself, ask them if they have a moment, and tell them why you're calling. Use a script to cover your points, but never *sound* as if you're following a script.

Hello, I'm _____
Point 1
Point 2
Point 3

Directory Cold Calls . . .

One telemarketer specializes in calling subscribers to expensive newsletters who haven't renewed after many notices from the publisher. He gets paid a commission only when he succeeds, so there's little risk for publishers. He gets business from referrals, but he also gets many of his clients by cold calling through the directory of the Newsletter Publishers Association.

Improving Telemarketing . . .

If your business requires a lot of outbound calls, you'll find that many of your telemarketers are not producing the number of calls per day that it takes to get the job done. Peter Belanger, telemarketing consultant, tells of one client whose reps were dialing only 35 calls a day and were averaging two hours of downtime, two or three minutes at a time between calls. To overcome this, at the beginning of the day every rep was handed a stack of 50 sheets each providing the details on one prospect in the database and were told to just start calling through them. This simple procedure doubled the number of decision makers they reached each day and cut wasted time in half.

Live Operators Only . . .

First Union Bank outlawed answering machines. Employees must have top-level approval to have voice mail or other automated systems. Twenty-seven live operators (about one per branch) handle about two-thirds of the calls, and refer the others. People hate being put on hold, and people hate voice mail when they want to get help or need a response. Since the bank started tracking customer satisfaction, the live operators have improved ratings.

Message-on-Hold Systems Can Help . . .

In an office with a lot of inbound calls, people get put on hold. They will generally put up with it for less than a minute before they hang up. Automatic messages, often humorous or educational, and even plugging your services, can make people more willing to hold on. A collection office of a Rhode Island hospital had 95 percent fewer hang ups after it installed a message-on-hold system. Chile Airlines' disconnect rate dropped from 26 percent to 7 percent after installing a system. New Jersey Transit had a 50 percent drop in abandoned calls.

"Nos" Are Good

When you're prospecting, getting people to say no can benefit you both. Be happy when you get a good no. That way you don't waste your time with people not open to contact, who aren't legitimate prospects.

NUMBER OF NOs:
~~IIII~~ ~~IIII~~
~~IIII~~ ~~IIII~~ III
VALUE OF NOs: $250

Phone Asks for Leads . . .

One answering machine strategy doubled a professional's mailing list in a year and added 8 percent to new business monthly. That was inviting people to leave their names and addresses to receive information about any specific topic. She had a variety of form letters in her computer which she then customized to answer their questions. Calls were also returned when appropriate, and prospects were added to her list for regular mailings.

> **Voice Mail Not All Bad**
>
> In one business study, 75 percent of calls were routine questions which voice mail could record for your later response. Set up your message so that people can push a button to skip voice mail if they need to, but can leave a message if they prefer.

Respecting Their Time . . .

Today, people are busier than ever, especially professionals. It helps to get straight to the point, whether you're telemarketing or writing a letter. When I call people, I generally start the conversation by saying, "I'm looking for people who want _____ (benefit)." If they don't respond, "Yes" or "Tell me more," that's the end of the conversation. None of their—or my—time is wasted.

Switch Over Your Phones . . .

If you're getting big-time telephone response, make sure you have big-time handling set up. The National Marrow Donor Program gets lots of calls to their 800 number when they run ads. These "spikes" cause busy signals and poor handling internally. Now they can switch calls to another company when peak periods come. This makes callers happier, and happier callers donate more. It also helps internal staff avoid stress. Even for "small time" you could use call forwarding to an answering service to get better handling when you're on all your lines.

Unique Business Card . . .

Prairie Systems has a picturesque business card. It shows a giant prairie dog over the company's headquarters. But what really makes it unique is that it's a phone card too, good for $10 in calls. So, it's a business card with a reason to carry it, a sample of what they sell, and a collector's item.

Mail, Then Phone . . .

How do you warm up a cold call? The standard way is to send a letter first. But timing is hard, and most prospects deny remembering it. So, send something novel. One ad salesperson sent a packet of grass seed labeled "Instant Customers." Then she started the phone discussion of how her advertising could grow customers for them. Prospects took her calls and made appointments.

· · · ACTION AGENDA · · ·

"He who hesitates is *last*."
—Anonymous

The longer you wait to put one of the 40 examples in this chapter to use, the less momentum you'll have for improving your customer service or marketing.

→ Here's a simple one for anyone. Call your own office and listen to the way your call is answered. Could you train your people to sound friendlier, or to say something different?

→ Now call your office when no one is there. Could you improve the recorded message? What about varying your message to make it more like one of the examples in this chapter?

→ If there's someone you've been meaning to call again, do it now.

→ Consider making calls early in the morning on a regular basis.

→ Are there new numbers or equipment that would be useful?

→ Can you hire someone to make cold calls for you?

9

Sales Techniques

"Selling is easy—if you work hard at it."

—Old sales saying

As mentioned in Chapter 4, traditional sales training that emphasizes how to overcome objections and "close," often with high pressure, is just plain wrong. You can make some sales that way, but building real relationships is far better for long-term service business.

If you're good at communication, or if you've studied selling, you know how to interact with people in a sales situation. Improving your focus on relationship building will help you sell better. It's also helpful sometimes to have specific examples of what people say or do in sales situations. This chapter contains many examples of more traditional sales issues, such as getting past gatekeepers, and asking for the appointment.

✦✦✦

Sales Psychology . . .

Basic sales wisdom says that people buy from motives of fear or gain—need or greed. Donald Burch says that when they won't buy after a presentation based on one side, he switches to the other. Either way, he can solve the prospect's problem.

Selling Risk . . .

If you're selling a high-risk investment, there are two ways to present it. One is to minimize the risk and build up the benefits. The other is to reverse-sell. When you emphasize all of the dangers in an investment or course of action, people naturally tend to think of the opposite positives. When you put the risks in writing, clients have been clearly

> **Reverse Selling**
>
> Some people naturally resist anything you try to push. With them, it's better to back off, play devil's advocate, and make them convince you that they're viable prospects who really can benefit from your services.

forewarned that it's a long shot. That's what the Thoroughbred Breeding Center did in a classic letter. They also got a sly plug in for the positives by noting there had been a lot of favorable publicity on racehorse breeding operations, and that's why they wanted to point out that only the most risk-tolerant investors should consider investing in their program. Then they set out net worth criteria and the like. This same principle of reverse selling can be used by a lawyer helping a client estimate the odds of going to court, a tree surgeon, a fertility clinic, or anyone else who is doing something when the odds are against success.

Publicity Feeds Advertising Sales . . .

Advertising and editorial don't talk to each other much at most publications. And editorial wants to keep a separation to avoid bias. But publications give free publicity for two reasons: to keep their readers up-to-date, and to demonstrate that their readers respond to "advertising." However, few publications use the free PR they give out well. The *Mortgage Originator* does. They did a review of my book and sent a note with a copy suggesting their low-cost classifieds. Are you following up completely when you have leads in totally different contexts (such as cards from a mixer)?

Help Them Buy Like Rich People . . .

When you're selling value, cite cases of rich people who bought from you. They become implicit referrals for you.

My favorite example is Malcolm Forbes Sr., the former owner of *Forbes* magazine. He had a whole staff of financial reporters. Who could get better information on beating estate taxes? He bought lots of insurance before he died and was able to pass his estate intact to the next generation.

Which Words to Use? . . .

Exactly what you say can make a difference. One consultant developed this phrase after he established that someone had received a referral to him: "_____ (name of prospect), do you have any situations in your company that our mutual expertise can solve?" He likes to use the word "situations" instead of "problems" so people won't deny having problems. And he likes the words "mutual expertise" to tell prospects that he respects their knowledge in the situation.

> ### Draw Them a Picture
> Pictures make things more concrete for people. An architect can show a computer model of a building. A beautician can show a computer rendering of you with a different hairstyle. If you can't use a real picture, "draw" a compelling verbal picture of the benefits of working with you.

Computer Presentations . . .

Sales presentations on computer are still novel enough that they get a lot of attention. For instance, one seller at a trade show found that people would stop and watch the "slide show" on a computer just because of the novelty. Another seller, when making pitches to grocery stores, has a picture taken of the grocer's shelf where the seller's product would go. Then, with special effects, he superimposes the display of those products onto the grocer's shelf. This gets serious attention and provides buyers more information about what things would actually be like if they bought.

Sales Proposal Pricing . . .

When you need to make sales proposals, you have to work hard to discover the budget they're really willing to spend. Sales pro Jack Sweeney usually gives companies three proposals. The lowest-priced one is the budget he thinks they can realistically afford. Most people take that one. The next two are each 12.5 percent higher. About 5 percent of the time, they take the highest one (which offers more service, of course) because they have the money and want a first-class effort. About the same amount of time, they negotiate below the lowest one. Other pros like to make the middle of three prices the logical one, so they get most sales there.

How to Ask for Add-On Business . . .

Paul Brosche of the Practice Builder Association suggests reminding people who talk to you that they may have other needs. Try adding the words "What else can I do for you?" after the primary discussion. It's basic, but it seems to add at least 10 percent to billing time or business.

Obtaining Long-Term Commitments . . .

Right after you've done a great job handling an IRS audit, arbitration hearing, or other problem is the time to sign clients to longer-term agreements. One CPA offers clients a discount for the extra commitment, which stabilizes his income too. Many consultants' retainer rates are as low as half their hourly rates.

Cross-Selling and Referrals . . .

When an agent writes an auto insurance policy, it's easy to ask about health and disability insurance. Dan Rust basically says, "This auto coverage is for payment of medical bills if you're injured in a car accident. If your bills were to exceed that amount, what other coverage would you have? And if you were unable to work, what income would you have?"

When you make a sale, what other services make sense? They don't have to be provided by you. You can get a referral commission or cross-referrals. For instance, when a plumber changes a toilet, a new floor may be needed. When a tree specialist takes out a tree, new hedge plantings may be in order.

Cross-Selling and Up-Selling

"Cross-selling" is showing people another service that may go logically with what they've bought. Or it may be an internal referral to another department in your practice. "Up-selling" is moving people up to a more expensive service that replaces the one they're used to.

Back-End Marketing . . .

Back-end marketing is what you do *after* the sale is made. It can include add-on selling, cross-selling, or improving customers' experiences. At Lands' End catalog, it's as simple as confirming that a customer's order is in stock and then telling the customer when to expect delivery. This is simple customer service that many companies forget. For a landscaper, it might be mentioning a plant special after the landscape job is sold. Not applicable to a dignified profession like law? How about offering your new clients a low-cost, client-only "checkup" of their other legal issues?

When Clients Exploit You

When you're delivering one service, clients will often ask you for other, free work. Budget a few moments for informal answers or a brief reaction. Then tell them that for more detailed work it will be an extra job which will require an estimate.

Add-On Sales of "Insurance" . . .

One accountant offered to "insure" clients against audits. For an additional 10 percent fee (minimum $50) he guaranteed free representation up to appeals court if they were audited. He offered it only to a relatively low-risk group. Half the clients took it. Only two were audited, less than 1 percent. He made a big profit on the extra fees.

Justifying Extra Business . . .

Automated Office sells training at client sites. To justify training costs in the first place, they say, "You're spending $1,000 to save $10,000." They also expect to find consulting business while they're there. Their instructors are coached in how to say no to solving extra problems, while still getting new work. To nicely put off solving extra problems, they say they'd like to help but their time is allotted to this specific problem today.

Anticipate Objections . . .

Allebach Creative wanted to sell new services creating websites. But customers weren't sure about the return on investment. Allebach addressed customer concerns up front, acknowledging their fears and pointing out the two key benefits—that they would get a head start on

their competitors in getting used to the
Web, and that the website could enhance other marketing. This created
great success in building trust *and* sales.

> **Better Negotiating**
>
> Pricing a complex service
> usually involves the "flinch
> test." If they flinch when you
> name a price, they'll want to
> negotiate. On the other hand, if
> they don't flinch, you may have
> a chance to add on other
> services.

Ask for the Last Turn at Bat . . .

One pro always asks prospects in the
first meeting to promise to give him a
15-minute debriefing on the problems
with his proposal if he doesn't get the
job. He figures it gets him more jobs because people
don't want to face someone they've rejected. Plus if the
meeting happens, he gets feedback and a chance to resell
the job.

Better Prospecting . . .

Often when an announcement is published that someone has been promoted, lots of people call to congratulate the subject and try to sell him or her more insurance,
and so forth. Ray Boose asks newly promoted people the
names of those who took their place. He's the only one
who calls the "other" promotees—until now!

Big-Time Bluff . . .

You are flattering customers when they know that you
want their business, but they can try to take advantage
too. Software company Simlinc had negotiations down
to the last minute to sell a $6.8 million software and sup-
port contract to Boeing. They wanted to close a deal in
that fiscal year with a big customer to help them in their
efforts to go public. Since Boeing knew that Simlinc was
eager to close the deal by a deadline, the company antic-
ipated that Boeing would take it down to the last minute
to see what kind of concessions they could get. Boeing
opened the final bid by suggesting that maybe they
would only take a small order for a few hundred thousand dollars worth of software. Simlinc's headquarters
won the face-off by calling their team home. When
Boeing negotiators saw a deal slipping away on software
that their engineers had already decided on, they quickly
went for the $6.8 million sale.

Dealing with Call Screeners . . .

Here are two ways Bill Bishop, sales trainer, uses to reach people by phone. If he gets a secretary, he'll say, "I want to ask _____ some questions. I can leave them on her voice mail, but I'd never get an answer soon enough. When can I call back with a better chance of reaching her?" This can provide you the key times to call, where you essentially have an appointment. His favorite is to leave a message like this, if he's referred in: "A mutual acquaintance of ours suggested I call, and I promised I would. My name is_____. My number is _____. I'll be in between _____ and _____." The message doesn't say whether you're buying or selling, or why you called, but it tends to get responses.

Writing Sales Proposals

Sales proposals can be a lot of work. Develop form material in your computer that can be personalized for each situation. Be sure to include a pool of references that you can customize for each type of client.

SALES PROPOSAL
SERVICES PROVIDED: _____
_____
SCHEDULE: _____
_____
_____

Don't Wait for RFPs . . .

Internet Systems Corp. targets the 300 largest banks in the world as their marketplace. If they waited until RFPs (requests for proposals) were issued, they would just be one of many bidders. Instead, they use an investment proposal format to show specific targets how they can improve profits in their businesses. Banks are very profit-and-loss oriented, so this approach fits their style, as well as the classic "consultative selling" approach recommended by Mack Hanan. Since they changed to this approach, Internet Systems says that it has cut their costs of sales and increased their hit ratio.

Let Them Help You Sell Them . . .

Phil Dorian likes this as a sales appointment opening: "What would you say to me to influence me to buy my services from you?" It's novel, it gets the other person thinking, and it may show you what prospects think the important issues are.

Fax Alert . . .

CareerTrack occasionally uses a fax update for last-minute notification of seminars in an area. It's quick, cheap, and actually easier to read than their general flyers which are much larger. Fax still has a lot of impact. To send a lot of them, use computer broadcast fax equipment or a service bureau.

> **ABC ≠ ABC**
>
> In old-line selling, ABC stands for *Always Be Closing*. Today the ABCs should be *Always Build Commitment*. In order to show your commitment to prospects and build theirs to you, build the relationship.

Out-of-Town Expertise . . .

There is an old joke that a consultant is someone who is more than 50 miles away from home. In my experience there is something to it. I have had 50/50 success faxing special offers to people in other cities when I was going to be visiting. About half the time, I've made the sale and given a speech inside a large firm in a distant city. From their point of view, you're a resource they cannot get normally, and they are saving money on transportation.

Fear Appeals . . .

Normally, I don't like negative, fear appeals. But I've seen two that may be OK, and work. First is the dust mite in the carpet. A carpet cleaner goes door-to-door and asks, "Is your carpet free of dust mites?" Most people have never heard of them. They look like real monsters when you blow up microscopic pictures of them. Then you show how your vacuum, treatment, etc. kills them. I just saw a network marketing (multilevel) postcard featuring a picture of the mighty mite! (They're in your bed too, and on your body. They eat dead skin. To get real creepy, there is even a type that lives on your eyelashes!)

In a similar vein (speaking of bodies!), Catherine Stevens, of Radiant Health Associates, sent out a form letter about different types of parasites that live in your body. She cited names I never heard of (flukes, *Giardia*, etc.). She enclosed an "objective" article by a doctor about all the health problems parasites can cause and how they sap your energy. Then she offered three ancient herbal cures you could buy. The cure could have also been nutritional consulting, colonic cleansing, or other services.

Finding New Prospects . . .

If you sell a service that everyone needs, such as banking, car repair, or insurance, then everyone you do business with is a prospect. One professional made a list of everyone she saw over one weekend, from the video store, to her child's softball game, to the grocery store, and came up with a big list of new prospects. If you do business with them, why shouldn't they consider doing business with you?

> **Wrong-Number Prospects**
>
> I've even had nice chats and gotten prospects when the number dialed turned out not to be who I was trying to reach! When you tell everyone you talk to what kind of people you help, some of them turn out to be qualified, or to know people who are.

Get Famous Help . . .

Travel agent Carolyn Kyle arranged for then USC Football Coach John Robinson to lead a group on a Mediterranean cruise. She invited people to a cocktail party to learn details and signed up plenty. Disc jockeys also lead celebrity cruises because they end up plugging it on their shows.

Getting Past Gatekeepers or Voice Mail . . .

When you call some big companies, if you don't know the name of a specific person, the switchboard won't put you through to anyone! Similarly for some voice mail systems if you don't know an extension. Jim Domanski, a Canadian telemarketing consultant, says try dialing random extensions. (If the main number is 5200, try 5201, 5202, etc. Or once into the message, try 224, 324, etc.) When you get a live person, just say who you are and what you're looking for. Usually people will use their internal phone directories to give you the right name and number or transfer you.

Information Helps Them Sell Themselves . . .

High-ticket information-driven products such as investments should offer as much information to prospects as they want. That's why Fidelity Investments was one of the early, big users of on-line services, CD-ROMs, and interactive discs. Insurance companies, mutual funds, and financial services firms should provide lots of information and allow consumers to interactively select specific types. This way, your buyers sell themselves just the way they want to be sold.

Partnership Selling . . .

A big sale illustrates marketing through partnerships: Forte Software provided the lead for a smaller company to land and will work with them on parts of the job. There's plenty to share, since it's a $5 million account!

Price Resistance

Many people get hung up on price. It's your job to show them that the benefits they receive will provide a real return on their investment. People need to make a "profit" investing in your services, or they won't buy.

Quality Loss-Leader Experiment . . .

The Spence Center for Women's Health is a chain of upscale clinics. Customers are greeted by name, and there are fresh flowers and bottled water around. The clinics lose money on the basic examinations that are reimbursed by the government. Spence hoped that the traffic would build business for profitable massages and Chinese herbal treatments. It didn't work, so the company added high-margin items covered by insurance, such as cardiology and bone density testing, which it had previously referred out. That worked.

Selling Value . . .

Sell value, not price. After Steve Springer sells policies for home or car, he says, "You are willing to spend x dollars to insure your tangible assets, such as your auto and home. How much are you willing to spend to insure your most valuable asset, your life?" It puts the cost in perspective.

How can you put your value in perspective?

Results-Oriented Sales Focus . . .

A publicity consultant approaches closing the sale like this. He asks, "When would you like to see results?"

If they want results soon, and aren't talking about committing money, don't take them that seriously as a prospect. If you can deliver the results, it's time to start talking about budget in a problem-solving, joint-effort way.

Sales Stunt...

Orvel Ray Wilson (*Guerrilla Selling*) recounts the story of a salesperson who just couldn't get through to the decision maker after lower levels had agreed to the value of the service-product package but said there was no budget. Finally, he sent a box with a homing pigeon in it. A note enclosed said, "I'll meet you any time, at the restaurant of your choice. Just put it in the capsule on the bird's leg. I'll be there." An entrepreneur had to respond, and the sale went through.

Sex Sells...

You may have heard about the survey that showed that 49 percent of salesmen admitted taking customers to topless bars. Five percent of saleswomen did. They claimed that in 70 percent of the cases, the customers proposed the setting. Forty percent of the men and 57 percent of the women surveyed said they felt that entertaining in topless bars gave male salespeople an unfair advantage over females in dealing with male clients. But a woman professional says, "Don't worry about it. There are lots of places to bond with male clients, from baseball games to golf."

Selling with Audiotapes...

Companies such as Southwest Airlines and J. B. Hunt trucking use audiotapes to sell their own employees on new ideas and company philosophy. You should also consider a tape to sell prospects. Many people like listening to tapes in their cars where they have time to be impressed. Tapes can work far better

Selling Tapes Two Ways

One consultant sells tapes to clients on a monthly subscription basis. The tapes help them run their business better. He also offers copies to the clients to give out to their own clients as a marketing tool to keep in touch.

than a brochure, or even in-person sales. They also make a novel mailer.

Show Them a Picture . . .

At a trade show, Cabletron lets customers travel through its cable TV network in virtual reality. Any engineer can let prospects "walk through" a design in 3-D CAD. The technology will be steadily advancing to impress prospects and let them "see and feel" what they're getting.

Stay in Touch When Sampling . . .

Business Matters does something clever when they send free samples of their software to build business. They call every customer during the trial and ask if they need help installing the software, have any questions, and so on. This starts building the relationship, and encourages people not to steal a copy of the software, since they wouldn't have support. They also sell add-on services with data updates that their software can use to perform better over time.

By being persistent in bringing people useful information, you can sometimes demonstrate the value of your service before people buy. How can you take the initiative by sending newsletters or clippings, offering seminars, and so on? And what can you add from other vendors that would help people benefit more from your service?

The Either/Or Close . . .

Sometimes closing techniques are appropriate—but less often than most traditional salespeople think. When using the either/or close (also known as the contained choice or alternate choice), one of Linda Fracassi's semi-

The Half-Nelson Close

When prospects keep asking you questions but you're not sure how serious they are, try this close: ask them if they would be ready to sign up if the answer is right. If they won't commit, they may not be serious buyers, they may have unexpressed doubts, or you may not have built enough trust.

nar participants pointed out, people have the tendency to pick the second choice, so put your preferred one there. (For example, "Do you want me to start on Monday or Tuesday?")

Up-Sell by Demonstration . . .

Fast Print, Inc., developed an inexpensive way to produce color proofs of black-and-white printing jobs. By showing people what color would look like, they up-sold many of them and doubled their sales of color copies. A graphic designer can show what sales literature would look like with extra colors. Architects can use CAD programs to show what extra design features would look like. Consultants can show examples of bigger research. By making it visible, you'll tempt many people into upgrading their service purchases.

Video Sells . . .

Tavco Marketing & Media specializes in making sales videos for collection agencies. They include testimonials which are very powerful. And they get watched.

· · · ACTION AGENDA · · ·

"Everyone who's ever taken a shower has
an idea. It's the person who gets out,
dries off, and does something about it
who makes a difference."
— Nolan Bushnell, founder of Atari and
many other companies

The 39 items in this chapter probably gave you a few ideas you could implement easily. Try writing down a couple and posting them to remind yourself to take action on them. A few steps you might consider include:

→ Make a list of the reasons people buy or don't buy your services. Include what they want to gain, and what they fear.

→ Test offering more than one price/service level in your sales proposals.

→ Develop a way to easily tell people what else you could do for them.

→ Develop a fax notice you can send out.

→ Can you use a video- or audiotape as a sales tool?

10

Managing a Sales Effort

> "A manager accomplishes things through the efforts of others."
>
> —Peter Drucker

*C*oordinating the efforts of others can make you successful. That's what management of any sort is about. Because salespeople can be quite independent and still do their jobs, some companies don't utilize them effectively. This chapter has a few ideas that can help you get the most out of your sales force, whether one or one thousand.

+++

Low-Cost Sales Reps . . .

The Photo Marketing Association hired retired executives from customers' companies to represent them all over the world, as well as to recruit new members. On a commission-only basis, this worked for both parties. Retired execs from your customers, or even competitors, still have contacts that can create business-to-business sales.

Network Marketing Strategies . . .

AT&T recruited Shaklee to sell long-distance services for them. This followed MCI working with Amway. Telephone networks using network marketing! It may sound novel, but did you know that in Japan many cars are sold with house calls? You may not be able to use multilevel marketing, but what it amounts to is paying people a commission for bringing you work and a smaller commission for finding other people to sell your services. Referral commissions are ethical in most service businesses.

Contest Drives Sales . . .

Incentive contests are designed to bring excitement to sales goals with prizes and fanfare. American General Finance wanted to increase consumer loans during the slow period of January and February. Twenty-three divisions introduced prizes to be won by their 1,300 branches and 7,500 employees. The theme was Aloha 500—The Race to Hawaii. Branch managers could win the trip. Employees could win 27" TVs and other prizes. Sunglasses were sent out midway in the campaign. Weekly communications were designed to add excitement. The campaign produced big results.

> **You Get What You Reward**
>
> Some professional firms don't want to reward people for bringing in business—so, many people don't bother. And the "rainmakers" often leave to start their own firms. They will make more money elsewhere if they aren't appreciated where they are.

Sales Contest Reward . . .

If you use in-house salespeople, a long-time contest prize is the "money cage." Companies even sell these. It's a box or bag that you can enter. A blower blows dollar bills around you and you have 30 seconds to grab all you can. It's crass, but people love it. If your cage is big enough, invite spouses in too. Friday at 5 P.M. is a good time, and salespeople have to make a sale after 3 P.M. to be eligible. That keeps people working up to the bell! (They also have less outside competition, since most salespeople knock off early on Fridays.)

Creative Sales Competition . . .

The Colvin sales team uses a clothes (as in clothing) "clothes the sale" theme pun every year. Each salesperson voluntarily submits monthly sales goals for the year. Each month, if you achieve your goal, you win an article of clothing that makes up a complete outfit. At the year-end sales meeting/party, the entire sales force appears on stage in however many (or few) clothes they've won that year. Participants get money orders for top-quality stores. Ninety-nine percent participate, and it's fun because everyone is working against his or her own goals, not each other.

Find Resellers for Yourself . . .

One creative printer sold to multilevel marketing companies. The printer helped customers develop catalogs to sell business cards, stationery, and marketing materials to their many independent salespeople and became the preferred supplier. In some cases, the printer became an OEM. (This means that the company's service is sold under the other company's name.)

Perhaps you have some services that could be represented by others to their markets. It can be done as a partnership with them endorsing you, or under their names.

Following Up Leads . . .

Many companies could double their profits if they actually used the leads they had. Study after study shows that trade show and advertising leads are not followed up properly—if at all! For instance, Performark, in one study of 10,000 advertising inquiries, found that 22 percent never received the information they requested. Forty-five percent received the information more than 65 days after their request; for 12 percent, it took 120 days to receive their

Building a Sales Culture

Most bankers hate to sell. NorWest is an exception. They give branch banks responsibility—and authority—for performance goals. They measure sales from each banker and reward tellers for referrals.

information. And 87 percent were never contacted by a sales representative.

Frustrated by Customers? . . .

In another study, women in sales reported that customers were their main source of work satisfaction. Men in sales reported that customers were their main source of frustration! While it's clear that customers can be both, you'll want salespeople who look at customers as a source of satisfaction and as fun to meet.

Marathon Sales Push . . .

The Westin Bonaventure in Los Angeles changed management at the end of 1995. The company brought in its top salespeople from its hotels all over the country to reintroduce the hotel to L.A. in a "marathon" event. They had special T-shirts, prizes, and lots of hoopla. It was fun for the visiting sales pros, it reached tons of local prospects, and it kicked off the "new" hotel in a big way.

> **More Contest Success**
>
> Professionals managing different offices of a large firm competed to produce new business. Prizes were given to everyone who performed. Quarterly results were up 34 percent.

Getting Salespeople's Attention . . .

If you have sales representatives selling for you, you need to get their attention and motivate them. There is a clutter of marketing to your customers, *and* to your sales reps. IBM used a mail piece featuring the cartoon character Dilbert to successfully get reps' attention.

Ongoing Sales Training . . .

If you have a big sales force in the field, they are not thrilled to receive reams of paper from your head office. Among other companies, FedEx has distributed quarterly multimedia disks explaining new programs to salespeople who can then view them on their computers. One user found a 29 percent increase in revenues per sales rep the first time the CD-ROM program was used. Multimedia has pizzazz, but audiotapes and videotapes have also been used successfully.

Pay Salespeople More Often . . .

If you have a sales force, it helps to pay them more often. For instance, every Friday at 5 P.M. will be more often than most other companies and will keep them at work until 5. If you have salespeople in close proximity, such as telemarketers, ringing a bell and paying somebody a bonus immediately upon making a big sale helps even more. It's one of the old rules of reinforcement: The more immediate the reward, the more effective it is.

Instant Sales Recognition . . .

Kathleen Christensen is the sales manager at a large health club. She understands the laws of reinforcement. She makes a point of giving employees instant recognition when they make a big sale. If they sell a two-year membership, she'll try to give them a gift certificate on the spot. They also have long-term incentives, but the immediate reinforcement has a big effect.

Sales Training Quiz . . .

Do you need to train a large sales force about new services? Every time Motorola releases a new product, it offers prizes for its salespeople to learn the product well. After sending out the information with the features and background on the product, the company offers a bonus if the salespeople call an 800 number and correctly answer seven out of ten questions. The questions are run by an independent firm and randomly generated on the computer. There are no penalties for wrong answers, so salespeople can keep trying until they win the bonus.

If you don't test people, you can't guarantee that they are learning what you want them to learn.

Traits of Successful Salespeople

Success traits include liking to win, enjoying what you do, believing in what you sell, and getting along with people. But behavior and sales numbers are the most objective way to judge ability.

— Number of letters sent
— Number of sales calls this week
— Number of presentations
— Number of sales

Optimists Make Sales . . .

Dr. Martin Seligman wrote the book *Learned Optimism.* An insurance company did a test. It took failed candidates who were high in optimism and accepted them based on Dr. Seligman's methods. The high optimists outperformed people who had been selected by the major tools developed over the years. You can train skills, but not attitude.

More on Selecting Salespeople . . .

If you're looking for the "holy grail" of selecting salespeople, here's a simple one. They can't build relationships and get business if they don't make calls! It's obvious, but many salespeople are reluctant to call strangers. Dudley and Goodson (*Earning What You're Worth? The Psychology of Sales Call Reluctance*) developed a paper-and-pencil test that predicts who will make calls. But the proof is in the actual behavior. You know when you make sales calls. Measure how much your sales staff does!

Sales Theme . . .

RMH Telemarketing Service Agency uses a movie and acting theme as a motivator. They award "Oscars," script performances, produce shows, and so on. Having a novel and fun theme enables them to motivate employees, as well as attract business. They credit their employee relations program with driving growth of more than 50 percent a year.

If You're Your Own Salesperson

If you're a one-person business and hate to sell, trade off with a friend in setting appointments for each other! It's much easier to call for others than for yourself. If you find the right buddy, this could be your marketing program.

Sales Presentation Training . . .

One of Ken Wax's training exercises is to give people a night to prepare a sales presentation with no literature, that lasts at least 15 minutes. They are not allowed to assume any details about the specifics of the prospect company's situation. They are encouraged to create visual aids on the spot.

His reasoning: if they can't handle this kind of presentation, it means that they don't have a good grasp of the benefits you offer.

Sometimes Others Can Sell You . . .

Most service providers want someone else to do their marketing for them. Westcon Services sells customer service training. A big part of its sales force is made up of independent computer consultants who sell for Westcon to their customers. Rather than commissions, the sellers get free training courses, plus status gifts from The Sharper Image catalog.

Virtual Team Support . . .

Access Graphics is a distributor that sells sophisticated systems through computer consultants (VARs). In order to help its partners sell bigger jobs, the company put together a team of consultants' consultants who will help any Access consultant handle the bigger deals. They work at volume rates, so they're cheaper than experts the consultants could hire on their own. Access has already let some consultants go after deals that the company wouldn't have tried for otherwise.

Systematically Working Leads . . .

Vanguard Technology has a system for pitching prospects up to three times before giving up. Normally, I recommend even more contacts over more time, but their system works for them. Their first call does a needs analysis on the phone. They ask prospects about how they manage their storage of data and whether they have an interest in a particular type of storage system. If prospects are interested, they are sent an information kit and are put in the file that triggers the next call.

On a second call, a systems engineer phones the prospect and discusses the prospect's needs in more detail. If the prospect still shows interest, but no willingness to make a commitment, the lead gets turned over to field salespeople who visit the prospect in person. Their deals range from $10,000 to half a million. Only if the field salesperson figures there is more potential would the lead be followed further.

Regular procedures encourage consistency. You can create a system that will work for you if *you* work it.

Reward Marketing Performance . . .

As this book shows, there are many different ways to market. An old principle of psychology is that you get what you reward. Too many businesses are structured to reward people based on seniority or technical skills, not for bringing in new business.

· · · ACTION AGENDA · · ·

"Behold the turtle. He makes progress
only when he sticks his neck out!"
—James Bryant Conant

If you manage a large sales force, one of the 22 ideas here can be worth hundreds of thousands of dollars to you. But it's up to you to stick your neck out and try something!

→ Ask your sales force for ideas to motivate them.

→ If salespeople are performing the way you want, reduce their paperwork.

→ Would tools such as laptops help your sales force? Most studies show they do.

→ Look for independent reps who might sell for you on commission only, or who can be paid for good referrals.

→ If you're a law firm, plumber, or other service business that doesn't have a sales-oriented culture, decide how to reward people for sales behaviors. When the rewards are there, they'll find the reasons!

→ Use a gift certificate or other small prize to immediately reward big sales.

→ Salespeople always want better—and more expensive—leads. Give the best new leads to the people who follow up the old leads best.

→ Develop a sales contest that everyone can win by improving performance.

11

Personal Mail

"The most successful people write personal notes regularly."

—Tom Peters

*T*he old-fashioned letter is almost gone. The thank-you note is hardly used. For people who like to correspond, E-mail has filled the void in many cases. Yet, personal notes and personalized mail are a very efficient—and effective—way to stay in touch. They have more impact with fewer words than a newsletter, because they are personal.

If you simply sent out three notes a day, that could be 1,000 contacts a year. Think what an impact that could have on your relationships with new and old acquaintances. In combination with deciding where to get new names, you could build an entire marketing program around this simple action.

The examples in this chapter are not all personal, but they all can make a personal impact for you.

+++

Thank-You Notes Work . . .

The owner of one auto repair shop makes a point of sending out at least two thank-you notes a day, and having three other staff members do the same. Forty notes a week add up fast to a more personal connection between you and your customers. And that generates the all-important repeat business.

Thank-You Card System . . .

The publication *Transport Topics* has set up a system for salespeople to automatically send thank-you cards each week to more than 250 advertisers in the trade publication. They simply log it in, fill out the thank-you note, add a personal message, and include a business card. It increases repeat business and strengthens the client-salesperson relationship.

> ### Written Magic
>
> "The difference in impact between verbally saying thank you and writing a personal thank you note is the difference between a lightning bug and lightning!"
> —Neil Simon, *Biloxi Blues*

Disaster Marketing . . .

There is a consultant for everything, including the after-effects of disasters, small and large. One disaster consultant sends a packet of information about consulting when asked, but always holds back at least one good piece to build in a follow-up for later. If you send people everything you have, they tend not to look at it. And it becomes awkward to send the same material later.

Personal Notes Pull . . .

Never underestimate the power of a personal invitation from the top. Frank Candy, president of the American Speakers Bureau, wrote 200 personal notes encouraging prospects to visit the ASB booth at a trade show. He used a greeting-type card. Thirty-seven prospects responded. The show generated sales worth 300 percent over previous years. "It was by far the most effective tool I've found in 15 years and hundreds of shows," says Candy.

Messenger Service Delivers . . .

The owner of Baron Messenger used to be able to walk from building to building handing out business cards. It worked, but he's far too busy now. His database keeps a record of every customer, the service used, plus where the delivery went. He now produces custom mailers when he runs a special—for instance, to people who've used his "911" emergency service when he's featuring it. He can also use the list of people who *received* deliveries as a prospect list!

A Personal Invitation . . .

Restaurants are a tough business. Here's a great opening letter that Murray Raphael sent to executives in the area around a new restaurant. The headline at the top of the letter is "Whoever said that there is no such thing as a free lunch didn't know about this letter." The letter then goes on to introduce the new restaurant, enclose a menu, and invite you to come in for a free lunch and be a charter member of its "Tasters Club." The letter was targeted to just 120 VIPs. The text flattered the recipients, saying that their names had been picked because they were prominent in the local area. The letter got about a 75 percent response rate. Half of the people who came in brought somebody with them. That probably paid for itself, plus exposed more people to the restaurant. And many became regular patrons.

A personal invitation like this will draw many people to many events. A phone call is even better.

Direct and Cute . . .

Here's a cute letter with personality that was effective for a carpenter/handyman. He sent it to lists you can purchase of new home buyers. After congratulations on your new home, he says, "In a shameless attempt to drum up new business, I thought I would take this opportunity to mail this letter to your new address." Then he goes on to explain his services.

Fax Cartoons . . .

Don West, a title insurance salesman, keeps a file of cartoons, illustrations, and other eye-catching items. If he wants to get the attention of existing clients, he simply sends a copy through the fax,

---

Use Waiting Time

Jay Conrad Levinson, author of many *Guerrilla Marketing* books, points out that you can convert wasted time to productive time by carrying notepaper with you and writing personal notes while you're waiting. He says, "You'll soon know that it was incredibly valuable time."

along with his note. He might also change the punch line or insert wording to personalize it. For instance, he has one cartoon of someone on a desert island with the word "HELP" in the sand. When he needs to get more material from the client to close a file, he might put a note that says, "Don't leave me stranded—I really need the information."

Paying for Attention . . .

One job applicant to a high-visibility employer got the standard-rejection form letter back, as did hundreds of others. He attached a check for $50 to the rejection letter and sent it back with a note that said, "I'd pay anything to work for _____. May I have an appointment to talk about it?" This got him the appointment, his check back, and a trial job. It was a nervy approach, but he had nothing to lose.

You could use the same idea to get a sales interview. You will certainly get people's attention by sending them a check, as long as it wouldn't be looked at as bribery to a specific individual.

Nostalgic Mailing . . .

Banks can tell from public documents what your interest rate is on your home loan. When their rates are lower, they solicit you for a refinance. The best one I got was a postcard from Great Western with an old-fashioned picture of one kid standing on the back of another to see through a knothole in the ballpark fence. The caption was, "Find out how much money you can save every month."

"Wish You Were Here" Cards . . .

Whenever you're on a trip, send postcards to clients. Frank Varone sends at least five and tells them that he "heard of

Cleverness Gets Attention

A customer wasn't responding, so the sales rep sent a puppy puppet with a note in its mouth that said, "I don't mean to hound you," "I hope you don't have a bone to pick with me," and other cute plays on words. The customer loved it and signed a new contract.

a great idea" and will call them when he returns. It sets up appointment leads while you vacation so you hit the ground running when you get back.

Steal This Idea . . .

My favorite postcard is one I received from Don Shapland. Out of the blue, I got a handwritten card from Yosemite National Park, using wording very similar to an example in my *Marketing Your Services* book: "Wish you were here . . . and you could be if you use our services," and so on. Sure enough, he *had* gotten the idea from my book. He handwrote 500 cards and sent them to the Yosemite postmaster to mail for him. He never had to leave home. He followed up with phone calls. Low cost for high impact.

Send Work Samples . . .

Photographer Lonny Kalfus hates to use the phone, so he sends a couple of new work samples every six weeks to his 150-name mailing list. They're all hand-selected as people he'd like to work with. He sends an unusually shaped package for memorability. Once a year when his assistant calls people to check the mailing list, work is often generated just because of the contact. He should get comfortable calling more often!

> **Writing Tip**
>
> When writing a note, try to picture the person in your mind. Then imagine a conversation with him or her, and write the way you would speak.

Congratulations Pays . . .

Lots of businesses send occasional letters of congratulations. Doing it systematically and offering something free in addition to congratulations can elevate your efforts above the rest. Canyon Cafes spends 45 minutes a day to find the names and addresses of workers who've been promoted in local papers. They mail about 30 letters offering congratulations and free wine to celebrate at two of their restaurants. Owner Jack Baum figures the program, which cost him $1,625, generated a 29 percent response, and extra revenues of $106,177. I'd say he's underestimating his costs, even not counting time. He counts on an average of three new visits per customer, which may be optimistic. But the program still looks great, especially if you get repeat business. Southwest Airlines employees responded so well that he bartered dinner passes in exchange for tickets to use in promotions for employees and customers, thus getting further "mileage" out of his program.

Rolodex Mailings . . .

Even though most people are computerized now, one salesperson noticed that customers still have Rolodexes on their desks. So, he sends out his business cards on a precut Rolodex card. It gets him in the right files.

Use Their Business Cards . . .

Caset Associates uses this small attention-getter that anyone could. Take your prospect's business card and blow it up on your copy machine, then trim it and use the back of it for thank-you and follow-up notes to that customer. You can also use a blown-up version of it to have notepads made, or to have it laminated, as a bookmark, or even a mouse pad. People like their own names, and this is novel enough that it will get their attention.

Mailing Series for Appointments . . .

Brian Jeffrey sells sales training. He uses a four-letter series mailed about three days apart to get appointments. Each letter has something of value enclosed, such as a sales hiring test, a profile of top performers, and a newsletter. The last letter sells recipients on taking his call and offers a special report on improving sales productivity. Prospects have to set an appointment to get it.

· · · ACTION AGENDA · · ·

"Luck is preparation meeting
opportunity."
—Thomas Edison

You can make your own luck in business by taking action. If you hate the idea of putting yourself forward, you may think that lots of the marketing ideas discussed in this book feel like artificial techniques. But you can find ideas for personal notes among these 17 that could not offend anyone. You do need to take the action, however!

→ Are you overdue writing a note to anyone? Would Mom like to hear from you?

→ Start with your customers and past customers and build a regular program of dropping them notes and other items of interest.

→ Have note cards and stamps prepared so you can dash off a note while you're thinking of it. Keep them in your car to use waiting time constructively.

Here are some reasons to write people notes:
→ to follow up a visit or phone call
→ to apologize
→ for an anniversary
→ on holidays
→ to offer welcome after a first purchase
→ to let them know about a change
→ to congratulate them after they are promoted or honored
→ to comment when you see an item on them, their company, or their family in the newspaper

Here are some occasions to thank people:
→ after a contract is signed
→ for a referral
→ after a final refusal (for their time)!
→ after getting great service
→ for helping you
→ for being a customer, on their anniversary with you

12

You Too Can Be a Junk Mailer!

"By the year 2001, direct mail advertising is expected to produce $346 billion from consumers and $238 billion from businesses."
—Direct Marketing Association

*I*f your service lends itself to mass mailings, like insurance, bookkeeping, dental care, taxes, or lawn maintenance, then you may be able to utilize this "sales agent in print."

Most people throw away a fortune in junk mail every day. You can obtain a good education in mass-mailing techniques just by opening and reading your junk mail. Look for the repeats that come over time. They're winners. *Reader's Digest* has probably tested 100 different letters to sell subscriptions over the years. And they can pay as much as $15,000 to have a letter written. When you're mailing millions of "pieces" every year, increasing response by a small fraction can be worth lots of money over the life of the customers.

+++

Flatter Prospects . . .

Small businesses seldom like their own banks. For good reason—they are usually neglected and have to play by

129

bank paperwork rules. Now local banks face big competition. Wells Fargo and others are doing mailings nationwide preapproving businesses for credit lines.

Clients will often pay more interest for the convenience and flattery of being solicited. If you make it easy for customers, they'll pay for your service too.

Hospital Fertilizes, Then Reaps . . .

Women's Hospital in Evanston, Illinois, has seen an 8 percent drop in births locally. But its deliveries are up 5 percent, its obstetrical calls are up 40 percent, and enrollment in childbirth preparation classes is up 53 percent. Here's how the hospital did it: It started with a blind mailing asking women in the area about their pregnancy plans; the mailing generated a 44 percent response. For the 3,500 who planned to get pregnant soon, the hospital sent more information, such as invitations to seminars, newsletters, and book offers. It's now positioned as the hospital most interested in helping new mothers. To start from simple lists of residents is tough. But the strategy of focusing in from a general group is widely applicable.

If you're a gardener, house painter, tax service, or the like, a general group may work. If you're more specialized, you need to start with a better list.

If You Knew Then What You Know Now . . .

Here's a letter from a realty company that could be used by any firm selling investments that have gone up in value over the last few years. The letter starts off, "Just suppose . . . that five years ago you had bought some well located land. Think about how different your life could be today . . . !" Then you go on to tell the benefits of owning the land, gold, stock, or other item. This letter then focuses on the location aspect and emphasizes that the services of a smart broker are going to be valuable to choose the right investment.

If you're doing a version of this letter, how about adding the old Chinese saying somewhere, "The best time to plant a tree was 20 years ago. The second best time is today"?

Classic Sales Letter . . .

This opening was used by *Newsweek* magazine for many years. "If the list upon which I found your name is any indication, this is not the first—nor will it be the last—subscription letter you'll receive. Quite frankly, your education and income set you apart from the general population and make you a highly rated prospect for everything from magazines to mutual funds." This approach both is flattering and tells people why they got the letter. For instance, a financial planner might say, "If the list that I found your name on is any indication, you understand the value of financial planning." This tells people that you've targeted them for a particular reason, and it tells them the benefit that they might receive right up front.

> ### Classic Headlines
> A mass sales letter can have a headline at the top, as well as on the outside envelope. Key words to try include "Free," "Secrets," "Revealed," "Magic," and "How to . . ."
>
> NEW!
> FREE!

Don't think this approach is limited. A handyman could use it to say, "If your address is any indication, then your house is a classic worth preserving." A dry cleaner could suggest that with the prospect's occupation, he or she has a wardrobe worth taking care of, and so on.

Follow-Up Mailings . . .

Champion Printing Company used this envelope that would be appropriate for any follow-up letter. The envelope said, "You asked for it. Here it is for the second time." It included a picture of time running out in an hourglass. The letter started, "Did you miss it the first time? It's just possible you may have been too busy or put off responding for some other reason. You requested _____ . We sent it. Here's another _____ , just in case it somehow went astray." Then there's a brief restatement of the benefits.

Selling Planning . . .

Bache Financial Planning sent a letter that could be used by anyone selling preparation or planning for business consumers. The letter started, "How would you rate a general who rushed into battle without a plan? A general who squandered blood, sweat, and tears, without a blueprint?" Then it went on to say, "You fight a tough battle every day, trying to preserve your financial nest egg, your home, those you love, etc." I think the second sentence could be improved a great deal by saying, "A general who squandered troops without concern for the lives involved?" Of course, you'd proceed to actually sell your planning services, or point out the benefits consumers will derive from your longer-term, more carefully considered approach.

A Standard Direct Mail Package

A normal successful bulk-mail package includes:

- "Teaser" copy on the #10 envelope (like a headline)
- An opening to the letter that gets to the benefit quickly
- A long letter with lots of details
- A P.S. that restates the proposition (this is often read first)
- Multiple items in the envelope
- A clear, simple way to act now
- A strong guarantee

Send Expert Guidance . . .

Mosinee Insurance sent out a free "Backache Prevention Guide" to business-owner clients. It reminded them that back injuries are the major reason for workers' comp claims and gave them tips on avoiding problems. Customers asked for more copies, and now Mosinee is sending the guides to prospects.

Contacting New Businesses . . .

New business owners often have to file a fictitious name statement, or dba (for "doing business as"), and/or register with agencies. Mailing lists with these names are available. Many bookkeepers, accountants, business consultants, lawyers, and others who can help new business owners call them or write them letters. One accountant made his offer attractive by including a free tax organizer for every free get-acquainted appointment and coupons for two free lunches for everyone who actually became a client.

Databases Create Direct Mail Success . . .

Capital One Financial Corp. was created by successfully soliciting people with credit card balances to switch to their lower-rate cards. They increased their balances sevenfold in six years. They are continuously improving their statistical model of whom to mail to. They have also brought in lots of money for high-interest CDs. The basic rule of this "database" marketing is to get as much information as you can and then test the influence of the variables on your responses.

> **Customized Mail**
>
> As companies improve their databases, they'll be able to deliver automatic mailings customized for specific groups of respondents. For instance, a bank could send offers of credit when the customer might need them: when moving, at the birth of a child, or after an overdraft.

Handling Bulk-Mail Problems . . .

The post office has lots of regulations. For instance, they rejected one 60,000-piece mailing for Club Med because it was marked "Bulk Rate" instead of "Bulk Mail." The ad agency that made the mistake asked for a special waiver so that they wouldn't have to cover the cost of tearing open the envelopes, reprinting new envelopes, restuffing the mailing, and telling the client they made the mistake. The Direct Marketing Association recommended that they whine a lot. They did, and the post office eventually let them have a waiver.

If you're doing mail in any quantity, get to know your local postmaster, and get to know the local processing center. Not only can they steer you right in the first place, but they also will usually cooperate to help you work problems out.

Less Selective Mailings . . .

Union Bank used its home-banking product to attract new customers. It preferred a broad mailing sent to new computer and software buyers because it didn't have time to select subgroups from the list. Frank Han said, "If I send out a mailing of 75,000 and only get a 5 percent response, I'm still better off than whittling the list down to 5,000 people and getting a 30 percent response." They also give referral fees to branch employees who sign customers up for home banking.

Loans by Mail . . .

Signet Banking Corp. is transforming itself into a national finance company through direct mail. This way it's not limited to results from its 250 branch neighborhoods. The centerpiece of the program is to send out checks by mail to prescreened people, selected based on information from databases. The checks become loans when cashed.

Hand Addressing . . .

Fasprint sends out its solicitations in hand-addressed envelopes and points out that you opened it, so your customers will too. The company sells hand addressing among other services! It costs more but does get opened.

Newspaper Flyers . . .

Betty's organic food delivery service has found full-page flyers delivered to specific zip codes by the local newspaper to be more effective than ads in the same paper.

Mailing Produces 120 Percent Return! . . .

How can you send out 1,000 mailers and get a 120 percent response instead of the normal one-half percent? The Acapulco Mexican restaurant chain sent 20-percent-off coupons to local businesses to give to their employees. The individual businesses' names were on the coupons, so it looked as if they'd made an effort to get the discount for their staffs. Because each mailing could reach dozens of employees, the total response was more than 100 percent. This mailing was cold, but a dentist, financial planner, child care service, or the like could call big companies to try to make the connection a bit

> **Newspaper "Mailings"**
>
> In order to compete with direct mail, newspapers are inserting flyers and distributing special-edition papers to people who don't subscribe. This way, they too can deliver whole neighborhoods that you specify.

stronger. As long as you make the company look good at no cost to them, many will promote your discounts.

Mass Coupons . . .

Val-Pak is one of many companies that mass-mail coupons to every household in specified zip codes. If you see the same people advertising in your envelope every mailing, you know it's working for them. For instance, dental coupons offering inexpensive teeth cleanings and carpet cleaning are two of the many services that these packs work for. Dry cleaners, chiropractors, and upholsterers also do well. Usually, they will allow only one of each type in the pack, so you have an exclusive. Costs are low, about four cents per household in groups of 10,000. And you can control the neighborhoods that you mail to by choosing the zip codes.

New-Home-Owner Mailings . . .

Stacey Lapuk Interior Designs has rented new-home-owners lists for more than five years—about 30 names a week. They mail a letter, articles about their firm, and testimonials. This nets them several clients a year. With a free introductory analysis or seminar offer, they could do even better.

Selling Exclusivity . . .

A classic example of reverse selling is the American Express card. They start their letter with, "Quite frankly, the American Express card is not for everyone. And not everyone who applies for card membership is approved." When you combine this with building up the benefits, you create a certain amount of snob appeal that can be very effective with an upscale or wanna-be upscale audience. The Marine Corps uses a similar appeal with its small, elite fighting force approach. The more you screen clients at the front end, the better the quality of customers you'll end up with.

Second Letters Pull . . .

In the days of carbon paper, you followed up your original letter with a carbon of it and a note saying, "Here's a copy of the letter I sent you a couple of weeks ago. You may have misplaced it. Now is the time to act," etc. Traditional experience said that this would pull about 80 percent of the response generated by the first letter. One such letter for Home Security Services generated a 1.3 percent response in the first mailing, and a 7 percent response in the second mailing! They used a two-week interval. Something like home security may take a little time to think about. Once you've sensitized people to the issue, they may begin to see more news about robberies in the daily paper, which will push them to act.

> ## Keep Mailing
>
> When lists work for you, don't stop mailing. For your best lists, keep mailing to them regularly until the response drops to the point where you can't afford to mail. Then after you "rest" them, try again.

Second One Free . . .

Free still works wonders in an offer. Direct mail guru Bob Stone is among others who've tested different offers like this: (1) Buy one year of service for $99, get the second year for $10; (2) Buy two years, get 50 percent off; (3) Buy one year, get the second year free. The actual price on all offers was $109 for two years, but the "free" offer—#3—pulled 40 percent better.

Selling Memberships with Envelope Copy . . .

The American Association of Individual Investors has been successful from the beginning as a nonprofit educational group. In one mailing, the association found that having the copy on the outside of the envelope in a larger type size increased response equivalent to $192,000 for the year. The group thinks its older target audience found the format easier to read. But the larger size may have attracted extra attention from everyone.

Tease Them . . .

Sales consultant and author Jeffrey Gitomer teases people with his enclosures. After he finds prospects who want more information, he'll:

- Fax them half of an article of interest, making them call for the other half.
- Send a letter that says something is enclosed, and then not enclose it.
- Fax a joke four days in a row, getting them to miss it and ask for it on the fifth day.
- Fax a question on Monday and answer it on Tuesday; do the same thing on Wednesday and Thursday; and then fax a question on Friday but not answer it.

He builds awareness and then relationships.

Simple Direct Mail Works . . .

One dentist had to commute hours to work for another practice two days a week for two years because he didn't get enough patients, even in an area with little competition. He said they don't exactly teach you how to do marketing in dental school. Most of the patients who did come in told him they hadn't even known he was there. After he started using a basic direct mail campaign, sending out letters introducing himself to people in the area, and so on, his practice more than tripled and he quit commuting.

Test Envelopes . . .

If you're doing lots of direct mail, you know that the envelope can make a big difference in getting your material opened. In one test, the difference between a printed message on the front of the envelope trying to interest people, and a handwritten message reproduced with printing was 10 percent in favor of the handwritten. That can add up to a lot of money when you're mailing by the millions, so it's worth testing.

> **Keep Testing**
>
> Your "control package" is the one you mail because it works for you. Once you have it, continue to test: test new lists, new envelopes, new headlines, new prices, new offers. You never know when you'll find a package that is twice as effective as the one that is now profitable.

SPRING MAILING RESULTS

Test #1 — 3.0%
Test #2 — 4.5%
Test #3 — 2.5%

··· ACTION AGENDA ···

"Many of life's failures are people who didn't realize how close they were to success when they gave up!"
—Thomas Edison

Doing mass mailings takes a lot of discipline. Fractions of a percent response can make a big difference in your profits. It is highly scientific. Companies that do it successfully keep careful track of every detail. The 24 examples in this chapter contain ideas that have generated millions in business. Why not see what they can do for you?

→ Check on the lists available to you. For national lists, Standard Rate and Data Service (SRDS) has most of them covered. For local lists, you'll have to be more creative. (But start with list brokers in your yellow pages.) The quality of the lists you mail to may be 10 times more important than exactly what you mail to them!

→ If you're writing your own sales letter, pick a classic to model such as some of those mentioned.

→ Set up a series of letters with enclosures that will help you get appointments.

→ Talk to companies that could give out discount coupons to their employees for you, thus leveraging your efforts.

→ Shop printing carefully. Costs can vary by 200 percent. Find specialists in mailing packages for best pricing.

→ Check whether a Val-Pak type of mailing would work for you.

→ Develop an information sheet you can offer free in your mailings.

13

More Unusual Mass Mailings

"A UPS delivery in a box will get through to any top executive."

—Stanley Marcus, of Neiman-Marcus

*B*ecause successful mailings can be worth so much, experts have come up with many creative approaches over the years. You'll find a lot of useful ideas here. And many of them can also be adapted to more personal mail. See if some of these could work for you.

+ + +

The "Wham" Letter . . .

Hershal Gordon Lewis, a famous copywriter, wrote a letter for a bank that started off, "Dear Homeowner" and then a large "Wham!!"—apparently handwritten—as the first word. The letter said, "That's the sound of a taxpayer hit between the eyes with the annual property tax bill." Then it went on to talk about loans and other kinds of assistance that the bank could provide. This letter could be adapted easily to be suitable for financial planners, accountants, bookkeepers, or lawyers. It could also be adapted for contractors pointing out the dangers of dry rot, or for exterminators, and so on.

Wanted Poster . . .

Creativity consultants, advertising copywriters, and other such professionals can have a lot more fun with promotional material than most of us. For instance, one copywriter produced a realistic-looking half-gallon milk carton with a headline on the side, "Have you seen this man?" His name, photo, and statistics were listed, along with a phone number to call if someone would like to meet with him. He could have also put a tag line on the carton that said something like, "For more ideas as fresh as this milk, contact . . . _____."

Striking Color Visual . . .

American Speedy Printing (good name for description and yellow pages listing order) mailed out a postcard solicitation with a zebra's picture printed in yellow and red. The heading was, "When you're used to seeing something in black and white, color can seem unnatural. Rather effective, isn't it?" Then they went on to sell their color capabilities. Altering colors could be an attention-getter for any advertising or mailing.

Attention-Getting Gifts . . .

For some businesspeople, a single account can be worth millions of dollars. When this is the case, there will be lots of other consultants, lawyers, and so on, trying to reach the decision makers. The West Coast trust division of a bank had been trying to bid on managing an investment portfolio for a doctors' group for years, but they couldn't get an appointment to make a presentation. They knew which doctors made the investment decisions for the group. So, they spent about $100 apiece on old-fashioned stopwatches and had them giftwrapped for each doctor. Then they hired a private detective to find their home addresses. Each gift was sent to the home, where it wouldn't be screened by an office manager. With it was a note, "Please time me with a stopwatch. I'd like to make a presentation. It will take less than five minutes and I won't take longer unless invited to say more." This dramatic gimmick paid off and the rep got the appointment.

File Yourself for Prospects . . .

The Institute for Business Technology is one of a few groups that send out their reference material with a labeled file folder. The Institute is the only one we've seen that sends it out with a regular file folder *in* a hanging file folder, so that you can handle it any way you prefer. Your material is more likely to be kept on file when it's "self-filing."

Put the End First . . .

Smithy Companies reversed its sales letter for the impatient. At the top, above the salutation, the letter said, "Would you like to enjoy _____ benefits? If so, call me at _____ . Cordially, _____ " (with a signature).

Then there was a P.S., "Just in case you're even busier than usual, I've given you the final summary of my letter first. If you have time, here's the rest." And then the normal letter started, "Dear _____." It gets attention for its novelty. It respects people's time. And it gives recipients a quick overview of what's happening.

3-D Mailing Shows Effects . . .

Allegiant Physician Services helps hospitals analyze (and cut) operating room costs. Its clever mailing using 3-D glasses won an award. When you put on the glasses, you could see costs listed in an operating room picture that weren't visible otherwise. And if administrators didn't know those breakdowns in

Novel Stamps

Many older postage stamps from the '50s are available from stamp dealers for about face value. To set your correspondence apart, you can either use lots of older stamps, or find one that has a theme related to your recipients' interests.

their hospitals, Allegiant showed them how to get them with its services. The mailing got a 10 percent-plus response when 1 percent is normally good.

Expensive Mailings . . .

The CIT industrial financing group used Harley-Davidson collectibles to get attention in an award-winning mailing. The targets were construction equipment manufacturers and dealers, so the Harley image fit. The first mailing sent free Harley sunglasses. The second sent driving gloves. And as a bribe for "taking a meeting" they offered a free Harley leather jacket! Of the 275 selected prospects, the response rate was a terrific 80 percent. While it was expensive, becoming the finance source for one dealer paid for the whole program. The rest was profit.

Show What You're Not . . .

A mailing by 3Com on computer communication wanted to emphasize speed. To make the point, it included a plastic slug with the caption "Once again, the competition is trailing behind."

This technique could be adapted anytime you want to emphasize your speed.

> **Lumpy Packages**
>
> An envelope with something lumpy in it will almost always get opened. Try a pencil, a key chain, or something tailored for your audience.
>
>

Wooden Cards . . .

One company that sells to construction companies cut two-by-fours into short lengths, stamped the company's name on them, and mailed them to 100 prospects with an invitation to a seminar. Thirty attended, two became customers, and the blocks of wood stayed on prospects' desks.

Any contractor could use this idea, or anyone selling to contractors.

Get Their Attention . . .

Convention and visitors bureaus are fighting for the attention of busy meeting planners just as you may be with your prospects. They are making their mailings more interesting than just dull background material on the city that planners might visit. They've used boxes of Cracker Jack with coupons inside, free weekend getaways, and contests for trips to major events such as the Kentucky Derby. The Providence, Rhode Island, Convention and Visitors Bureau sent brownies to 450 members of the International Association of Convention and Visitors Bureaus. The note inside said, "Score Brownie points at your next meeting. We'll call you next week with our recipes for success." Follow-up calls generated 21 serious leads and 60 prospects for meetings.

Picture It . . .

If you were selling indoor air quality, how would you make it "concrete." One trade publication soliciting advertising sent out a clear plastic cube with a person at a desk inside. When you shake it, you see "snowflakes" fly around. The campaign produced 6 percent more ad revenues than the prior year's campaign.

Ben Franklin Mailing . . .

The most novel mailing I've gotten in a long time was approximately the shape and size of a dollar bill, with the face of a hundred-dollar bill printed on one side of the light postcard stock. It had a 20-cent stamp, and on the backside said, "We have a great offer for you. You'll make one of these 'Ben Franklin's' every hour of the day. Call toll-free, 24-hours. If you're not interested, check your pulse for signs of life. Otherwise, leave your name and phone number and we'll get back to you." Postcards have to meet certain size criteria. This one seemed too narrow, but it came through. So, check your local post office and then consider trying it if your prospects would respond to the picture of a hundred-dollar bill.

Blatant Curiosity . . .

The biggest problem in sending out bulk mail is getting your envelope opened. If people decide it's junk from the outside, you'll never get a chance to make your pitch.

One saleswoman, who sells services to bars and restaurants, rubber-stamps a pair of lips in red on her envelopes to owners. She has a lot of luck getting appointments.

Another Rubber Stamp . . .

Ross Murphy, a direct mail consultant, rubber-stamps a picnic basket on the outside of his envelope. The picnic basket has the head and tail of a fish sticking out from under a checkered cloth. It has nothing to do with the mailing, but he thinks it makes people curious and more likely to open the envelope.

Brainteasers . . .

Jean Padula sent out a series of three brainteasers in direct mail pieces. They featured picture puzzles that asked people to find what was wrong with the illustration, or find the hidden picture. After each mailing, the company got lots of requests to quote on projects and many orders. Other people just called to find out the answer, which provided another contact. Padula happens to be in the printing business, but this could work for almost any business, where you make the teasers about your industry or service area. They add a fun, humorous image to the campaign.

> ### Don't Trick People
>
> Be careful about making people mad with misleading envelopes. For instance, Ross Murphy also recommends putting "Check enclosed" on the outside of an envelope, and then inside saying, "Thanks for *checking* the *enclosed*." I think this is bad policy. Since people think of direct mail as tricky in the first place, you don't want to come across this way.

Spreading the Light . . .

Most junk mail looks like just that— junk. Most marketers should send only smaller batches of more personal mail. MailAmerica sent a small tube. Inside was a return-address envelope and a sales letter, plus a very small candle! This raises your curiosity. Then they tie it together in the letter by saying they can shed "light" on your next mailing package. Their letter takes until page two to say, "we realize you are busy." You can do better by keeping it shorter, but the general idea is good. You may never use bulk mail, but in small batches, you can afford to make a big impression.

Empty Envelopes . . .

Getting attention in the mail is harder and harder. Insurance agent Don Howard mails an empty envelope and then follows up with a call. Prospects say there was nothing in the envelope. Don says that's why he called: What would happen if their paychecks stopped coming because of illness or injury?

Fake Express Mail . . .

One way to get your mail differentiated from the crowd of other junk is to use fake express envelopes. You can design your own, but one place that sells them is Golden State Envelopes (818/865-7940). Theirs is a half-size "Next Day Letter Express."

Fold Your Letters Differently . . .

Target Marketing magazine and Ted Kikoler spend a lot of time trying to figure out if one little detail on how you mail things can increase your response a tenth of a percent. That can be the difference between profit and loss on a million-piece mailing. *Target* likes what's called "the Z fold." The letter is folded accordion style, so that the top panel is the first thing that people see when they open the envelope. That means that you insert it into the envelope backwards, facing the back of the envelope where they will open it. This fold creates some problems in mechanically inserted mass mailings, so Kikoler suggests that you use a regular three-fold, but with the typed part of the letter out, rather than in.

> **Don't Be Slick**
>
> People appreciate clever items in the mail, but avoid being too slick. The ideal item is personal enough that they know you're not mailing it to everyone.

Give, Then Follow Up . . .

Chris Clark Epstein gives out Pez dispensers at her seminars and talks. That's memorable. Then three weeks later she follows up with a mailing that includes a Pez refill and further information on services. That's clever.

Mailing "Hogs" Attention . . .

In today's advertising clutter, you have to stand out. There are dozens of professional speakers for every one job. The same is true for consultants and many other services. That means buyers get overwhelmed by solicitations. When one meeting planner told Joe Bonura her desk was full of speakers' brochures but to send his anyway, he sent a big piggy bank with his brochure stuffed inside. He included a hammer with a note, "Inside is the secret to helping your members make more money in _____. Break me!" In a follow-up call, the secretary recognized him as "the pig guy," and he got the job. (P.S.: They couldn't bear to break the bank.)

Novel Envelope . . .

A translucent envelope with a clear label caught attention in one office (it looked something like wax paper). It had no return address, and you could just barely see a large "Hey!" through the envelope on the card inside. It happened to be from a computer service, but you could adapt it for anything.

Novel Packages . . .

Unusual packages get attention. A company called Message In The Bottle (815/877-4069) will sell you the same. (And their name follows another rule for good names—it describes what they do.) You could probably make your own message in a bottle and tie it to nautical or "help!" themes.

> **Sandwich Mailing**
>
> The Bank of New Zealand mailed a special box to students entering college. The pieces made up a fake sandwich with "meaty" offers "to guarantee you won't go hungry as a student."
>
>

Novelty Letters . . .

One of the all-time great series of funny letters was from a hotel, directed to CEOs. It started with an engraved letterhead from the "Office of the Chambermaid" and said, roughly, "I'm the chambermaid. I take care of the rooms here. We have great restaurants and other facilities, but the newly renovated rooms are the heart of the hotel." It ended with something about, "You can see that if they would spend the money engraving this stationery for me, they were happy to put millions into upgrading rooms for you. Please come and see for yourself."

The second letter in the series was from a vice president who said he normally wrote the letters but that in the interest of staff morale he had let the chambermaid write one. She'd gotten lots of response, which may make his job unnecessary, so he wanted to point out that they have other facilities. All she did was talk about the rooms, but they have meeting facilities, and so forth. Then the next letter, naturally, came from the chambermaid, who said that the vice president got so upset he almost fired her and that people were beginning to suggest that they change jobs. Then she went on to cover the other attractions.

The next letter was from the chambermaid again and said that the vice president was so successful that he got promoted and now she has to train a new vice president. And the last letter was from the vice president, who said that she was exaggerating, and while they appreciate her zeal, they would prefer that she stop writing letters. They enclosed cards for special visits, the nightclub, and so forth.

> **Reverse Sell**
>
> Here's the opening of a letter sent by a client company for its service provider: "If your lawyer remembers that YOU are hiring them, returns your calls immediately, meets all deadlines, knows your industry, happily answers any questions, keeps it simple, and never surprises you with their bill, THEN YOU CAN STOP READING HERE." Get one of your happy clients to send a letter like this for you, and you'll do well too.

Party Mail . . .

A service firm had a beach party in the middle of winter. To get even more attention, the invitation included a plastic bag of sand and miniature dark glasses, hot dogs, pop bottle, shells, beach umbrella, and palm tree. They got a 40 percent response rate and won an award for creative direct mail. Even people who didn't come remembered the invitation and passed the toys along to their kids.

Phone Gets Past Gatekeepers . . .

Getting through to some people is impossible unless you go all out. One woman wanted to get a big deal with

Subway Sandwiches. She sent a *telephone* with all the speed-dial numbers set for her number. She got the deal.

Pizza Delivery . . .

Viking Office Products sells products but really takes a service approach. One clever promotion the company used was to send a pizza box to prospects. The box said, "Get your office supplies nearly as fast as pizza . . . without the calories!" Inside were a few samples such as Liquid Paper and message forms. This approach combines value provided by their vendors with a clever campaign that gets opened and gets attention.

Telegrams Still Work . . .

Getting through the clutter of regular mail, E-mail, and voice mail is getting harder. Unless you scream, many people figure your message is not that important and put it in a pile they never get to. The old-fashioned telegram still works. Many people have never received one. Don't use phone delivery; send the cheaper one they deliver by mail that looks traditional. Be sure to have a clear, simple message asking for a simple response. It works when it's past time to trim their roses, send in tax documents, make a dental appointment, and for many other occasions.

Theme Mailing . . .

For travel agents, rental cars are a commodity, so their relationships with the car companies are based on service and making the agency look good with its clients. Budget Rental won an award for a mailing campaign that focused on its top agents. To stand out among the clutter, the company used a colorful "educational" theme (grades, report cards, etc.). The two main strengths were that Budget kept the program going to build stability and empowered agents to give unhappy customers *of other car companies* free Budget rentals. They also had the usual personal bribes for new business generation.

"Mousy" Cleverness . . .

Here's an idea for a clever series of letters that comes from an old set by Robert Silverman. The letters are typed in all lowercase letters and use no punctuation except periods and commas. The first letter started with, "i am s. mouse of _____ company and im the boss when the regular bosses leave at night im in charge." The mouse goes on to explain that he has the run of the office, and that the previous night he answered the phone and spoke with someone who wanted to place an order, but he forgot to get the caller's name and address, and now he feels like a "rat." He explains that he is sending this letter to everyone who might have called in the order, in hopes that they'll call again.

This first letter didn't get a great response, but it was followed by a second letter. In the second letter, the mouse explained, "im s. mouse and the reason i dont use capital letters is because im tired a man called this evening and asked why my letters look so terrible i said that if you tried standing on the shift key and stepping on another letter at the same time you'd skip capital letters too. Plus he kept getting thrown off the keyboard by the springback! The letter goes on in this vein and then says, "Please call during the day and buy something. The other bosses never 'mouse up.' When they take their orders they get them straight. And they can type letters better too."

If silly, creative letters like this fit your style, they not only get through to the boss, but often get copied and faxed around the country to give people a quick laugh.

· · · ACTION AGENDA · · ·

"The world makes way for the man who knows where he's going." [And women too]

—Ralph Waldo Emerson

Successful marketing takes more persistence than creativity. But there are some fun opportunities to be clever. If you know where you're going, among the 31 examples given here you'll find some you can use. How about these?

→ If you work with big accounts worth a lot of money, consider the really dramatic items that you could send. Many companies use watches with their own names on the dials. What about sending a watch with the prospect's name on it?

→ Can you start your sales letter at the end to get to the point and attract attention? How about hitting them between the eyes with a "WHAM!!"? Something in a box?

→ Would puzzles fit your image? Quizzes? Trivia? An empty envelope? Fake express mail? A telegram?

→ Can you get a client to write you a strong testimonial letter emphasizing how much better you are than other service providers they've worked with?

14

Using Newsletters Effectively

"Newsletters get you recognition, build your
image, provide specific reasons why prospects
should choose you, and should tell readers
how to take action."

—Elaine Floyd, *Marketing with Newsletters*

*N*ewsletters are an effective way to keep in touch with your audience while building your credibility. Newsletters can amount to a kind of sample of your services on the advice side.

Quarterly is the recommended interval for publication. However, monthly can be effective for some uses if you keep it short. Unfortunately, many companies put out a newsletter that is too technical and not reader-friendly. Or it is sloppy, does not reflect their unique character, and so on.

Sometimes newsletters do not create much response in the short term. Make an effort to include items in each newsletter that offer further information, such as a checklist. This stimulates calls and gives you a chance to talk with a few readers and gauge their interest.

In most cases, you'll give your newsletter away free. However, you can require information about prospects in return for the free subscriptions. And if your newsletter is a real success, like some of the cases mentioned here, it may even become a subscription- or advertising-supported profit center in itself.

+++

Long-Term Newsletter Results . . .

R. Bruce MacDougall, of Matz & Son Insurance, had tried to get through to a top exec at a high-tech company. No luck. Then, out of the blue, the exec called him because of an article in the company's newsletter which he'd been receiving. When a problem came up, the exec remembered Matz & Son. Newsletters build your image and remind people of what you can do for the long term.

> "Forget information overload. All people crave information and, even more, being 'in the loop.'"
>
> —Tom Peters

Newsletter Style Idea . . .

Severson & Werson's newsletter on intellectual property (copyrights, trademarks, etc.) has good information. Many other professionals do decent newsletters as well. Newsletters build your expertise, remind prospects and clients of you, and so forth. But most legal letters look dull, and read that way too. Get help. Try making yours like *Forbes* magazine. *Forbes* has great editing and keeps most stories short!

Mail Before Phoning . . .

One professional uses his newsletter to warm up cold calls. He sends an issue every month or so to prospects he's never met who use services like his. After six months, he calls them. People feel as if they've known him for years and take his calls for appointments.

Keep Mailing . . .

Your mailings don't have to be fancy, just consistent. Blue Brick Design keeps regular postcards going out when the firm doesn't publish its newsletter. Of course, these can also be a work sample for the firm. When you remind people of your business, they also remember to give you referrals. Aacorn Graphic Design adds flyers, reprints of work, and articles of interest to the mailing mix to prospects and clients to stay "under their nose on a regular basis." Aacorn also tries for a clever, light air.

Group Marketing Newsletter . . .

The Business Marketing Notepad is an eight-page newsletter that's been coming out for years. It has good articles on direct mail. Lots of consultants do something like it, but the unusual feature is that this newsletter is a joint effort of half a dozen experts in different parts of the country. As they say in direct mail, it must work, or they wouldn't keep doing it.

When several of you each send the same newsletter to your clients, you all get cross-exposure. What sort of team would it make sense for you to work with?

"Stock" Newsletters . . .

CPA Dave Levinson buys a "stock" newsletter from another company. He selected it carefully to represent the quality he wanted. Mailing 350 quarterly, he keeps his name in front of people and has gained new clients, referrals, and add-on business.

> **Express Your Personality**
>
> The best newsletters express who you are. Write yours like a personal letter to your friends in order to build relationships over time. Include "irrelevant" personal asides. If people haven't met you, they should still feel that they know you from your newsletter.

Send Personal "Stuff" . . .

Don Dible, a speaker, provides this example. A professional in Rochester, New York, subscribes to 50 publications relevant to her clients. She has her secretary clip articles that would interest clients and prospects. She sends them out with a personal note that says, "I thought this might interest you. You need not reply." The note is written on her card which is double-width to leave room for the message. This is much more personal than a general newsletter. It's a great tool to let people know you're thinking about them, and a natural if you read a lot.

More on Personalizing Your Newsletter . . .

Bullet Graphic Center sends a monthly newsletter. That's for mass marketing. But the top 20 customers always receive a personal note and a clipping of an article from another newsletter or magazine. This creates a personal "newsletter" for each client, which is always better than mass marketing.

Newsletters by Fax . . .

Faxes often get more attention than letters. So, faxing a newsletter instead of mailing can make sense. The same can be true of E-mail for clients who are on-line. You can also fax unsolicited newsletters if you give people an easy way to get off your list. One accountant who specializes in retailers sends one-page faxes out about accounting for inventory during changes in the seasons. He also offers free phone consultations about the issue he features "only if you call this week." Nice touch. This adds a little urgency.

More on Fax Newsletters . . .

One professional services outfit publishes a weekly fax newsletter to 4,000 people. It features tips that are updated every week. The newsletter produces 10 sales leads a month, and people call to add their name to the subscription list. Using fax broadcast software makes it less expensive than print and easy to distribute.

Audio Sales Newsletter . . .

Want to rev up your sales force? Send them an audio newsletter they can listen to in their cars. The National Speakers Association uses an audio newsletter in addition to its regular magazine. It works for a big trucking firm with its drivers, as well as for many national sales-driven companies. The CEO can have a fireside chat about the state of the company. Even better, interview top sales producers every month to inspire others and recognize the top guns.

Send Your Newsletter to the Top . . .

After a lawyer got his newsletter going, he sent regular copies to state supreme court justices, big firms, and other stars. Many responded with notes and compliments. It raised his profile. Large firms approached him

for joint work. He could say that major judges were subscribers, and he even had an offer to purchase it.

Cooperative Marketing Magazine . . .

Harvey Simkovits is one of 15 speakers in Canada who
shared their lists of people who book speakers and created a glossy magazine to send them. They each write a
column and share costs. They even have 500 paid subscribers. They allow free reprinting, which gives them
further exposure. And their material is on-line.

Teamwork like this can give you a much bigger image
and marketing results. It also encourages mutual referrals within your team.

Getting Newsletters Done . . .

Emanuel Equipment provides assembly
services. They traced at least half a
dozen new customers to their quarterly
newsletter soon after they started sending it out. They had had trouble getting
around to doing a newsletter, so they
hired someone to produce it for them.
Another way to make it happen.

> ### Creating a Partnership
> A novel way to build a relation-
> ship with a bigger firm is
> offering to take responsibility
> for getting out a joint newsletter
> on the area you share. It builds
> your relationship and gets you
> associated with them in the
> recipients' minds. This tactic
> could be used, for instance,
> by an independent medical
> service provider wanting to
> connect to a health care group,
> or a small law firm connecting
> to a big firm.

Holiday Newsletters . . .

Sending Christmas cards for the holidays is trite and largely lost in the clutter. Far better to send Thanksgiving cards like Harvey
Mackay (*Swim with the Sharks* . . .) and others. One
young consultant sends out a newsletter at Christmas
suggesting that the tips included will "help you have an
even more prosperous" new year.

Newsletter Lag Time . . .

Federal Heating sends 30,000 copies of its newsletter
twice a year to prospects in its service area. Since both
central air conditioning and heating are expensive, the
company knows that it often takes several years to close
a sale from a lead. The newsletter reminds prospects of
their seasonal heating or cooling needs.

Newsletters Pay Off...

EvaluMed, medical services, sends its newsletter out religiously. The writers strive to make it helpful, which includes printing a schedule of when the service's doctors will be where. The company gets responses to every issue immediately, as well as helpful questions and feedback.

One-to-One Newsletters...

In the pharmacy area, more than 10 million newsletters have been customized for prescription drug users in the last year by one company alone. Book Pharmacy allows Health Resource Publishing to hook into its computer.

It can read prescription numbers and create a customized newsletter for each of the pharmacy's patients. The letter covers articles about the drug purchased as well as the medical condition the drug is used for, and includes ads for related products (which is how it is funded). The pharmacy can also customize aspects of the letter, such as including special coupons. The program is free to pharmacies, and customers see it as a personalized service for them. The front of each newsletter even has the name of the person for whom it was custom-printed. About 900 pharmacies, mostly from chains, are current users, but more will join in. Other industries could do this as well.

> **Small Newsletters**
>
> A newsletter doesn't have to be big. A number of professionals use postcard newsletters packed with 10–20 short tips, quotes, and jokes.
>
>

Selling Advertising...

Signal Graphics is able to produce a free newsletter for a local residential complex because one page of space is reserved to sell advertising. The company now makes about three times what it costs to produce the newsletter by selling ads. Signal also promotes its services in the space to the residents.

If you're an editor, a graphic designer, or a printer, using this approach can increase your business.

··· *ACTION AGENDA* ···

"If you think you can, or if you think
you can't—either way you're right."
—Henry Ford

If you've been wanting to do a newsletter, go for it! If your prospects get lots of newsletters, you know your competition. Make it your goal to stand out from the others. It shouldn't be hard to do something more creative, easier to read, or more entertaining. Be sure to include an offer for further information that will show you what recipients are interested in reading about.

Newsletter deadlines come around fast, but you can do a good one if you want to. One way to make it easier is to gather material regularly, so that deadlines find you with material to use. Another technique is to dictate items when you think of them. Editing is easier than writing for most of us. A third approach is to buy a stock newsletter and add personal inserts.

From the 19 items in this chapter, here are a few ideas to consider for your action plan:

→ Decide if you want to do a newsletter, and if you'll do it yourself or pay someone else. Look into the "stock" newsletters you can buy.

→ Can you start a newsletter as a one-page letter on your stationery?

→ Start gathering material you'd want to cover in a newsletter. You can always use it to write a stand-alone article instead. (See also Chapter 19.)

→ Who could you do a newsletter with?

→ Start collecting articles you can send to specific clients for a more personal "newsletter."

→ How about a fax update to clients and prospects?

→ How about a newsletter on your website? (See Chapter 21.)

→ Could you sell advertising in your newsletter to support it?

15

Low-Cost Guerrilla Ideas

"If you have a modest amount of money for
marketing, handle it with big ideas and low
cost, guerrilla tactics."
—Jay Conrad Levinson, *Guerrilla Marketing*

*G*uerrilla marketing, *street-smart marketing*, and *underdog marketing* are all terms that suggest substituting your brainpower for money to make your efforts more successful. Ideas that can be done at low or no cost are included in every chapter of this book. Here are more examples for you to consider, from postcards to window displays.

+++

Old Postcards . . .

Postcards have advantages because they're mailed first-class, they're inexpensive, and they get their message across without people having to open them. Here's a clever one from Storage Dimensions. It's that old picture (off copyright) that you see of a plane with five stacked wings trying to take off. They added, "Engineering says this baby can really fly." The card then says their approach is better designed!

Cool Postcard . . .

Jay Levinson is a big advocate of postcards. He liked one from Triple A that had a tasty picture of an ice-cream cone. It offered you a gift certificate at Baskin-Robbins for requesting an insurance quote.

I bet Baskin-Robbins would give them to you free just for the extra business they would generate when you took the kids in. For a summer theme mailing, anyone could use this idea.

Lower Postage Too

If you keep your postcards to the size limits, you spend about a third less on postage than with first-class mail. You're getting first-class delivery for about bulk prices.

Famous Mailings . . .

Resco Print Graphics in Wisconsin got a lot of mileage from a series of cards featuring famous people and quotes. They sent them out to 1,200 customers. The cards were popular enough that the company got calls from clients who wanted Resco to print a similar series for them.

Postcard Shotgun Marketing . . .

Here's a simple but effective realty postcard. The picture side has a graph of "Who Sells the Most Land in Marin?" which shows the firm highest by far in "sales per agent." (Choose the graph that makes you look best. Since there are only two people in this firm, they may specialize in this area but still not sell that much total!) The address side has an extra message hand-printed, "We have CA$H buyers looking for lots—Please call us to sell your land!" They covered every household in selected cities and found many lots that hadn't been listed for sale. This is a case in which a shotgun, mass-market approach can be useful. A dentist might do the same thing offering teeth cleanings, since everyone needs them and many more people skip them than have them.

Pretty Pictures . . .

You don't even have to mail them out to use postcards for marketing. Maxracks charges companies $3,500 a month to give away 50,000 postcards in racks around the country. People pick them up because they're free and colorful. If people actually mail them to others, you reach their friends too.

Postcards to Websites . . .

NYNEX phone service targets generation Xers with radical-looking postcards distributed in hot clubs or student newspapers. The postcards promote NYNEX's collect-calling service (used largely by the young) and direct people to its website. The site is full of "extreme" sport information, like jumping out of airplanes with a "surfboard" and so on. Popular with generation Xers because X marks the spot when you hit?!

> **Barter**
>
> You can often barter your services for marketing help on publicity, brochures, or sales training. This gives you a way to turn your unused time into productive marketing.

Promotional Mailings . . .

Ink Inc. sells printers direct mail programs they can use in their service areas to build business. Here are a few examples of the company's postcards to stimulate your thinking. One is a picture of a coffee cup that says, "We offer a special blend of quality copies and expert service." Another is an old photo that says, "If only old photos could talk . . . they'd tell you where to find the best copies in town." A third shows a jungle and says, "It's a jungle out there . . ." on one side and "But the path to our copy shop is clear!" on the other. In the jungle picture is an "explorer" wearing a shirt that says, "Which way to great copies?"

Marketing by Billing . . .

One dentist realized that a number of his patients were going to other dentists for services that they weren't aware he provided. In order to deal with this, he designed a custom billing statement which added a four-line message:

> Dr. _____ also provides a number of services, including (list the services—dentures, cosmetics, tooth whitening, and so forth).

This could also be done as a separate sheet included in your billing envelope. The initial response was an 8 percent increase in additional services purchased by patients.

Blowgun Marketing—Not a Pygmy Idea . . .

Ray Wilcox markets construction services in expensive neighborhoods. Typically, the houses are set back from the street and surrounded by gates. Many contractors and landscapers tape their cards to the mailboxes. Maids or butlers simply throw them away. Wilcox rolls his card into a tight cylinder and attaches it to the back of a hand-made paper dart. He slides the dart into a two-foot length of half-inch PVC pipe and uses it as a blowgun, sending his card as much as a hundred feet over the fence to the doorstep of the mansion. He gets lots of curious calls wondering how he got it through the fence. He says, "It is helping me develop a clientele base. It's not glamorous, but it works."

Inside-Out Mailing . . .

Glen Gardening took a novel approach on one mailing. They used an 8½″ × 11″ piece of paper with their name and logo on the left in the top third. They wrote a brief note on the other two-thirds. Then they folded the page into a self-mailer so that the type was on the *outside* rather than inside. Much as with postcards, readers don't really have to open this format. Put a label on the top third, and it's ready to go, and ready to read.

Ride-Along Mail . . .

Conventional wisdom is that selling more than one thing in a single letter leads to confusion and reduced response. However, a few companies are experimenting with mailing two companies' offers at the same time to reduce costs. The second offer is connected to the main offer, which may help avoid confusion. For instance, a mailing for car insurance includes a Tylenol package and says, "Get quick relief from car insurance headaches." Another combination is long-term health-care policies and Red Lobster discount coupons: for at least a year, these combined mailings have beaten control package response rates and also have reduced costs 10–15 percent from the ride-along paying its way. The free sample inside (mentioned on the envelope, or lumpy)

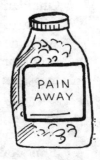

probably also increases the number of people who open the envelope in the first place.

Share Mailing Costs . . .

Many service businesses send out newsletters. If the cost of printing and distribution is holding you back from sending out more, consider selling brief ads or other listings in your newsletter, such as a resource directory, or include postcards or coupons for other vendors who want to reach your database. Oftentimes, these are enough to pay the entire costs of your mailing. You can also exchange plugs by trading your mailing for someone else's mailing to reach a new group of clients. Several insurance agents and others who send out magazines use this approach.

Trade Mailing Lists

A good mailing list of local buyers is a valuable asset. Once you build up a list of local prospects, you can often trade it with other people for their lists. This can be beneficial in groups as small as 25 people if 1 in 10 might buy your services.

Door-to-Door Persistence . . .

Mike Sabin couldn't find a job but knew how to paint houses. He picked an upscale suburb that had lots of homes that could use painting and knocked on 30 doors, 30 days in a row, six hours a day. Not one person would hire him because he had no references (being new in town). He pushed himself to make one more call, and he finally got a job. The "Smiths" said he could use their name as a reference all around town. His wife suggested sending them a dozen flowers, since they were his first customer ever. The next night one of the Smiths' friends called, and he got that job. For the next 30 years, he got jobs all over town. It can all start with just one.

Marketing Confetti . . .

Getting the word out about your services everywhere means everywhere, if it fits your image and you have the nerve. Joe Girard, a famous salesman, throws out bunches of his business cards after a touchdown at a football game. He figures if only one person picks it up and calls, it pays. And they already have their interest in sports in common.

A Roadside Solicitation . . .

Chris Westall decided that with his background in marketing, he should get out and market any way he could. For two hours on a busy downtown street, he put up his cardboard sign. Instead of saying, "I'll work for food," it said, "BS, Business Management, determined, results-oriented, six years of experience; please take a résumé." He then proceeded to pass out 250 résumés, one of which resulted in a call, a job interview, and a possible offer. It's a numbers game. You'll never use this extreme technique, but if you get out there, things happen. (And see the next item for someone who does use it!)

Create a Distinctive Image

You don't have to stand by the side of the road to get big attention. A distinctive image can take the place of a big marketing budget. Gateway 2000 uses a cow motif to emphasize its Midwest roots and stand out from the crowd.

"Will Work for Food" . . .

When Greg Taylor is short of work, he stands in front of the local hardware store with a sign that says, "Need Work Now. Pager Number _____." He wears a hard hat and carries a weed-whacker to make it clear what sort of work he's looking for. It's effective. He spends a lot more time working than he does standing with signs.

Living Signs . . .

Anytime you're willing to wear a funny costume and look silly enough, you can get some free publicity. (The media are so nice that way!) In southern California, real estate agents and developers are starting to hire people to do it for them. People in bright costumes hold signs by the side of the road to announce open houses or grand openings. One provider of "bodies" hires out-of-work actors and dancers who like to play to crowds at red lights.

For most nonprofessional services, this can work well. Simpler ideas include temporary signs alone, balloons, searchlights, and so forth.

Pick Up Old Phone Numbers . . .

An accountant picked up the phone number of a closed accounting office, with the permission of the prior number holder. Because the closed office had had a large yellow pages ad, the phone company wanted her to pay for the ad, but sharp bargaining got the cost down to a minimal level. The other person's ad brought in less business than her own regular yellow pages ad, but the cost was low, and she set herself up to own the phone number for the new phone book. In another case, a roofer picked up a retired roofer's number free, after the six-month waiting period, with similar good results.

Consulting Classified . . .

Here's a classified ad that focuses on the benefits. The headline is "Product Returns Solved." Advertising in a software newsletter, the consultants then lay out their services and explain why they are specialists in the distribution consulting area. Unfortunately, the ad gets a little long, saying things such as "help you better understand these problems," and "compare your situation to other producers." Those phrases are too generic and uninteresting. The ad should focus more on specifics like "generate substantial cash from these returns," or offer a performance guarantee. The free offer of a guide in this area, which it does include, almost gets lost.

Unique Envelopes

A British bookseller that mails to the U.S. types the opening of its letter on the *outside* of the envelope above your name. In America, you often see "teaser" copy to the left of the address, but this starts with "Dear Sirs" and goes across the envelope like a letter.

Distribute More Coupons . . .

Few people do this obvious one. Place coupons good for a free something or a big discount on your service at merchants near you. Gold's Gym uses a "free workout for you and a friend." They also place coupons away from the gyms by targeting stores that appeal to fitness buffs, such as bicycle shops and ski shops.

Local Shopping Exposure . . .

A dentist had an office across the street from a busy shopping center. He did his dry cleaning there and realized that many other people in the area did too. For $100 a month he got a hangtag message put on the hangers that the dry cleaner used. In the first month alone he got several responses. Business continued to build over time, as people were reminded by new hangtags and realized how close and convenient he was.

Lowest TV Media Rates Available . . .

Some small radio stations and cable systems will make tremendous deals, half their rate card or less, when the time would otherwise go unsold. But many deny it. Here's how to find out their real lowest rates. Legally, broadcasters are required to give politicians near election times the lowest rates they give anyone. Find that rate. Preparing your commercial to run on an "as-available" basis (only when the time would go unsold) also can get you big price breaks. On one small TV cable system, commercials were as little as $2 each, in batches of a hundred! (A rate of $10 to $100 is more average.)

Per-Inquiry Yellow Pages . . .

The R. R. Donnelly Corp. guarantees its yellow pages. The company charges only half of the ad cost for advertisers who aren't satisfied with the results. This policy helps to improve each customer's perceptions of the book's value.

> PER INQUIRY (PI): Paying for advertising based on the number of actual inquiries generated.
>
> PER ORDER (PO): Paying for advertising based on the number of actual paid orders generated.

For national advertisers, a number of publishers now have per-inquiry yellow page rates that require you to pay only for sales calls generated by your ad to a special 800 number. This is to encourage you to test advertising in more books.

More on Per-Inquiry . . .

In one survey, 11 percent of TV stations said they were willing to work with advertisers on a per-inquiry basis. Since many don't admit it, this means that you have a pretty good shot at arranging radio and TV commercials and pay only for responses generated.

Remaindered Yellow Pages . . .

Re/Max New England bought remaindered, odd-shaped yellow pages space in all hundred directories throughout their area. Most of the spot ads were outside of the realty category. They felt that the price was worth it nevertheless, and some of the ads fell into areas such as furniture and moving companies that related to real estate.

Low-Cost Brochures . . .

PaperDirect and many other companies sell preprinted material for brochures. For instance, an 8½″ × 11″ sheet will have four-color designs printed on it. You add your black text with your computer printer, and you have a color brochure. The trouble with these preprinted papers is that people may begin to recognize them if you use a common design. So, look for one that's not "in stock" at your local copy shop or office superstore.

Temporary Signs . . .

Some services have retail locations where signs or balloons can attract business. For instance, Discount Travel parks its car in front of its office with a sign on the trunk visible to a major flow of traffic.

Turning Want Ads into Business . . .

Bookkeepers, desktop publishers, and consultants have answered want ads in the paper to get work. Someone who advertises to hire an employee for the service you provide can be open to a consultant. Such people may not pay your going rate, but they'll often pay a flat fee for the work they need. And because you're better than someone they'd hire, you make more. It can be steady work to get started with.

Ambush Marketing Publicity . . .

Your cause is what you make it. Kodak was the official sponsor of the Olympics and paid big bucks for the privilege. Fuji practiced "ambush marketing" by buying billboards around Atlanta featuring track athletes from its much cheaper sponsorship of the Track and Field Association. Thus, Fuji gives the impression of being an Olympic sponsor. 30 Minute Photos service in Texas got publicity for themselves by asking for a boycott of Fuji for its tactics. Another PR opportunity exploited by all.

Neighborhood PR . . .

The Barry Insurance Agency has a sign in its window reminding people to donate used eyeglasses to the Lions Club. This is about the lowest-cost PR you could get. It helps the charity and makes the agency look good with passersby. And it builds goodwill with the Lions, who also need insurance.

Cold-Call Cross-Selling . . .

A Miami copy business distributes messenger service cards, and vice versa. When they cold call in any large building in Miami, they come away with two or three customers, just covering part of the building.

Guerrilla Flyers . . .

In the parking lot of a hotel hosting a business opportunity seminar, someone hit the windshields with a flyer saying, "Financial Freedom. Are you tired of working for someone else? Do you want a better life for you and your family? If the answer is YES, then here's an opportunity," etc. It was a multilevel company of some sort. But its cost to target 100+ expensively developed prospects was almost nothing compared with the

Posters

A poster is very low cost. Here are some ways to make them stand out:

- Use a big headline, about half the page.
- List benefits prominently.
- Direct people to call for more information.
- Attach slips that people can take away with your contact information and key message.

newspaper and TV ads by the seminar promoters to get people there!

Delivery Sales . . .

Quality Printing has its delivery driver give out a notepad, Rolodex card, and promotional piece shrink-wrapped together to businesses located on each side of the customer to whom the delivery is made. The driver also brings back business cards from these establishments for the salesperson. The driver receives $5 for every first order from these new customers. This simple approach has generated a lot of business. The salesperson gets about 20 leads a day this way, and his calls get a warmer reception because of the gift. There is also an implied referral involved, since the prospect's neighbor uses Quality's services. Any service like plumbing, pool, or gardening can use a similar approach successfully. Your gift item can be as simple as 10 Tips on How to Use _____ Service, Maintain Your Pool, Maintain Your Lawn, and so on.

Sharing Retail Spaces . . .

Many banks have set up small branches in supermarkets. Now Wells Fargo is leasing space in its banks to drugstores, with upscale coffee shops and copy centers on the horizon. Even if you're not into retail locations, you can place a small informational display, or your flyers, in many retail locations such as banks, dry cleaners, and restaurants.

> ### Underdog Marketing
>
> "An underdog stakes its reputation on such characteristics as innovation, remarkable customer service, best price or highest quality. It then communicates to its customers whichever is the strongest of these attributes."
>
> —Edmund Lawler,
> *Underdog Marketing*

Targeted Flyers . . .

One gardener developed a specific flyer offering to trim your roses. If you don't care about roses, the flyer would leave you cold, but if you do, it's dead on. It talked about avoiding fungus and disease, and proper timing for pruning. It could have been better laid out and more lively. It could also have scared you a bit by giving you a quiz about threats to your roses that would be hard to answer. This one was distributed by the newspaper but could also have been done door-to-door. Expensive ads can also be targeted to specific concerns of your prospects.

Cut Service Delivery Costs . . .

Practical Computer Solutions saves money on facilities and delivers better service by taking its custom software training to customers' sites. Similarly, the Microsoft Online Institute delivers training more cheaply on-line.

Donations for Visibility . . .

If you have the time, give services away to charities that are visible. Calfo/Aron, a design firm, gets both satisfaction and credits from work on annual reports, newsletters, and the like for nonprofit organizations. The printed credits expose them to corporations and patrons of the arts, add to their portfolio, and get them leads. Not all nonprofits try to help those who donate services. Select ones that will give you exposure and referrals by introducing the topic when you're negotiating how much to give.

TV Donations

If you donate a gift certificate for your services to the local public broadcasting station, you'll often get repeated exposure. Usually people who buy your certificate either won't cash it in or will buy more services to complete a bigger job. You win either way.

Employee Cards . . .

Many companies give all their employees their own business cards—but not enough. If you send work out—such as printing—the person who did the job can include his or her card. This builds relationships. And in social situations, when your employees tell others where they work, they can give people a card for more impact. Basic cards are cheap (as little as $10 per 500). If you can afford the expense, consider ones with employees' pictures for more personalization.

Ask for the Tough Ones . . .

One Prudential Insurance agent began his business with no client base in the New England area. He asked other agents to give him all of their problem cases. Some of these were late payers, some had unresolved claims, some were just plain difficult. Since he had no one else to work with, he started providing outstanding service and built a good practice.

Backroom Partnering . . .

There are more ways to partner with your competitors than the obvious marketing cooperation. The Bank of Nova Scotia and Canadian Imperial Bank of Commerce are staunch rivals, but they're combining their backroom operations to achieve efficiencies of scale. It will lower both their costs but not reduce their competition in the marketplace. Of course, if it works, it also makes a merger easy!

Barter for Clients . . .

A consultant bartered marketing expertise for a used computer system. She also helped her hairstylist with publicity in return for services. Barter not only cuts your costs, but also can get you a beginning client base who can then provide referrals and testimonials.

> **Client Reminders**
>
> Provide an extra-reminder service to get more ongoing business. Florists can remind customers of upcoming birthdays, anniversaries, and other special occasions. Mechanics can remind customers about oil changes and scheduled maintenance. What can you remind your clients about?

Long-Term Appointments . . .

Hall Hollister, of the Practice Builder Association, says that the rap on accountants has always been that they aren't proactive enough. One way to take the initiative with your clients is to preschedule key meetings. For an accountant: it might be a midyear review, an end-of-year checkup, and so forth. Scheduling appointments far in advance tends to lock the clients in to you. It also keeps your mind on servicing them so that they don't fall through the cracks. A user of this method reported a 21 percent increase in billings over the prior year from this practice alone.

Mock Advertising . . .

One firm was a small player in a field dominated by giants. They couldn't afford a magazine ad, but they decided that they could afford a four-color flyer. They designed it to look like a magazine ad, with other text printed in black on the back, as you would see on an ad reprint. The flyers were sent to customers and prospects. All salespeople handed them out as well. They made a good impression, and since the piece looked like an ad, people "remembered seeing them in trade magazines." It gave the firm the image of a big advertiser without all of the expense.

> ### Prove Yourself
> Sometimes you can sell a sample of your services at a very low cost. Devon Direct proved its worth to MCI by running a test mailing campaign. The campaign worked so well that MCI mailed 150 million pieces in the next two years.
>
>

Pay for Performance . . .

DialAmerica has broken ranks with other professional telemarketing firms that charge about $35 an hour. They charged Intuit (Quicken software) only for results. This "per-order" method puts you on the same side with your clients. Obviously not applicable everywhere, but a real competitive advantage if you can do it.

Sell Your New Marketing Material . . .

Express Press is so good at marketing, they developed another business to help other printers market by using their mailings. Accountants such as Chris Frederiksen have done the same with seminars and tapes for other accountants. Ideas, ads, and material you develop can be traded with people in other parts of the country, even if you don't have enough to sell regularly.

Send Your Cards Everywhere . . .

Randel Thompson of MicroTech reports getting several thousand dollars worth of business from simply including two business cards with everything he mails out. Speaker Tom Hopkins reports having received a similar response as a real estate agent when he put his card in every bill he paid!

Window Displays . . .

It's easy for printers like Hillcrest Copy to create window displays of work samples. For instance, they showed color Xerox copies of photos, including reductions of larger originals to strips of $1'' \times 1''$ copies. If you're a dry cleaner with a window, put articles about yourself, tips on how to care for silk, or pictures of customers of the month in your window—anything to attract the attention of passersby. If you have an office but no window, create a wall display of items that will attract people's interest while they wait.

Send Reminders for Repeat Business . . .

When car service stations put a sticker on your car door noting the mileage and the date your next oil change or checkup is due, it doesn't make much of an impact. But when that information is put on a transparent sticker on your front window, it is a constant reminder.

What can you do to help people and sell at the same time? Florists could remind their customers of secretaries' day, their mothers' birthdays, their anniversaries, etc. A realtor could remind you about heater maintenance checks. Offer something to all your customers to encourage repeat business.

Great Names . . .

A witty business name can attract attention. Here are two names that won a business magazine contest for wit and also describe what the businesses do: All Bugged Out is an exterminator service, and Great Impasta is an Italian Restaurant.

Multiple Billboards and Barter . . .

Cruises One is a huge agency that books $60 million in cruise-line business each year. They bartered cabin space for billboard ad space, where they featured a low-price cruise with an 800 number. In three weeks they counted $85,000 in incremental sales. Cruises One also uses an "aerial billboard," which flies over major events and advertises their toll-free number. At the Super Bowl it resulted in the sale of 47 cabins—people even called from their cellular phones in the stadium!

Help Your Competitors . . .

Gameday sells customized T-shirts as advertising items. The company went out of its way to help Hawk Specialties, a partial competitor, get started and make contacts. Gameday used Hawk as a subcontractor and couraged them to join a networking group at which they gained greater exposure. If you're small, talk to big competitors. Sometimes they'll mentor you. If you're a bigger company, developing smaller partners and sub-contractors can keep you in touch with new developments and help you get referrals to the bigger jobs.

· · · ACTION AGENDA · · ·

"To achieve, peak performers focus on
only a few things at a time."
—Eugene Garfield, *Peak Performers:
The New American Heros*

To get something new done on your marketing, what few ideas can you apply of the 51 discussed in this chapter?
How about:

→ Find or print an interesting postcard you can use for quick notes.
→ Can you do a postcard mailing to prospects?
→ Add a message to your bills mentioning other services you offer.
→ Look for people you can share or exchange mailings and mailing lists with.
→ Call all the listings in the yellow pages for your service to see which numbers are out of business that you might obtain.
→ In what local places of business could you put a flyer?

16

Brochures

"Of all those arts in which the wise excel,
Nature's chief masterpiece is writing well."
—John Sheffield, *Essay on Poetry*

Writing a great brochure isn't easy. A brochure can create an image for you: it can make you look big, expensive, clever, solid, zany, and so forth. Some companies have to have brochures. Some shouldn't invest the money. If you're in a visual business, such as architecture, in which people like to see before-and-after pictures, you probably need one. However, in many cases you may be able to use pictures and other printed material that is not in brochure form. A good rule of thumb is that if your competitors have brochures, or your prospects ask for one, you need one.

Many businesses don't need an actual brochure. Nevertheless, all services can use written material like that in a brochure. Make sure you have a backgrounder on yourself, testimonials, a client list, your philosophy, benefits you offer, articles you've written, and other material that demonstrates what you do.

Brochures can reassure prospects that you are established. They seldom will make the sale for you, however. They are useful to document information, and as a handy reference.

But too many brochures talk about the provider (features), and not about "customer benefits."

If you're going to invest in a brochure, make sure you can do a better job than your competitors. The examples here should give you some ideas.

✚ ✚ ✚

A Better Brochure . . .

The Wyoming Tourist Board made these changes in their brochure and got increased results. They flipped the orientation from 8½″ × 11″ to 11″ × 8½″ (sidewise, or "landscape"). This gave them wider pictures, made them stand out from competition, and made the brochure look more like a coffee table book. They also created eight special pockets inside that can have custom material inserted for different markets without reprinting the whole brochure.

> **Features versus Benefits**
>
> Features say what you do, but benefits say how you help people.
>
> Features = What's So
> Benefits = So What?

Use Your Cover . . .

Too many brochures waste their covers. Covers are like headlines that have to entice people into opening the piece. The Universal Triathlon Alliance's brochure originally had only a large logo with their name on the cover. When copywriter John Mora revised it, he added: "You Train Hard. You Race Hard. Why Not Join a Multi-Sport Organization That Works Hard for You?" By shrinking the logo, they created plenty of room for this concise benefits question that draws readers inside.

Sell to Their Worries . . .

Apex courier service put a dialogue—from the point of view of a secretary—on the cover of its brochure. It highlighted the point that Apex knew that secretaries would take the blame if a package was late. Many new customers said they identified with the situation portrayed as they signed up for service. Apex also made the brochure a keeper by including a rate chart on one page.

Can you include useful industry statistics in a brochure that recipients will want to keep?

Include Testimonials . . .

The most valuable element in a brochure is testimonials. The most common item that is missing in brochures I analyze is testimonials. For instance, Alan Corey Advertising has an elegant folder/brochure with four-color work samples, gold stamping, and so on. But they provide no testimonials, or even a client list.

Pictures of Your Work . . .

Hair By Rainbow in California paid $3,000 for a CD-ROM brochure with special effects. It covers their offerings from massage to aromatherapy. They mailed 3,000 discs out to local businesses which would have computers to play the disc. Instead of a 1 percent response for an "average" mailer, they got 7 percent quickly and a few more percent over time. They also played the disc in their shop window 24 hours a day to attract passersby.

Word Pictures

Many services can't be pictured easily. In that case, it's up to you to draw a word picture for people so they can "see" themselves hiring you.

Picture Your Results . . .

People need your help to picture the results you'll produce for them. Bel-Jean Printing has targeted color copying for realtors. They send a promo packet showing the same photo of a house for sale in black-and-white and in color. Color sells them. Reds Printing sent color-printed mouse pads out which kept their name in front of graphics people who produce the color originals that need copying. They were very well received. Even better are mouse pads customized for specific customers with tips on them, such as how to save Postscript files. Perfect Image Printing up-sells customers to color by pasting in color pictures on their brochures to demonstrate the difference.

Hairdressers have computers to show what new hair-styles would look like. Architects and contractors have CAD. What could you use?

Mail, Then Phone . . .

One way to warm up cold calls is to get attention with your mailing first. One big professional services firm had an impressive brochure. When it was mailed with a good letter, prospects called for appointments!

Fax Brochure Publicity . . .

Thomas Greber shows people how to construct fax brochures. Naturally, he has a fax brochure on creating fax brochures. He gets a reasonable amount of publicity just because of the novelty, and for using his own recommendations.

> **Collateral Material**
>
> What material can you collect (such as testimonials) or produce (such as tip sheets) that you can send out or leave with prospects? Start on it now, and you'll be further ahead.

Highlight Your "Leave-Behinds" . . .

When you're making in-person sales calls and you can't get by the secretary, you need to leave "stuff" (a technical marketing term!). Typical brochures often get tossed. One salesperson leaves a flyer and a one-page letter with yellow highlighting on relevant key phrases. She figures they get attention and she often gets through on the spot.

Your brochure and other "leave-behinds" are salespeople in print. Can you highlight them for each prospect to make them work better for you?

Your Sales Album . . .

A binder or album full of testimonials is a great tool for many service providers. You can do it better by including more. An architect could include before-and-after pictures of jobs. A consultant could include pictures of the factories where she's brought total quality changes. Pictures add variety and give people a reason for turning the pages. And don't forget tip sheets from you and publicity about you.

Computer Pictures . . .

One way to make a "brochure" stand out is by making the medium unusual. Direct Marketing Services in England created a multimedia presentation on a PC disk. Then they put it on a CD-ROM. It got a lot of publicity and created some immediate new business. As technology changes, there will be other approaches that will work, such as sending out custom Internet browsers.

Disk Brochures . . .

Big companies such as Ford have spent hundreds of thousands of dollars developing brochures on disk or CD-ROMs. Digital One Sheet produces 1,000 disks with your picture on the label. For about $2,000 they even write it for you. It's easier for the average person to look at the contents of a disk than a videotape. It's also more novel than a brochure. And it tends to be saved for that alone as well as the perceived value of the disk. It can also be copied and sent to others for extra exposure at no cost to you. Speakers and real estate agents are big users. (Digital's number is 303/850-9999.)

More Multimedia Brochures . . .

Island Hideaways is a rental agent for fancy Caribbean getaways. They started using a CD-ROM "brochure" and stood out from the competition's "mere" four-color printed brochures. People even pay for the disk, which covers production costs. Users get 2,500 pictures, 200 pages of information, plus maps and more. It's easy and fun for them to select a vacation spot.

Features versus Benefits . . .

Printers are probably the most guilty of promoting features when they give you a list of all of the equipment that they own, and send a few samples of their work—bore . . . ing! Classic Graphics breaks the mold on using printing samples by putting together a spiral-bound book with each page showing a type of service. Potential buyers can understand what they see better than they would by simply being told what different equipment can do for them. The company figures the piece costs $20 a copy, even doing it internally, but it increased sales 30 percent the year after it came out. If you can't show pictures or work samples, your testimonials and literature should paint word pictures of benefits, not features.

Display Folders . . .

Skyline Displays has a brochure with pockets. It includes lots of expensive bound-in pages with pictures of displays the company has done. The pockets allow the company to put personalized information in the front and back. Another novelty is a tab cut on the edge so that the brochure can be stuck sidewise in a file system with the Skyline name showing.

You can create custom brochures for each important prospect by gathering individual items (your picture, testimonials, backgrounder, etc.) in a nice folder with your label on it.

Benefits of Benefits

Everyone talks about emphasizing benefits, not features. But often you have to think it out further to get the right benefit to emphasize. Often the first benefit you think of provides another benefit that is the key one. For instance, hopefully your clients save or make money by hiring you. What they use the money for may be the real benefit they seek.

BENEFIT 1

BENEFIT 2

BENEFIT 3

Prefab Minifolders . . .

You can now buy preprinted brochure paper in various styles. One that is still novel is the size of a #10 business envelope. It has a pocket and a flap so you can insert sheets of paper with your brochure material on them. When things change, it's easy to change the inserts.

Video Brochures . . .

A well-done marketing video can increase memory retention by 50 percent over print ads and increase buying decisions by 72 percent, according to a study at the

Wharton School of Business. And they can cost less than a four-color printed brochure, depending on their length and complexity. Some things to include on a video are satisfied customer testimonials, a deadline for response, a reason for watching (such as a contest), and an 800 number. Add a response card and a trackable discount or other coupon. One user found a 30 percent increase in response. Tell people at the beginning that it's brief. A video shouldn't have to be longer than five or six minutes.

Video Nostalgia . . .

Brown University sent out a videotape loaded with nostalgic items about the school. It successfully increased donations from alumni.

Video Fundraising . . .

The Disabled American Veterans is one of hundreds of worthy causes that have to compete for donations. They decided that the next best thing to being there was to include a nine-minute video in a mailing to high-level executives at 900 major corporations to raise money for a sports clinic. The video showed what the clinic did and the benefits to the veterans. The mailing was preceded by promotional material and testimonials for the sports clinic. This campaign not only won awards but got 10 major new corporate sponsors and raised $280,000—almost twice the prior year's mark.

Standardized Services Offer Benefits . . .

Moore Graphic Services in Minneapolis created a software program that features brochure templates. Customers simply input their information, and they can get a custom brochure quickly and easily. Can you offer a standardized, limited-option service that will assist your customers?

··· *ACTION AGENDA* ···

"For all your days prepare,
And meet them all alike.
When you are the anvil bear,
When you are the hammer strike!"
—Edwin Markham

It's your choice whether you are acted upon by the marketplace or whether you take the initiative to strike. If any of the 20 examples here appeal to you, now is the time to take action.

→ Gather before-and-after pictures if they would be appropriate.

→ Collect more testimonials you can use.

→ Start a sales album to hold good material.

→ If you're going to do a printed brochure, find examples of others that you like. Look for color schemes, formats, and content.

→ Consider the preprinted paper for brochures if you can find designs that are not used by others. (Paper Direct at 800/272-7377 is one of many sources.)

→ Would a video brochure make sense for you?

→ How about an audiotape?

→ A computer disk?

17

Advertising

"Advertise, or the chances are the bankruptcy court will do it for you!"

—P. T. Barnum

"I know that half my advertising is wasted. The trouble is, I don't know which half."

—John Wanamaker, department store founder

*A*dvertising is defined as mass-media paid marketing. It is the most common form of marketing outreach that most people think about. It can also be the most dangerous if you don't know which "half" is working!

With advertising, you pay your money and take your chances. You seldom know how well it will work until *after* you've paid. And even then, many companies don't track their advertising's effectiveness. This makes it important to test ads inexpensively before you commit to major campaigns.

As mass marketing, advertising can be a great way to reach lots of people quickly and make a big impression. And advertising can be closely targeted by using specific trade magazines or other outlets with defined audiences. It can also be used as a direct-response medium by including coupons or

"800" numbers. Unfortunately, it seldom is used this way, so most companies never know how effective their ads are.

Warnings aside, there is some great creative advertising out there. And with the advertising clutter hitting people from every direction, you need to be memorable and attractive. Here are some ways to do it.

+ + +

Checking Advertising Effectiveness Early . . .

What's the quickest and cheapest way to test whether it makes sense to advertise in a particular place? Here's a tip from a clever couple, the Hoffmans. Look at the publication vehicle (radio, TV, etc.) and note the specific people advertising from your category, in your size, and so forth. Then write or call them and ask them how *they* did! Most will tell you. You get a much less biased picture than you would from references the media salespeople give you, who are usually selected to be positive. The Hoffmans saved a lot of money and also got some suggested new places to advertise. It's obvious, but few people do it.

Advertising Your Free Report . . .

The Eastern Credit Corporation has an effective ad for its services. First is a big "Yours Free" headline. Then a picture of a depressed-looking businessperson handling paperwork to collect debts. Then Eastern offers a free report covering what a collection-letter series must have, third-party letters, contingency efforts, bounced checks, tele-collections, and using collection agencies effectively (surprise!).

You wouldn't go too far wrong following that model— strong headline, visual, and report outline covering the topics people care about (which you can test for).

Money Advertising . . .

In general, ads with handfuls of dollar bills in them look "low class." But the oversized $500 bills that are used by one mailer do get your attention. There was also an ad in the newspaper that looked roughly like a bill, with dollar signs in the corners ($) and the seminar presenter's picture in the middle. (Text is in the other areas.) Since it's for a seminar on how to make money, the format works, as well as gets attention, even in black-and-white.

Efficient Advertising . . .

It's difficult to get attention with small ads in cluttered media. If anyone can do it, it should be marketing consultants like Tom Meyer. His ad features his picture, which attracts the eye. The main line is "Give me your tired, worn out control packages—I'LL BEAT THEM!" Then it gives a good credential for him. The main line appeals to experienced companies that already are mailing (that's what *control* means), so he doesn't waste time with dreamers. The ad seems to promise performance but doesn't commit him to a guarantee—he decides on that after he talks with prospects. There's also the likable familiarity of his key line sounding like the words on the Statue of Liberty: "Give me your tired, your poor . . ."

Magic Words

The "magic words" for advertising from one classic study include:

• New	• Introducing
• Now	• Unique
• At last	• Free
• Amazing	• Breakthrough
• Fast	• Sale
• Easy	• Special

Advertising Contrasts . . .

American Express employed a great example of visual contrast in one of its ads. It featured Willie Shoemaker (the jockey) standing back-to-back with Wilt Chamberlain (the basketball player). It caught attention beautifully, as any contrast is intended to do. For instance, Roper Starch Worldwide Research shows that a black background can increase the visibility of the foreground material as much as 50 percent.

Better Legal Advertising . . .

Most legal advertising is dull. It focuses on the firm (features), not on helping readers (benefits). Here's a good ad used by Miller, Mailliard & Culver. It began, "We would have been Galileo's law firm." It went on to say that Galileo's views changed the world, and he would have needed a law firm as bold as he was. The ad used a long, thin format all the way down the side of one page, dominating the page without incurring the cost for the whole thing. The firm appeals to prospects who feel they have something important going. The ad appropriately lists intellectual property as the lawyers' first specialty.

AIDA

A common formula for structuring an ad is AIDA:

A = Attention (they have to know you exist)

I = Interest (you have to show why they should care about what you offer)

D = Desire (they have to want the benefits you offer)

A = Action (unless they take action on hiring you, nothing happens)

Color Advertising . . .

Research from Roper Starch Worldwide suggests that a four-color ad is noticed 45 percent more than a comparable black-and-white ad. Depending on costs, even adding one color to an ad can increase its value more than the expense.

Competitive Headline . . .

Here is a good headline for competition-oriented people: "Find out what your competitors are spending on advertising." The high-tech ad-tracking service that runs the ad can tell everyone what everyone else is doing. The headline gives the message very clearly.

Free Offer . . .

Profit Boosters has an ad that gets attention. A big headline says, "Free. $500 . . ." Then in slightly smaller type it adds, "analysis of your direct mail package." They go on to make claims that they can double your response, and so on, but the benefit is that they will give you a free analysis with 10 specific suggestions to improve your response at no obligation. Their use of a photo by the "Free $500" headline at the top gets some attention, but it's rather dark, and the person isn't smiling or particularly inviting. This drawback notwithstanding, putting a price on your free analysis, free get-acquainted meetings, and so forth is a winning strategy.

Negotiating with Ad Agencies . . .

If you're buying marketing services, ad agencies are one of the traditional places to go. It might be useful for you to consider the following general guidelines on rates from The American Association of Advertising Agencies. In one recent survey, 14 percent of advertisers paid the old, traditional 15 percent commission on media purchased. This method has been declining for many years. Paying for consulting at a fairly high rate is more common and was used by 35 percent of clients. But 45 percent of clients got some sort of reduced-rate commissions. Some of the remaining 6 percent had special arrangements based on performance.

Picture Your Service . . .

Destiny Marketing sells computer solutions. One of the company's ads uses a picture of a computer disk behind all the words (in a light color or screen). It's a way to instantly show what you do. A dentist could use a tooth, a consultant something relevant to clients' industries, or a bookkeeper ledgers.

Classic Headlines

Here are some other classic headlines that you can adapt to your situation:

"Six Types of X—Which Group Are You In?"

"Now Any X Problem Can Be 'Duck Soup' for You"

"Do You Make These Mistakes About Your X?"

Prefab Advertising . . .

In most fields people will sell you marketing material with an exclusive in your area that you can use. For instance, Barren Publishing sold once-a-week dental columns using a Q&A format. You stick your picture and name in, and put it in your local paper. You save time and, presumably, have proven columns. Unfortunately, if suppliers are producing new ones every week, they may not have tested the actual effectiveness, but practitioners using the program say that it does get attention. Prairie Moon has one such cartoon service for printers, and there are lots of others.

Who Else Needs . . .

"Who else needs X benefits?" is a proven headline. It nicely implies that you've helped lots of others. For instance, "Who else needs an editor who enhances Annual Reports?" Or "Who else needs a lawyer who listens?"

Stylish Advertising . . .

Talk about boring ads. Look in any newspaper at realty full-page ads. They're a repetitive checkerboard of pictures and data. Get creative! Nan Allen has an artist do a large sketch from a photo and uses a picture of that instead. Later, she presents the original sketch, framed, to the new owners. It reminds them, and all their guests, of her forever! Great for referrals.

If you can't afford an artist, try one of the computer programs that can convert a scanned photo into a drawing.

Creative Advertising . . .

Here's another way to change the boring "checkerboard" realty ads full of houses for sale. Decker Bullock specializes in really expensive houses, few under $1 million. They used an ad in which all but one house shown were already sold. Then the last square said: "The market is good—let us put a SOLD sign on your house too." A good way to attract top listings.

Ad on Ad . . .

The TeleMatch Company provides a service that matches addresses and phone numbers. Whichever you have, it can provide the other. The company has a clever series of ads featuring what looks like an entry torn from the page of a dictionary, defining its name, "TeleMatch," as the services it offers. The ads have a picture of a telephone and are "pasted" down on a white space. It gets a lot of attention as display advertising because it's different.

Clever Car Repair Advertising . . .

Here's a 2″ ad that stands out. The headline is "WANTED for Porsche & VW Service" (nicely targeted as a specialist). Then there's a picture of the mechanic in two poses like a criminal holding a license plate frame with his name and "VW Technician" in front of him like a prison number. (Maybe the criminal connotation is too close to reality for some customers thinking about mechanics!) But S CAR GO (clever name, too) confirms that the ad did real well for them.

Advertising Your "Farm"...

Christina McNair is a real estate agent specializing in a particular neighborhood ("farming"). She organized the neighborhood garage sale and then advertised it in the classifieds with her picture. This provides a service to her area and publicizes her.

Dyno Advertising...

It's always a challenge to make a small ad stand out in a publication (or a big ad!). Since the Contemporary Group is a marketing firm, they *should* come up with a good approach. Their message is on six strips of plastic labels that you make with the little "Dyno" label makers. They're different lengths and crooked. Very distinctive among all the typeset ads.

> ### Don't Get Bored with a Winning Ad
>
> You see your ad a lot more than prospects do, and you'll get bored with it sooner. Consistency is a big advantage in advertising. Don't change a successful ad until you can tell it is less effective. And even then, after a brief rest it will probably be good again.
>
> B-O-R-R-R-I-N-G

Front-Page Newspaper Advertising...

Want front-page coverage in your paper? They usually don't sell ads there. But major papers are beginning to attach Post-it note–like messages to the front page of newspapers when they are delivered. Normally you'd refer people to a bigger ad inside.

Front-Page Magazine Advertising...

A few magazines are now adding extra front-pages with ads over the regular front page. Or they're splitting their front page so it opens to an ad. For instance, Positive Response Television, a media buyer for infomercials, got the September 1995 cover of *Response TV Magazine*. Other methods include a single fold or a sticker advertisement.

Novelty Advertising Gets Attention . . .

A Norwegian company, FH, originally advertised for a "hard-working, friendly salesperson." They got no responses. When they advertised "Tiresome and boring wholesale company seeks indolent people with a total lack of service mindedness for a job that is completely without challenge" they got tons of responses.

The first thing your ad needs to do is get attention. Humor or sarcasm is one way, as is blunt honesty. If either fits your style, go for it.

Resume Ad . . .

Einson Freeman used a clever ad in the form of a resume to promote their marketing services in a magazine. They put these typical resume headings down the left margin: Candidate, Personal Data, Education, Hobbies, Working Philosophy, Career Objectives, Primary Activities, Employment History, Additional Achievements, References, Compensation, and Interview. Opposite each heading they included information about themselves and their clients, with a little bit of humor. For instance, under Hobbies, they listed "think tank" diving. And, of course, under Employment History they listed large customers they'd had. They could have improved it by using a typewriter typeface for the resume part, and giving it a headline other than "Confidential Resume" so that the reader would more quickly realize their point. For instance, the headline could have been something like "You Can Afford Big-Time Marketing Help."

Be Different

One of the common elements in many successful ads is that they take a fresh approach that surprises people and gets their attention. Try honesty—or anti-BS—it can work wonders.

"Adver-torial" Results . . .

For professional service providers, writing an article and inserting it as paid advertising can be your most effective advertising. For instance, one accountant wrote a brief article focusing on the importance of researching investments before you invest. In about a 20-line article, he simply explained the service, pointed out the dangers of acting on investments from hot tips and people who are trying to sell you something, and then offered a free, get-acquainted meeting and information on the service. He ran the ad four times in his local business section and got 39 responses. Of those, 22 people became clients.

Adver-torial Plus Ad . . .

LifeSearch provides competitive quotes by computer on many different insurance policies from different vendors. But their advertising approach could be used by anyone. They bought a full page in a business journal and used about half of it for a column with a picture that looked very much like a standard editorial. The column wrapped around their ad, which had pricing and sample premiums laid out by age and number of years. Articles get lots of attention—probably five to ten times more than an ad. These adver-torials do well alone. And the inset ad allows people to see an immediate example of the service. Thus, it's going to appeal to people who like pictures as well as those who like words. And it's going to have more of the editorial appeal than an advertising appeal.

> ### Use "Newsletter" Formats
>
> Few people want to read ads. You have to make it easy for them to become interested. When you're writing an advertorial, use subheads and short paragraphs to make it easier for readers to get your point when they're skimming. Most good newsletters are written that way.
>
>

Q&A Advertising . . .

One marketing firm buys space in targeted magazines such as *Upside* (for high-tech executives). It presents an ad that looks like a column, called "Ask the Professional." The format is to present one question and answer from each lawyer, which, of course, focuses on the services the lawyer sells. The format has been so successful that the firm now sells it to search services, graphic designers, acquisition specialists, and accountants. It will work for any service and looks more like editorial.

Case Study Advertising . . .

Birk Marketing Research took a half-page ad and used the majority of it for a case study description of how they helped a specific client solve a problem. They then added that they were action-oriented and results-oriented. The ad could have been improved by making it more readable or more skim-able. There were no subheads, and the layout was an odd shape that was hard for the eye to follow. However, they did underline some key phrases that at least gave you an idea of what it was about.

Give Your Ads Personality . . .

The only time I ever advertised as a consultant was a 1″ ad in the local business journal classified section. The ad said something like "impatient, irascible, brilliant consultant available to solve problems." Because I said some negative things about myself, I was able to get away with claiming to be brilliant. The unusual approach generated a lot of interest and some work.

> **Plan Good Ads**
>
> Don't rush your ad together just before deadline. The yellow pages and most publications will design your ad for free, but it will look like everyone else's unless you give them direction and make them redo it until you get what you want. Take your time: you may have to live with it all year!

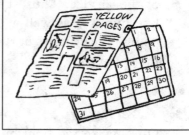

If You've Got It, Flaunt It? . . .

Mortgage lawyer Rosalie Osias flaunted sex in her ads to mortgage bankers. One ad showed her lying on her desk in a miniskirt with a flirtatious grin and said, "Try this nonconforming law firm." She felt that the mortgage banking market was an old-boy network and she needed something sexual to get their attention. By the fourth ad, male bankers were running to introduce themselves to her. Her closings went from 5 a week to 40 or 50.

Personalize Your Advertising . . .

In a full page of eighth-page ads in *TeleProfessional* magazine, Kathy Sisk's ad stands out because she is the only one who includes her picture. You can often see your competitors' ads before you advertise. Make yours different. She also uses a reverse at the bottom of her ad to make her name and address stand out: another good technique in moderation.

Better Yellow Pages . . .

Nelson Personnel Services does two smart things in their yellow pages ad. Years ago they were rated number one by a local paper. They're the only company that features this in their ad. (What happened to the other years?) And they are the only one that says they specialize in IBM and Mac word processing. They've "preempted the truth." What other computers are there? And word processing has to be the first thing most employers are looking for! Why wouldn't every ad feature them?

Better Yellow Pages Ads

Here are some things that can make a better ad:

- Use a large headline
- Put your offer in the head
- Include testimonials
- Have empty space to set off your message
- Use a border to set yourself off from other ads

Naming Yourself for the Yellow Pages . . .

If you depend on the yellow pages, use a name that's early in the alphabet to be noticed. Try putting "American," "Better," or "Alternative" before your business name. If you can build a benefit into your name too, so much the better. Here are some good ones: ComfortCare for a heating oil dealer; Coach Kraft for a body shop; Accountants on Call for temporary accountants.

Newspapers Outperform Yellow Pages . . .

Bertotti Landscaping advertises weekly in two major local papers. Few competitors do. Bertotti features photos of work in its ads and notes its awards. The company tracks more qualified leads from the newspapers than from the yellow pages for the same level of expense. Test, test, test!

Co-Op Advertising . . .

If you're in a service business that uses parts or also sells equipment, co-op advertising could work for you. Many manufacturers have money available to pay for local ads.

You just have to mention their products or logos. Ask your suppliers. Many co-op funds go unused every year.

Yellow Pages Pictures . . .

Yellow pages research says that if you offer a professional service, your picture in your ad boosts response. Two reasons are that it's novel and pictures get attention. It also makes you more "personal" when potential clients are picking from an impersonal source such as the yellow pages. It can work in other advertising too.

YOUR PHOTO
HERE
LEE'S
POOL
SERVICE

Unique Yellow Pages Listing . . .

Jeannie Davis in Denver found an unused category in the yellow pages that fit her consulting service. That way, she was not only first in the list—she *was* the list. You can sometimes get the phone people to create new categories. But start by asking for a list of what's already approved.

White Pages Listings . . .

Some advertisers don't like to refer people to their yellow pages ads because it exposes buyers to their competitors. If you have multiple phone numbers, use your white pages listings strategically. When people don't know where to look in the yellow pages, what would they call your service? Recently I looked up "Illustrations for Books" in the white pages and was surprised to find someone listed that way.

· · · ACTION AGENDA · · ·

"Your attitude, not your aptitude, will
determine your altitude."
—Zig Ziglar

Your success with advertising will come from your can-do attitude, and keeping track of your results. You don't have to come up with 10 great ideas. You only have to keep looking and testing until you find one pretty good idea. Then you can improve it over time.

A good place to start looking is in this chapter. Hopefully, you've already marked a dozen of the 37 ideas to consider further. For instance:

→ Write an article that you could have published as an advertisement.

→ Since headlines are so important, write 20 and test them with people you know. Then keep the 3 best and write 20 more!

→ What kind of dramatic picture would fit your ads?

→ Who sells proven ads in your field? Ask your national association if you're not sure. (If you still can't find any, call me and I'll see what I can do!)

→ Make sure you track your ad results. At the minimum, always ask callers where they heard of you.

→ Build a testimonial into your ads.

→ Pick out yellow pages ads you like as models and start designing one you can use.

→ If you have multiple phone lines, list in the white pages in several different places.

18

TV and Radio Commercials, Billboards, and Other Advertising

> "Doing business without advertising is like
> winking at a girl in the dark. You know what
> you're doing, but nobody else does!"
>
> —S. H. Britt

*E*very day, people are inventing new ways for you to pay them to advertise your services. Some even work! After print, television and radio commercials are the most common methods. There are many more.

Use these examples to give you ideas you can apply.

+ + +

Consistent, Creative Advertising . . .

For many years, TV commercials for Washington Mutual Bank have featured spokespeople such as a log-rolling accordion player, a precision lawn mower drill team, and a trained squirrel. The theme is "That's different. That's Washington Mutual." It's increased consumer recognition tremendously, and the consistency of the campaign has caused the response to "keep getting better and better," says a spokesperson.

197

Moo(ving) Ads . . .

In Britain, dairy farmer Harry Goode started selling ads mounted on the sides of his cows near a major highway. For $40 a week, Ben & Jerry's ice cream was a logical taker. This is worth arranging as a stunt just for the publicity if you can find a local farmer with a sense of humor!

Big Time TV on a Budget . . .

AdExchange recycles television commercials! They are a tool that you could use if you want to do quality television commercials for 90 percent off. AdExchange data banks have thousands of commercials from financial institutions, insurance companies, hospitals, and other service and nonservice providers. Some originally cost $100,000 to $350,000 apiece to produce. For instance, one award-winning, three-commercial campaign cost $500,000; you could probably license its exclusive use in your geographic area for $20,000, give or take (it depends on the size of your marketplace). Banks such as Evergreen Bank and hospitals such as St. Mary's are among the many users of these commercials. You have many options with the recycled visuals. In some cases, you might be able to use the exact script and voice on a commercial, just inserting your name and phone number. In other cases, you can take a commercial intended for one purpose and, by changing the words, totally restructure it to your marketplace without having any cost for this quality of work. If you are spending real money on commercials, your ad agency commissions might be as high as your entire cost for these commercials. (AdExchange is at 415/777-2330.)

> **Effective TV**
>
> If you can't afford big-budget special effects, you may need to do something to set your commercials apart. How about a talk show format? Changing the color balance to surprise people? Using some black-and-white? Involving children or animals? Calling yourself "Crazy _____"?

Low-Cost Network Television . . .

One professional firm sponsors *Washington Week in Review* (PBS) in their local area. It's the type of image they want with the prospects they want to appeal to. Local ads on many cable channels such as TBS or ESPN are also quite inexpensive.

Police Advertising . . .

A county sheriff in Illinois needed to raise money for police cars, so he sold an ad for $6,500 to a local alarm company. He put the ad on the police cars. It's a nice fit, since it implies an endorsement from the police. Other places around the country are following suit, so expect more ads on police cars. Maybe bail bondsmen can buy ads in jail cells next!

Ads, Ads Everywhere . . .

Ads are sold almost everywhere, but only recently on the floors of stores. In supermarket tests, floor ads increased sales of the items by 19.2 to 29.1 percent. For your service business, how about on the sidewalk near your office? For instance, one restaurant had painted footprints on the sidewalk leading to its location around the corner. This is probably one of those areas where it's better to ask forgiveness than permission!

Don't Abdicate Responsibility

Don't give up responsibility for your commercials to "professionals." David Packard (of Hewlett Packard) says, "Marketing is too important to be left to the marketing department." Take responsibility for testing your commercials to see if they're effective.

Elevator Billboards . . .

A dentist realized that in elevators, to be polite, people avoid making eye contact, so a sign might be just the thing to grab their attention. For $100 a month, he got the rights to put an 18" × 24" public awareness poster inside the elevator of his building. It mentioned that to get dental care, you didn't even need to leave the building, and that he had convenient early and late hours, lunchtime service, and so on. Every month or so, he would change the sign to deal with a particular issue—such as gum disease. All of the signs offered a free first examination. He now gets an average of 12 new patients a month from this one simple sign.

With persistence, you could probably arrange for signs in neighboring buildings as well.

"Fresh" Marketing . . .

Breaking news is what many people watch television for. Commercials can be used the same way. Denver sports teams have started using same-day advertising to fill last-minute seats. Silvi's Mexican Restaurant, which has a fresh theme, films commercials the same day they air: one commercial might show the tomatoes being picked fresh in the field at dawn and then delivered to the restaurant and chopped into salsa.

By making your message more immediate, you get a sense of urgency and surprise customers who are used to the same old stuff.

Winning Radio Advertising . . .

A Kentucky radio station produced a "bingo" game to sell advertising. Each of 12 advertisers got one square on the card. When listeners heard a sponsor's ad on the air, they circled the respective square on the card, noting the time and date. When they got bingo, they sent in the card for a drawing. The promo lasted six weeks, with new prizes each week. One of the winning advertisers was an accountant who doubled his tax practice during this period.

You can suggest it to your local station.

Attention-Getting Puzzle . . .

Speaker Susan Stephani sends out an item that looks like a luggage tag to promote her services. It lists her speech topics on one side with information on how to contact her. It has a string attached. The string has little rings too large to go through the tag hole. The copy says, "Puzzle: Get string off without tearing tag or string!" It also says, "Puzzled about finding a speaker who can motivate, educate, and entertain? Maybe Susan is the answer?" I'll bet a few recipients call just to find out the answer and end up considering her to speak.

There's a similar pencil with a loop attached that's not long enough to go around the pencil. Magic/novelty shops would be a place to find this kind of item.

Host a Syndicated Show . . .

You can be your own *Home Improvement* TV star. Since Holigan Homes began hosting a syndicated TV show featuring tips on home improvement, it's grown more than 100 percent. Most of the company's focus is on selling new homes, but the same thing would work for any contractor.

Be a Local TV Star . . .

One business consultant hosts a talk show, interviewing people in a 15-minute or half-hour format. In addition to showcasing your own expertise and status as the host, you can feature professionals who regularly refer clients to you. Another person charged guests $500 or $1,000 for an appearance as advertising. Guests also received a copy of the tape to use as a marketing tool.

Advertisers Pay Consumers . . .

FreeFone, in Seattle, has the technology for the ultimate in one-to-one marketing. Consumers who sign up are paid to listen to advertisers' five-second pitches. Every time they pick up their phone, they can activate quick plugs and make 15 cents. They can also get coupons by mail if they authorize it. Subscribers answer a survey about their interests so that ads can be customized to them. Ultimately, if you dial a competitor of one of the advertisers, a custom ad could come on asking if you'd like to change your call to the advertiser.

School Advertising Plus Demographics . . .

Cover Concepts found a new place to sell advertisements: book jackets given out free to millions of students across the country to protect the covers of their textbooks. That was enough to attract advertisers such as Nike and Gatorade. But the way the company attracted more than 90 advertisers and doubled its business sales every year was by building extensive demographic data from the Department of Education and the Census Bureau. It could tell advertisers what percentage of each school was what ethnic group, and so forth. If an advertiser wanted fourth-grade classes, 25 percent Hispanic, Cover Concepts could do it.

Better Than Welcome Wagon . . .

One service provider distributes his gift certificates to moving companies. He even imprints the certificates with the moving company's name. It makes the movers look good to give them out. His is the only certificate they give away, so he reaches people sooner; it has more impact than it would if it were distributed with Welcome Wagon and it costs him less.

If you set this up, you could sell space to other services and have your own extra business!

Advertising as Poetry? . . .

Landscaping contractor Bill Brady has used a jingle successfully in his commercials and personal presentations for many years: "Throw away your gardening boots. Give the job to Roots and Shoots. If you want your yard to look like heaven, dial 499-1177." As a speaker, Denis Waitley (*The Psychology of Winning*) is also know for long, customized poems about an audience's specific situation.

If creativity fits you, poetry adds a distinctive flair.

Realty TV Is Reality . . .

Kirt Donaldson, a realtor, proposed a show on local cable access in his area. It's a small cable system, but it makes him the star in his area. And in case no one watches, he gets newspaper publicity about the show anyway!

Billboards After Billboards . . .

Law firm Goldberg and Osborne had a huge billboard in Phoenix with their name, the phrase "The injury lawyer," and an eagle logo. Right behind it was a

---

Outdoor Advertising

Billboards are referred to in the advertising business as "outdoor." Sometimes they are very cost-effective for the big exposure you get.

much smaller one that said, "The discount accident lawyers," advertising the firm of Hastings and Hastings. Both were effective: one for big attention-getting, the second for guerrilla marketing.

Service Billboards?

You don't see many billboards for services. This means you have an opportunity to be unique if you can come up with a good one.

Another great mini-billboard setup is to copy the old Burma Shave format with five small placards in a row, spaced out a hundred yards or so, that create a little rhyme. It strikes people as clever when they are not familiar with Burma Shave, and it makes them feel nostalgic when they are. For instance, a chiropractor could use, "Too much commute, Causes lower back pain, Give sore back the boot, And you'll sing in the rain." And then the last sign says, "Joe Chiropractic." You can most likely do better with some thought.

3-D Billboards . . .

If you're using billboards (outdoor advertising), a good way to get attention is to have three-dimensional objects on them or coming out of them. One billboard for leasing by GMAC used a 3-D model of a truck on top of the headline "Don't let a truck payment break your budget." And the billboard underneath was broken into three parts—very eye-catching.

Sneaky Billboards . . .

Hawaii is one of many states, like California, where you can't put up billboards. But many billboard-free states have "Adopt-a-Highway" programs—you can get your name on a sign for adopting a mile or two of highway and paying for its upkeep.

Truck Advertising . . .

If you have trucks, they should be moving billboards. Office Depot's clever trucks are a great example with the pictures that look as if a person is standing in them, while advertising some of the brands they carry (which probably pay for the exposure through co-op funds). And if your trucks go downtown, paint your name on the top, as one contractor did, so they can be read by high-rise denizens.

Better Job-Site Signs . . .

Contractors use job site signs listing their name, the architect, and so on. It's advertising, but not much. David Wood, a consultant on construction marketing, says smart clients add more information to their signs; for example:
* The dollar value of the project
* The number of jobs created
* The local materials purchased
* The number of jobs the new facility will create

Visual-Proof Billboard . . .

This one's worth mentioning because it's so creative. The asthma, anti-air pollution people in England put up a billboard coated with clear glue. As pollution stuck to it, you could read the message to "call 800 . . ." to make a contribution! Creative but not applicable, you say? A chimney sweep could use a small card to demonstrate dirt in the chimney, or in your house. A car wash could attach one to the car after a wash to show when it was due for another. A computer consultant could show you why you should clean your computer. And an asthma M.D. could have one in his or her office to show local pollution.

Winning Billboard . . .

The accounting firm of Eskew and Gresham had a winning billboard for growing businesses. It said simply, "Beyond Bean Counting" at the top, with their name at the bottom, and "Certified Public Accountants." Running from left into the center was a series of beans, with the last few sprouting green, bigger and bigger as they moved to the right.

What Will They Keep? . . .

The best *advertising specialties* for business customers are items they keep on their desks because they're too good to throw away. The small rectangular letter opener with the little razor in the corner is one. The Rolodex card slot puncher invented by Bob Merrick is another. Simple calculators are a third. Mouse pads are popular nowadays. One advertising consultant sent prospects a computer mouse pad with a built-in solar calculator.

Better Specialty Advertising . . .

A major hospital used to give new mothers a cheap diaper bag filled with unhealthy food. When they switched to a better bag in bright corporate colors filled with useful items such as eyedroppers, electric plug safety caps, and a holder for hospital instructions, the mothers' connection to the hospital was enhanced and produced more referrals and repeat business.

ADVERTISING SPECIALTIES: Useful items that you give away with your name on them. Calendars and pens are the most common, but almost anything can be used.

A Better Promotional Calendar . . .

Calendars keep your name in front of people all year around. But items such as calendars and pens tend to get old fast because people get so many of them. One professional noticed a small calendar displayed in several homes that he visited. It was a 4″ × 9″ single card with all 12 months printed on one side and holidays listed at the top. The card had a hole punched at the top, making it easy to hang in different places. The next year he had a similar calendar made for his business and mailed it to all of the homes within a mile of his office. He included an offer for a free first visit. It immediately brought in five new patients, and many more people saved the calendar.

Specialty Ad Paper . . .

You know how people in restaurants make notes about their business plans on paper napkins? The Boulevard Restaurant in San Francisco is one of the few eating establishments that use a specialty ad item that looks like a book of matches but has handy pieces of paper in it for customers' use.

Sports Schedules . . .

If you can't print up your own sports schedule to give out to fans or alums, Positive Promotions will imprint your name on pro football schedules for the season, and other sports (800/635-2666).

Specialty Water Advertising . . .

With the craze for bottled water, someone finally provides custom labeling of sports bottles for you to give away. And their name follows my advice to say it all, Custom Label Spring Water Co.

. . . ACTION AGENDA . . .

"Failure to hit the bull's-eye is never the fault of the target. To improve your aim—improve yourself."

—Gilbert Arland

You can advertise anywhere. Some media, such as radio and TV, may seem too big for small service providers. But that may be how you *get* big. Whether it's a simple sign on a fence, or network television, review the 30 ideas in this chapter and decide what target *you* can aim for.

→ Call your cable access TV channel and see what the rules are for getting a show on.

→ If you like TV commercials, check the cable provider about buying inexpensive local commercials on ESPN, TBS, Nickelodeon, and other national channels.

→ Radio is fast and can be targeted narrowly depending on the station you buy. Could it work for you?

→ If you don't know what advertising specialties might work for you, call a few reps from the yellow pages and ask them for ideas and to see their catalogs.

→ Could you put up a sign somewhere? How about exchanging small signs with another business?

Publicity Builds Your Image and Business

Publishing Your Way to Fame and Fortune

"The biggest complaint of editors was not the number of press releases they received, but that they weren't well targeted to their audiences."
—From a survey of editors

If print advertising is paid mass media, publicity is its free twin. It is defined as free mass-media exposure. PR stands for public relations. That field covers more than getting publicity, such as crisis management and investor relations. However, for our purposes here, *PR* and *publicity* are used interchangeably.

THE MEDIA NEED YOU

The major media of interest to you are probably newspapers, trade magazines, radio, and television. The same media that you would buy an ad in will give you free exposure if you meet their needs. They have a need to obtain interesting content so that people will want to "read" them, but they don't have big budgets to spend on searching for interest-ing stories. Because I've been a journalist for a number of years, I can also say that we are generally swamped with press releases and other material. So, we have the somewhat arrogant (or lazy) attitude that the news will come to us. In other words, the easier you make it for them, the more likely they are to feature you.

If you look at your local newspapers, you will see that most of the business stories come off of the national wires. This means the publishers need your help in finding interesting local stories like yours! Television is similar: most features they present about companies come from video press releases, unless breaking news is involved. Even the *Wall Street Journal* relies largely on press releases and calls.

So, do the media a favor. Help them publicize you to their audiences.

+++

Good Publicity from Complaints . . .

Mark Twain said, never pick a fight with people who buy their ink by the barrel! Many magazine editors have complained about service, been ignored, and then written scathing editorials about the idiot companies in their own publications. The opposite can happen too. UssA Insurance got a big plug in the *Wall Street Journal* in a guest column because the company took good care of a customer. The writer wrote and complained. He got a quick callback, an apology, and the problem fixed. The follow-up call to check on satisfaction, plus a letter with a gift certificate for his phone bill, turned it into a story to retell! A complaint is a chance for you to shine, not something to dread!

Good PR Column . . .

Doing a column in your local paper is good publicity. Karen Ussery, a professional organizer, wrote one on how to find things that you file.

What could you write that would help readers?

PR Hooks . . .

To get big publicity, it helps if you can provide a "hook" for the media to tie you to a bigger story. Elaina Zuker wrote a book on influence styles. But she could have used her typology to get publicity without a book. She analyzed the influence styles of the mayoral candidates just before a big election, using media stories about them. (The media may have also found being used as a research source appealing.) She got a major PR story explaining her system, as well as rating the candidates.

PR About Failures . . .

Yet one more way of tying to current news. A major story featured a consultant to law firms, and focused on the recent collapse of a major firm.

If you consult to any industry, and occasional companies fail, a general press release on causes of failure will be a nice hook for the local media or the trade press. Everyone wants to know why businesses fail, even though many times it's not generalizable. You can prepare the article ahead of time and start building your media contacts for when a story breaks of a major failure.

5 Ws Plus H

All journalists are trained to look for the *Who, What, When, Where, Why,* and *How* of a story. Be sure you answer these questions in the first paragraph or two when you go for their attention.

Develop Novel Publicity . . .

To get publicity, you need a novel angle that a reporter hasn't heard about. Speaking of hearing, did you know that restaurants, bars, and other businesses can be designed to create a certain level of noise? Consultant Eric Engstrom says it's part of the dining experience. When open kitchens came in, noise also went up. People want to hear a level of excitement. Noise tells you it's a popular place and others are enjoying themselves. An architect and a restaurant owner can also be the source of this story. Add a picture of a decibel meter, and a reporter has everything he or she needs for a unique feature story on a slow news day!

Using Your Clients for Publicity . . .

Featuring your clients is a great way for you to get repeated publicity. Here's one that any limo service can use where there are commuters. Luxury Limo cut a deal with three very ordinary women who had a long commute. For little more than the cost of a van pool, the three women get big-time service to and from work. They save a half hour each way and get to be stars when they pull up at work with champagne in the car. It generated at least one major feature story for them all.

It works the other way around too. Your consultants, accountants, lawyers, bankers, and other professionals can be a source of publicity for you. Tell them that anytime they get covered for publicity, you'd be happy to add a client's-eye view to round out the story on them. To make it easy for them to use you, provide a nice written testimonial with media readers in mind. To help them do it even better, lend them this book so they'll know how to get publicity!

Marketing by the Book, and Newsletter . . .

Many consultants and companies have gotten business from books they've published. For instance, Inquiry Handling Services did a book on direct mail issues, sponsored by the American Management Association. It's still the single greatest lead tool they have.

Writing for Customers . . .

A sales manager attracted lots of business in the securities area because he wrote articles for various industry publications. Articles don't always bring leads, but you can also reprint them and use them to build credibility with your own prospects and customer base.

> **Easy Book Products?**
>
> A book may not be as hard to have as you think. If you know your field, the basic material for a short book can be dictated in about 10–15 hours. Ghostwriters will do one for you for $10,000 to $20,000; or if you can get nine other people to write chapters, you can have a joint book.

Write Like a Journalist . . .

Christina Dochtermann of American Signature printing did a good job getting publicity by following the rule to write like a journalist. In a major trade publication that goes to her customers, she writes about how to build relationships with your printer to benefit from their long-term input and consultation. Then she quotes a number of big customers such as *Reader's Digest* on how working with American Signature developed new capacities for them to reach their readers, and so forth. Throwing in a few color pictures added to the big-time media coverage.

Tip Sheets for Publicity . . .

To get publicity, sending tip sheets of your advice works well. You make the tips available if people contact you. The same material can also be sent to prospects, as Management Services does. In their case, it's tips on how to get publicity. They work on a guaranteed-results basis for book publishers.

Checklist PR Ideas . . .

Tim Connor is a speaker and an author. He gets publicity by producing checklist-type articles and offering to send people more details. He has articles such as "Sales Strategies of Six-Figure Income Salespeople." When you request one article, he also sends a list of articles, books, and tapes available, and some self-tests—such as his Management Success Questionnaire and Sales Success Questionnaire.

> **Ask Journalists' Advice**
>
> If you're not sure what type of story might be good for publicity, call a few journalists and ask them what they recommend for your area. They'll often be glad to tell you. They usually recommend information of value to their readers.
>
> PRESS RELEASE

Publicity Is Not an Interruption . . .

Newsletter News and Resources gives an example of how PR was mishandled. A small business owner's name was given to an editor of USA Today as a source. When the editor called, she said that she had too many customers and didn't have time to talk, so she blew the chance of publicity. Here's how it could have been handled. Ask the editor to hold for a minute, and then tell all of the customers that the editor of USA Today is on the phone and wants to interview you. They'll feel as if they're in on the news as it's happening. Then get customers into the interview. If the editor asks a question that customers can give a testimonial about, bring them on the line. If the customers get quoted, they'll be even more thrilled. Editors are often on deadlines and in a hurry, but you may also be able to schedule a slightly later time that you could call them back.

Seminars, Books, and Letters . . .

Marcia Yudkin attributes most of her clients as a consultant to seminars and books she's done leading to word of mouth. She's also gotten publicity and clients from letters to the editor.

You could easily get letters to the editor published every week if you wanted to. Why not set a goal of one a month? As an incidental benefit, you'll have a reason to keep up on your reading (or skimming) which will find you items to send to clients.

Write Letters . . .

The letters are the most widely read editorial part of the paper. For instance, lots of people comment on how terrible it is to go to the dentist. One such slam gave a local dentist a chance to write a letter to the editor explaining that, yes, it was common for people to dread going to the dentist, but here's why it was actually not bad, and why dentists did certain things they did.

In a way, the more criticism your profession gets in the paper, the more excuses you have to get free publicity. Just don't come across as defensive. Work to make your profession look good, and you'll look good in a modest, indirect way.

Holiday Blues PR . . .

If you're a therapist, every year you have a chance to issue a press release on holiday depression. You can get quotes from police about how things are busier then. There are holiday neuroses and Sunday neuroses. Times like Christmas, when people tell themselves they should feel close to their family but don't, tend to precipitate depression and other problems. Involve suicide counselors for quotes, and people from medical schools near you. Do the work of the reporters by putting together a list of suicide referral agencies as well. And, of course, include tips on how to cope.

More Holiday PR . . .

The Christmas holiday was the "hook" for customer service consultants and authors Karen Leland and Keith Bailey to get major publicity with tips for merchants on how to deal with customers. And the nice thing about a "news" tie-in to a holiday is that you have all year to plan for it!

Publicity Pictures . . .

Most media like interesting pictures. Here is an example of one that makes a conceptual point while attracting attention. To make the point that advertising on the Web is analogous to billboard advertising, InfoSeek staged a photo of CEO Bill Peck sitting on a billboard holding a portable computer. It made the cover of *Web Week* for major publicity. Most PR photos tend toward stunts that are somewhat ridiculous.

Temp Surveys . . .

To be seen as an expert in your industry, produce new information. The results give you publicity which identifies you as the expert. The temp industry really uses surveys to get publicity. In the same week, here are three across my desk. Accountemps finds that 96 percent of senior executives favor mentoring. OfficeTeam finds that 84 percent of execs allow at least one casual dress day a week. And Robert Half finds that 43 percent of execs expect to expand, while only 8 percent expect cutbacks.

The other great benefit of this approach, besides some information you can use personally, is the excuse to contact your prospects to ask for their participation in the survey, then to thank them, send them a clipping of the article, and so on. They'll know you well after a couple of quarterly surveys!

Possible Holiday PR Themes

Here are some timely themes for publicity throughout the year:

- New Year's: Any service can talk about starting the year off right with your bookkeeping, cost control, and so forth
- Valentine's Day: Restaurants, massage therapists, dating services
- Spring, Easter, May Day: Landscaping, beauty salons, carpet cleaning
- Fourth of July: Event planners, travel agents
- Back to School: Photographers, parenting seminars
- Christmas: Financial planners (end-of-year planning)

Taxing PR . . .

If you are an accountant, a bookkeeper, or a tax attorney, every year you can send a press release on "Tax Freedom Day" to your local paper. This is the day that people can quit working to pay their taxes, usually sometime in May. The Tax Foundation put a novel spin on this concept in a press release that made the Associated Press nationally. It says that the typical American works almost until lunchtime to pay federal, state, and local taxes, before earning a penny for food, clothing, or shelter. This is an idea you can adapt to put a different spin on your local press release next year.

Worthy Disease . . .

A local oncology center (cancer) got a major newspaper spread and a letter of commendation from the local congresswoman. It was in response to a breast cancer awareness and alternative treatments campaign. It's a worthy cause and it also promotes their services.

Be a Reviewer . . .

Good reviewers for computer programs were hard to find for our computer construction newsletter. The ones we found got free programs and referrals from us to readers who wanted more information. This can work for other professionals too. Pamela Kelly is a lawyer who reviewed a negotiation program for *Inc. Technology* magazine. Sam White, a researcher, did the same for a custom news service program.

Use Your Newsletter . . .
Your newsletter can help you build relationships with the media as well as your clients and prospects. Put them on your mailing list. Then when you call them, they'll remember you.

Be Forward . . .

One newspaper had a list of the 96 Most Important People for the year 1996. A number of the people who made the list had gotten friends to nominate them. The paper used the same list as the basis for the next year's list. One bit of attention leads to others, but you often have to get the ball rolling.

Trade Show Press Kits . . .

If you're displaying a press kit in the press room at a trade show, it's usually one of hundreds. Having a fancy folder with your name on it does not stand out from the crowd. For that situation, it's better to put an identification of your services on the cover of the kit. Better still, put a brief headline and two-line summary of the news aspects. This will cause more people to pick it up.

The Press Kit

A press kit is a folder that contains a press release plus other material that helps the reporter write a story, such as photos, interviews, brochures, and background information.

Flextime Publicity . . .

Bonadio and Company, a 55-person accounting firm, got great publicity in the local media by announcing a formal flextime program for CPAs. They believe the program will allow them to keep employees who need flexible hours. And, by keeping employees, they'll be better able to keep their customers (who like continuity of the people they work with). There's almost nothing to lose for a company instituting a test flextime program. It improves morale, and also gets publicity.

Wall Street Journal Publicity Tips . . .

Wall Street Journal editors Ann Podd and John Brecher say that the *Journal* is built from the bottom up. By that, they mean that ideas come from reporters and then get pitched to editors. At many organizations, it's the other way around. However, even at top-down media, you can pitch individual reporters. This gives you a chance at several, and you can still try the editor if you fail. Research what the reporter has written lately. And a little flattery never hurts!

Great PR Picture . . .

Here's an example of a great photo getting big-time PR. Bill Dayton made the cover of *Inc.* magazine for August 1995. He dressed in a coat made of charge cards which he used to originally finance his business. It's a little silly, but that exposure is probably worth $10,000 to $20,000.

Humor Index Sells . . .

Malcolm Kushner is a business consultant who has compiled "The Cost of Laughing Index" for a decade or so. It's composed of the price of rubber chickens, Groucho glasses, *Mad* magazine, and 13 other items—such as comedy club ticket prices. Every time the Federal Reserve comes out with its Cost of Living Index, he has a good chance of getting publicity with his Index. It helps him get speeches and consulting on humor as a management tool.

> **Use Publicity Later**
>
> Remember, PR is worth more for you over time if you use it than at the time it appears as one shot. Be sure to get a clean copy of anything in print, reproduce it, put it in your office, send it to your prospects, add it to your newsletter, and so on.

Low-Cost PR Photos . . .

Most press releases don't have pictures. Visibility Public Relations in New York is experimenting with scanned photos printed out with a normal press release. Editors like it because it gives a sample picture, and they can request a better photo. We get dozens of press releases a day, and I don't think we've seen one done this way, so it will add distinctiveness to your press release, and at a much lower cost than including a photo with everything.

Make It Easy for Journalists . . .

Entrepreneurs Express rented offices to small businesses. To support small businesses and attract prospects, they ran mixers and seminars. Their local paper published a weekly guest column on small business. They wrote a column, and it was accepted. Surprisingly few local consultants and others are submitting guest columns to the paper. Another consultant appears often because he sends them groups of columns at a time. When the paper has a choice between a column in the hand and recruiting one, they use what they have.

Give Them Lots of Material . . .

One speaker/consultant starts his publicity process by talking to editors on the phone. Once he makes a connection, he sends them 10 or 20 articles on disk in the format and length they prefer. Many of his pieces get used just because they are there and available when a deadline approaches.

Media Modality Preferences . . .

Here's advice from a journalist on how to cultivate journalists. When you develop a media list of specific individuals, find out *how* they like to be contacted. That is, some prefer faxes, some prefer regular mail, some prefer E-mail, some prefer the phone. Also find out *when* they like to be contacted. This depends on their deadlines. They also will have a preference for lead times: how much notice do they like before they get a story? Of course, if they're initiating a story, they'll want your material immediately!

> **Selling to the Media**
>
> "The media is your customer. In today's environment with more competition and more media, the press can be an ally."
>
> —Tom Peters

Decorator Publicity Ideas . . .

Here are two local publicity stories that won big for an interior decorator. Feed them to your local newspaper. Interiors for a Song did a one-day makeover of a room. The same woman, in the same paper, got a plug for "10 quick fixes for rooms." This would work for landscaping, but also for boat maintenance, a legal checkup, and almost anything else if you're creative.

Get Paid for Your PR . . .

Deloitte and Touche put together a 64-page personal tax and financial planning guide in conjunction with the American Association of Individual Investors. Because the latter is a nonprofit they got lots of free publicity and were able to sell it for $6 a copy besides.

Rate Your Competitors . . .

Ronald Dans, founder of QuickCard Systems, provides a clearance service for checks over the phone. Getting a trade article published, covering 12 points on how to select a check clearance provider, is not only perfect PR for him, but also provides the system by which his competitors will be evaluated! Wouldn't you imagine that his own company passes his checklist with flying colors? Any service provider can do the same by running consumer-oriented articles explaining how to choose a lawyer, how to choose a landscaper, and so on. It might even be worth doing as a paid advertisement in editorial form.

Politically Correct Publicity . . .

If politically correct publicity works for you, use it. Chin, Wright & Branson is a law firm in Boston with few white male attorneys. With their broad client mix from different demographic groups, they're a natural to grab publicity, as they did from the *Boston Globe* Sunday edition.

Politicians Are an Easy Target . . .

A psychologist, an anthropologist, a sociologist, an economist, or anyone else who can comment on the body politic can almost always get some publicity. For instance, a British psychologist, David Cook, was quoted on the difference between politicians and psychopaths. He said, "Psychopaths lie easily. They get pleasure from duping people, whereas politicians lie for a purpose." Heck, why couldn't lawyers, tax accountants, or almost anyone else who deals with the government also comment on politicians?

PR for PR . . .

The Holton Company in Washington gets a lot of inquiries and publicity by letting publications know about its free "Beginners Guide to Public Relations Tactics." It's a good qualifier for prospects too.

PR Tie-Ins . . .

Andrew Harper's Hideaway Report is a newsletter, and thus a product. But the example it offers of PR tie-ins to news is so cute that I can't resist sharing it. Nicholas Leeson is the man who brought down Bearings Financial by losing billions of dollars trading, and then fled to avoid prosecution. He was found in the Shangri-La Tanjung

Aru Resort, on Borneo. Harper points out that suites there go for as much as $600 a day. "Only a pompous twit would secrete himself in a 500-room chain hotel where his mug pops up on CNN!" Harper then goes on to "advise" white-collar fugitives how to escape better. In Southeast Asia, they should go to obscure upscale retreats like Aman Wana on Moyo Island. There are no phones, radio, or newspapers. Since Harper specializes in exclusive, small, expensive resorts that give five-star service, this is a perfect tie-in, as well as cute for the journalists to pick up. *Forbes* magazine did, among others.

Predictable PR Tie-Ins

In addition to holidays, here are a few other regular events for which you can plan year-round publicity:

- Sporting Events: Super Bowl, opening games, Kentucky Derby, and so on
- Seasons Changing: longest day, shortest day, spring, Groundhog Day
- Elections: national and local

"Private" Press Releases . . .

One type of publication that always needs material and will accept almost anything is local volunteer-run newsletters of associations or groups of professionals. Company newsletters sometimes also fall into this area if they are not big-budget items. One local professional targeted press releases to large employers in his area. His news was useful for the employees of the companies. This could easily be an article on maintaining your teeth by a dentist; individual tax issues by an accountant; or making a will by a lawyer. The first such release delivered to big companies generated five articles in the company newsletters and 46 inquiries. From these, 21 people became new clients after a free consultation.

Promoting to Editors . . .

Seminar speaker Gordon Burgett sends a one-page sheet offering 10 different articles that might be of interest to a publication in which he is trying to get exposure. An editor can just check off any article he or she wants to see, and get it in hard copy or on disk. He also offers a review copy of his current book. On the back of the sheet are various plugs for the book.

Publicity Advice from the Horse's Mouth . . .

Here's some advice from an editor on how to get more publicity. Feature stories are a one-time event. If you want repeat publicity, you need to build a relationship with the media. You become their source to be quoted on stories in your area. To build a relationship, you have to talk to them when you're not pitching a story. Take them to lunch when you have nothing on your agenda, or give them a lead that has nothing to do with you. Also, send thank-you notes. They seldom get them.

Publicity Humor . . .

Speaking as an editor, I can say we're a very jaded group. We've seen a million angles. If your press release looks just like everyone else's, it better have something important to get any attention. One press release for a company at COMDEX, a big computer show, got off to a good start by calling the recipient a "Dear victim/attendee." Anyone who has been to COMDEX, which is a huge zoo, agreed. This opening got editors chuckling and, as one editor said, got them to read the rest of the release. Out of letters to 700 editors, about a hundred stopped by the exhibit as a result of the release.

Use Your Clients

The more interesting your clients, the more publicity you can get for the two of you. Show how your service helps somebody famous—or unusual—succeed. Plus, they'll appreciate your efforts to get them exposure.

Publicity Pays . . .

Albert Prior of Erdman Anthony engineers wrote an article on "ADA and the Workplace of the Future," showing how the Americans with Disabilities Act would affect companies. It got published in 28 engineering and business magazines and newspapers. The best one alone generated 60 leads.

Realty Publicity . . .

Here's another angle you can use to "hook" the interest of your local media. Every place likes to think it is different. One newspaper asked locals to nominate unique homes for sale in the area. What a setup for real estate agents!

You can suggest the idea. Reporters always need them.

The Best of Food and Drink PR . . .

Media are always looking for new ways to cover things their readers care about. That's why you should help them with ideas from this book! In my area, there are newspaper features on the best bars, the best restaurants, the best bars with views, etc. If those don't work for you, how about best ethnic food, best one type of food, most unusual drinks, best on the water, best retro atmosphere, or the like. Or have your own contest at your facility for best bartender, waitress/waiter, quick chef, or whatever.

Silly Publicity . . .

When the media are out of fresh ideas, they'll go for anything new. San Jose State University has to compete in football with the big schools—and they seldom win. The school's marketing consultant put out the word that it was looking for someone with the "evil eye" to put a hex on its next opponent! Stupid? Yes. But it got a story in the major metro paper.

If it fits your style, ask for volunteer witch doctors, psychics, witches, warlocks—whoever it takes to get the media's attention.

More Event Tie-Ins

Here are some other events you can expect that will create publicity opportunities:

- Mud slides or flooding for a gardener
- Major lawsuits or crimes for a lawyer
- Changes in the tax laws for a bookkeeper or CPA
- Global warming or weather shifts for a windsurf instructor or event planner

---

Tailoring Your PR . . .

Margie Seyfer, a telemarketing consultant, writes articles especially tailored for each industry. For instance, in the auto business, she'll use repair shop examples of her general points about how to answer the phone better. People like to read about people like themselves. Her customization makes her come across as an industry insider they'd want to use.

Tie an Old Technique to a New One . . .

Mindy Aleman got publicity by writing a guest column about trade show marketing. She opened it in an unusual way, talking about on-line marketing as the current "cool" way to go. She segued directly into savvy marketers knowing that there are benefits of promoting their services directly and personally via trade shows or events. Then she went on to write the basic article about trade show marketing. This is a kind of publicity hook, where you pick something that is popular and then tie your item to it, as discussed in other items on using holidays as tie-ins.

Stunt Photo . . .

An eye-catching photo is always valuable. One stunt is to have miniature people doing something relevant to your service. For instance, a miniature person could be holding a huge pen signing your contract. Or a person can sit in the world's largest upholstered chair. It's corny, but it always attracts attention.

Research Creates Publicity . . .

Become a recognized expert in your area by doing research. For instance, Empire College, a school that trains its students for jobs in local businesses, does a "what's hot in job skills" survey. Local newspapers run stories based on the survey results on topics like computer use, job responsibiilities, and the most valuable skills an employee can have (which Empire just happens to train people in!). Besides being able to personally profit from the knowledge gleaned from the surveys, a research approach offers the opportunity to recontact survey respondents to thank them, send them a summary of the results, and send them copies of any resulting articles. Besides increasing your name recognition, your customers and prospects will think of you as an expert after a couple of surveys.

Tie Publicity to Outside Events and People . . .

When you tie your publicity efforts to outside events and people, your news becomes of interest to a wider audience, and is hence more likely to be picked up by the media.

DriveSavers is a service that recovers data from computers. They tied one publicity effort to news of a big power outage. Tying your publicity to clients who are more interesting than you also works. DriveSavers placed PR stories about how they rescued the data of a famous group of rock musicians. It was news because of the clients—the same story about recovering data from the hard drive of a teacher would not have been picked up by the media.

· · · *ACTION AGENDA* · · ·

"When you're young and having fun,
time flies. When you're older, time flies
whether you're having fun or not!"
—Anonymous

You'll never be any younger than you are today. Isn't it time that you enjoyed the success and acclaim you deserve? You'll have to make it happen by taking action. If you're a big company, you may have internal PR staff. Or you can hire outside professionals. They'll find many ideas in this section of 51 tips.

→ If you're getting started, I'd recommend that you call the media you're interested in. Give them your idea, and ask for their input. Many will say, "Send a press release," but it will be useful to talk to them and "pitch" your idea directly.

→ As with most marketing, being referred in is best, because of the implicit objectivity. When your acquaintances say they know about an interesting service, it has more credibility than when you try to pitch yourself.

→ Some media are very friendly and really need material. Volunteer newsletters put out by trade and professional groups often fit this category. Weekly community newspapers are another candidate. If you're a beginner, get your practice with the easy ones that know they need your help.

→ There are lots of levels of publicity. You don't need to get a front-page feature about yourself to reap a payoff. Calendar listings and letters to the editor have been very effective for many service providers. Where can you send a letter now?

→ Save a clean copy of any publicity you get; it will build your credibility to get more later.

→ A research survey builds your image and contacts. Make it a short phone survey the first time with 3 to 10 questions.

→ What interesting customers could you build publicity around? For which of your service providers could you be the featured client?

→ What holidays can you tie a press release to?

→ Develop a list of company publications that might use your material.

→ Can you create an interesting photo?

20

Publicity in Many Forms

From Stunts to High Tech

"In the future everyone will be world-famous
for fifteen minutes."

—Andy Warhol

*C*hapter 19 covered more traditional ways to get publicity, such as writing a column or being featured in your local paper. This chapter covers publicity in other media.

While you should target a particular outlet for your publicity, ideas are not always media specific. The same item might be covered by television and the newspaper. So, some of the ideas here can be adapted in many ways. That's the usual case for marketing. It can be done many ways, for many results. Your job is to decide what you want to accomplish and get it done.

✦ ✦ ✦

TV Interview Tip . . .

To look your best on TV don't stare directly at the interviewer. Instead, hold your head still and look back and forth from one of the interviewer's eyes to the other. This causes the whites of your eyes to change shape, which makes your eyes appear to sparkle on camera.

Tap Dancing to Publicity . . .

Every year on Labor Day, tap dancer Bessie Bair tap dances her way across the Golden Gate Bridge as a holiday tribute to workers everywhere. The idea tires me out. And yes, people still tap dance—one of my kids took lessons. (For what I don't know!) If you're a dignified professional, you might use such a stunt to raise money for charity. If you don't worry abut your dignity, go for it just for crass publicity!

CD-ROM Sampler . . .

The Mac Temps Office in London put together a CD-ROM showing available temporary employees and samples of their work. This was appropriate, since their placements are mainly in creative industries, such as advertising and publishing, where multimedia and work samples are popular. Because of the novelty, it was also featured on the cover of a British magazine in time for a trade show. Plus they integrated the disk with publicity for their booth and gave copies away at the show. Calls since then have been up 30 percent. They say, "We've had more coverage from this CD-ROM than from anything we've done since we've been here."

Tie Yourself to the News . . .

To appeal to any media, you need to provide news that their audience will care about. A PR strategy is to tie to current events. Radio host George Chamberlin received a press release after a number of bad fires in his region. The local real estate agent's release talked about how the fires affected local property values. That got him an interview.

Charity Partnerships . . .

New Lamps for Old! Service Merchandise joined with Goodwill Industries to give people a discount on new items if they brought in usable household items for Goodwill. Service got publicity and a tax deduction for the donation. Goodwill got publicity and more stuff to sell. Goodwill even has a special department to encourage

---

Be Different

"I don't care what you do," campaign strategist James Carville once told presidential candidate Bill Clinton, "just make damn sure it's big and different!"

partnerships (301/530-6500). They promise access to their 21 million donors and 63 million shoppers.

Advertising for Publicity . . .

If you're a speaker or national expert, advertising in various directories of experts such as the *Radio-TV Interview Report* brings a few media calls. The average seems to be about one call for $100 of advertising. And saying you were recently interviewed by a station in some faraway place can sound impressive to local media and audiences.

Give to Receive . . .

Giving money to charity is usually good for a little publicity and goodwill. Everen Securities makes its anniversary a "Community Commitment Day." For instance, one office donated 10 percent of its total revenues for the day to the local historical society. Across all its offices, Everen has donated a quarter of a million dollars to local charities. That was enough to get the company a nice mention in one paper.

Award-Winning Publicity . . .

Ruppert Landscape has specialized in winning awards to gain publicity. They spend about $6,000 a year (10 percent of their public relations budget) on entry fees and other costs for award competitions. It has helped build them to their $22 million size. They've won local beautification awards and national association awards. They figure they get twice the publicity from each award because they issue a press release when they win and so does the award giver.

They trace three or four general stories every year in major magazines or newspapers to awards as well. Ruppert also uses contests to enhance visibility in markets where they are not well known.

Publicity from Adversity . . .

The UC Davis swimming team couldn't fly to its meet because of fog at the airport. So, each team swam at its own pool

Publicity from Entering

You can get publicity just from entering contests, especially national ones. Send out a local press release, then you win whether you win or not.

PRESS RELEASE
JOE GARCIA
NOMINATED
FOR
CONTRACTOR
OF THE YEAR

and exchanged results via faxes! The event got way more publicity than a usual meet.

What long-distance contest could you stage?

Crazy Stunts . . .

Sam Walton, the founder of Wal-Mart, said he would do the hula on Wall Street if employees made 8 percent pre-tax profits. They did, he did, and the company got major publicity. You can't do this every month, but Herb Kelleher, CEO of Southwest Airlines, showed that you can do it fairly often. He's full of regular stunts that pull in big publicity.

Photo Publicity for Charity . . .

The media like pictures. Here's great photo publicity in a major paper. One hundred bikers came across the Golden Gate Bridge together to deliver "toys for tots" to a charity. Take pictures yourself, if needed, to get later coverage. This also illustrates tying to a charity and looking for a pictorial "hook." Any group of your association members and their friends would do, delivering holiday turkeys, toys, clothing, and so forth. Do one better by involving the media as an additional sponsor. Then they're guaranteed to cover you and the charity.

Publicity Stunts

In the old days, publicity stunts included antics such as marathon dances, sitting on flagpoles, and swallowing goldfish. Times haven't changed much: any silly stunt can still get you publicity if it provides a good photo opportunity.

Create an Award Today . . .

Do you want publicity? Create an award or list in your local area. Mr. Blackman's Worst Dressed List is a big hit. More business-oriented lists include Messiest Office by an organizer, the Worst Boss contest, and the Top Ten Most Humiliating Public Relations Gaffes by Fineman Associates, a PR firm. The professional car washing and detailing association rated cars based on how washable they were!

"Crappy" Donation Gets Attention . . .

There's always some local publicity to be had by donating a gift certificate for your services to local charity auctions at schools, public television stations, and so forth. A landscaper donated a delivered truckload of horse manure to an auction. He wasn't sure how it would be received, but it got its share of bids, and more attention. Since manure is available free, he uses it regularly now. And when he delivers, other possible work is usually discussed.

Get Certified . . .

Certification won't always build your business, but there are a number of cases where it does. For instance, if you are a software consultant, getting certified by the software vendor will make it easier to sell software to customers, says Bolder Designs, even if you don't really need the training.

Graffiti Publicity . . .

The Abruzzo sons help their mother sell million-dollar homes in one of the most expensive counties in America. They became crusaders against graffiti partly because they traced the loss of one sale ($30,000 in commissions) to a buyer's being afraid that the graffiti she saw meant there were gangs in the neighborhood. Every Sunday the brothers spend a few hours at freeway overpasses with buckets of paint and rollers, making graffiti disappear. It's a great example of how self-interest helps the public. They've gone further to launch Teens Against Graffiti (TAG) in order to get young people to join the fight. A local bank has even provided a $500 grant to help the group get started, which gives the bank publicity. You can add to such an effort by signing up other sponsors against graffiti who would publicize it.

Double Stunt . . .

With a name like Doubletree Hotels, maybe it is logical to have a publicity stunt hiring people who are doubles of film stars and sets of twins. Doubletree had a casting call in its parking lot before

---

Public Service Publicity

Here's another publicity tip for the aggressively civic minded. Reator Rick Thurber makes it a point to tear down any illegally posted sign in his city. "I'm not going to rest until this blight is removed," says Citizen Thurber, dramatically quoted in the local paper. What can you crusade about?

one hotel opening. Lots of people want to be stars. More than 700 identical twins, mostly cute children, and 50 celebrity look-alikes auditioned. Local TV and newspaper photographers took tons of pictures and gave the hotel lots of publicity. The grand opening featured a greeting line of celebrity twins who looked like Clark Gable, Marilyn Monroe, Bill Cosby, and other celebrities. The result: "It was the most successful grand opening in the chain's history."

Employee PR Ideas . . .

Kaufman & Broad gave each of its employees a company T-shirt and challenged them to get publicity exposure from it—legally. The winner of the campaign would get a weekend for two in New York. Two hundred employees got the company publicity during the six-week contest. They varied from wearing it skydiving, to sending it to a gondolier in Italy to wear (sending a picture back). One winning entry marched 100 employees in T-shirts to an overpass, causing traffic jams. Another put together a mock magazine with computer-generated images of Michelle Pfeiffer in the T-shirt. I like the one that enlarged the T-shirt and had it put on an elephant!

Fixing the Vote . . .

If your trade association or local newspaper has a contest for the best of _____ , you should consider trying to promote yourself. One accountant won the Best Accountant in the County Award one year because everyone in his networking group voted for each other, effectively stuffing the ballot box. Guy Kawasaki won a similar industry award for a small software company he was working with because he sent letters and even ballots to all of its customers soliciting their votes for the product. He was so successful in turning out the votes that giant Microsoft, which had a competing product, protested.

Political Publicity . . .

During elections, a local restaurant offered free soup to anyone with a voter stub. Guess what: that's illegal in a federal election. But it is permissible for local elections between federal years. And the restaurant got extra publicity because their offer was illegal for the federal election!

PR by Fax . . .

Gaughen Public Relations has a fax-on-demand system. They offer both information for the media and information on how to do publicity for book authors and others. As with many other fax-on-demand systems, an activity log records the callers' fax numbers and the documents they order. This gives the company a targeted list they can use to send people relevant follow-up information.

> ### Fax on Demand
>
> Want to try some fax-on-demand numbers? Try these:
>
> - U.S. Commerce Department Hotline: 202/482-1064 (for trade information on the Near East)
> - Para Publishing: 805/968-8947 (for information on self-publishing)
>
> Just dial the number and follow the instructions to get documents sent directly to your fax machine.

Publicity Alchemy: Lead into Gold . . .

Bad press can be a chance for you to get *good* exposure. A local TV station had run stories on telemarketing scams. Ralph Reese, owner of a telemarketing firm, invited the station to send a crew in to show viewers how to determine if a call was fraudulent. (Consumer education is a perennial way to get publicity because it helps the media's customers, not you.) Naturally, it showed the company's call center to advantage. Similar publicity points could be gained by a lawyer decrying frivolous lawsuits, a roofer educating consumers on how to avoid rip-offs, or a plastic surgeon pointing out that changes in the face can help self-esteem.

Publicity Cause . . .

Regian & Wilson advertising and publicity is winning recognition for hiring and advancing women—about half the company at all levels. They show their own PR skills by getting awards from women's media groups and local publicity for their efforts. This is also an example of tying to a trend or current news.

Publicity Culture . . .

Redwood Landscaping does lots of clever things that get it publicity and help employee morale—such as sponsoring the wedding of two employees on the company parade float (getting the employees lots of presents from other firms too) and deploying its precision lawn mower drill team for parades. Golden Gate Disposal also has a precision drill team for parades. It's a kick.

Publicity for Possibilities . . .

A pawnshop in Atlanta got free publicity during the Olympics by tying to the event. They put a sign in their window: "Gold medals pawned!" No one took them up on it, but they got the publicity.

Publicity Stunt Is for the Birds . . .

There's a saying that any publicity is good as long as they spell your name right. A Scottish insurance company, Scottish Life International, sent out 77 homing pigeons in England to news media promoting investments. Plus they offered a prize to the organization whose bird returned home first. People complained to the SPCA, and even the Racing Pigeon Association said it was a bad idea. Associated Press (the big wire service) didn't mind. They released theirs and reported the story on the international wire. It certainly got attention, which is the point of a stunt!

Sidewalk of Fame Brings Publicity . . .

Express Press has its own "Walk of Fame," like Hollywood Boulevard. Hand and foot imprints from 90 celebrities now appear on the sidewalk outside the company's plant. Every new imprint is new publicity.

Rather than wait for celebrities, you could start with people in your town who deserve recognition, from the chamber of commerce person of the year, to the largest donor, to a charity event you cosponsor.

Publicity from Your Own Contest . . .

Here's another "contest" to get publicity. San Jose State University has a bad writing contest every year. You get publicity at the front end recruiting entries. Then you publicize yourself and the "winners" at the end.

What contest could you sponsor?

Publicity from Spouting Off . . .

"Cheaper!" is a chain of discount food and cigarette stores that is doing great. They publish libertarian-type rantings on their bags against things like taxes and intrusive government regulations. The bags are so popular that they've been gathered into at least one book, *Bagatorials*. If you're willing to be radical or controversial, try something daring on your napkins, bags, bills, etc.

Ridiculous Stunts for Charity . . .

If you can launch a contest to get people to do stunts to raise money for charity, you get all of the publicity without having to be ridiculous yourself. One company offered bartenders a trip for two, a two-thousand dollar cash prize, and trophies for raising the most money for charity, tying into their services. The bartenders parachuted, competed in triathlons, and ate sacks of raw oysters on the steps of City Hall wearing diapers. They got lots of publicity for themselves and the company—and raised lots of money for charity.

· · · ACTION AGENDA · · ·

"If a man can write a better book, preach a
better sermon, or make a better mouse-
trap than his neighbor, though he builds
his house in the woods the world will
make a beaten path to his door."
—Ralph Waldo Emerson

I refer to Emerson's quote as "the world's fourth biggest lie" because in this world of overly busy people, advertising clutter, and intense competition, the world *won't* notice you unless you help them—repeatedly! Many of the 29 ideas in this chapter can get you attention. But, as usual, you have to apply them.

➜ Can you have a contest for your employees to get your
company publicity?

→ Can you create an event to raise money for charity?

→ Can you combine the first two and compete with other companies, such as your suppliers, customers, or competitors, to use events to raise money for a charity?

→ Can you give an award, or create a top 10 list?

→ Can you take on a cause, such as graffiti or litter?

→ Is there a contest you can win?

→ What stunt can you create for publicity?

21

On-Line Marketing

"Success in the on-line marketplace isn't a sure
thing . . . [but] nothing we've seen so far
comes close to its potential."
—Jay Conrad Levinson and Charles Rubin,
Guerrilla Marketing On-Line

*A*fter 20 years of quiet development among academics and
nonprofits, the Internet exploded onto the scene in the
mid-90s as an "overnight" success. One of the intriguing
facets about on-line is that it has characteristics of most other
forms of marketing. Websites are like billboards and catalogs.
On-line can include advertising, publicity, mail, video, the
telephone, customer service, research, networking, and most
other aspects of marketing. In many ways, it is integrated marketing by itself.

As a mass advertising media, on-line has been disap-
pointing. However, as a new form of communication—E-
mail—it has been a big success.

E-mail combines many of the best features of the telephone with mail. At its best, it can be an intimate, immediate
way to build connections between people, without the frustrations of voice mail, delays, and so on.

One of the exciting—and distracting—features of on-line
marketing is that every week new tools are being developed.

235

Just remember that marketing is not about techniques; it's about building relationships with customers and prospects. On-line is simply another way to do that. Whether your website sings and dances may not be the major concern of your audience.

This chapter offers many ideas that you may find useful. It is important that you develop your own hands-on familiarity with on-line. If you're interested, go on-line and judge the current state of the art—and the aggravations—yourself.

+++

On-Line Customer Types . . .

Demographics divide people by objective criteria such as computer ownership. Psychographics divide people by attitudes and psychological variables. From a study by Odyssey, a market research firm, here are some demographic/psychographic groups and how they relate to on-line and high-tech usage:

- *Enthusiasts* want to be on the cutting edge of technology. They'll pay a premium, but they want high performance. These people would respond to a website that sings and dances.

- *Hopefuls* have attitudes similar to enthusiasts but don't have the money necessary, nor the technological knowledge, to be on the cutting edge. They'd like to be involved with on-line, but it has to be on a budget.

- *Satisfied households* watch a lot of television and are quite satisfied with it. They are somewhat positive about new technologies but see no real need for change. This group will gradually become more on-line oriented.

- *Old-liners* don't want to be involved in new technology. To promote a service to them, you should make it look easy to use, and not cutting-edge.

- *Independents* are not particularly interested in technology, even though they have the means to pay for it and the demographic profile for it. To attract them, on-line would have to fit their interests outside of media and technology.
- *TV households* have mixed feelings about technology. They watch a lot of television but don't enjoy it. They have high incomes, but they are cynical about business and concerned about privacy issues.

There are many other ways to slice up people's attitudes toward technology and media use, but this sample should give you ideas of what might be useful as you market on-line.

Networking for Introverts . . .

Many business users have made friends, found clients and suppliers, even fallen in love on-line. On-line chat rooms, forums, and various clubs are a good way to network if you're shy about meeting people in person. You share an interest—the topic of the forum—and you can take your time typing in your responses.

On-Line Advertising with Attitude . . .

On the Internet, having an "attitude" is cool. So, when PSINet took a full-page ad that said, "Having more experience than any other Internet service provider doesn't mean we're better than they are. (Aahh, screw it. Of course it does!)," it fit the on-line style. Since the ad was in *Forbes*, which is more conservative, it got even more attention.

E-Mail Sales

Spamming is the sending of unsolicited messages to people you don't know. Here are ratings of whom customers would be willing to get unsolicited E-mail from:

- From a company I do business with — 60 percent
- From a magazine I subscribe to — 48 percent
- About my interests and hobbies — 48 percent
- From a company I know but haven't done business with — 14 percent
- From a company I don't know — 9 percent
- From none of the above — 27 percent

Better Meeting Information . . .

Perhaps the World Wide Web's best use is as a customer service tool. Meeting planners and travel agents are now posting material on their websites for prospects and customers to look at. This can be anything from floor plans to directions. Why shouldn't any service provider post educational material—on teeth for a dentist, food for a nutritionist, or keeping out of contract trouble for a lawyer?

On-Line Service . . .

An architectural services firm found that competition and high costs were cutting into profits. To improve service and cut travel time for meetings they helped their clients go on-line. By making plans available in real time on the client's computer, the firm could discuss them, cut down cycle time, and improve service. They started with six clients who were technologically ready, and they are gradually introducing it to the rest.

On-Line Sales Leads . . .

Kaufman and Broad, a big home builder, tracked 32 sales to its website at *New Homes* magazine's site. Because they're exposed to more detailed information such as floor plans, on-line prospects are probably better qualified than other leads.

Free Samples Get Them Hooked . . .

Www.submit-it.com is one of several websites that will register your site with many indexes and search engines, thus helping you market yourself. They make their money by selling deluxe services that do even more for you. You can give out samples of your expertise at your website and in chat groups.

On-Line Flattery . . .

Michael Swartz of DNA Software surfs the Web to find sites he can say something nice about. It's a good way to start a "conversation" and a relationship for business.

Better On-Line Listings . . .

The search engines for your category typically provide only the top 20 sites at a time, and most browsers don't look beyond those. The trick is to find the rules the search engine uses for listing the top 20. Most often it's based on recency of updates, or newness of the pages. In order to exploit that, Stan Rosenzweig, owner of a computer business, hired student interns to surf the net for his firm and post listings to his site, make changes in content, and update the page in order to keep it consistently in the top 20.

On-Line Focus Group . . .

WP-Studio wanted to conduct focus groups with broader representation than the company could get by itself with traditional methods. It used Cyber Dialog (212/804-1170) to do on-line focus groups. Cyber Dialog has a large database on which to draw, and not only were the on-line sessions cheaper than regular focus groups, but also respondents seemed to be more frank, since they could all type anonymously at once. Results were also faster.

> FOCUS GROUPS: Groups of about 6 to 10 people selected for their interest in your service. You use them to get customer or prospect input, judge reactions to new services or advertisements, and so forth.

On-Line Cards . . .

You can create an on-line business card using free software from www.versit.com. It attaches your card, complete with picture and/or sound bite, to your E-mail.

On-Line Mortgages . . .

Eastern Mortgage Services got 50–100 home equity loan applications a week from its website within months of creating it. Plus, the applications are for higher average amounts but cost Eastern only $10 to handle on-line, versus $100+ the traditional way. The company approaches its offer as it would any other direct mail solicitation by making it to the point and easy to read, offering free 24-hour approval, and calling for action. To attract people, Eastern employs the "traditional" on-line marketing techniques of registering with search engines and linking with more than 200 other sites.

Phone Cards Plus Internet . . .

What's as hot as on-line marketing in some circles? Phone cards. So, naturally there are phone cards for on-line access instead of long distance. The first to create one was Interactive Media Works. One of the first to use it was the Junior League of San Francisco. A cute promo item or fund-raiser, but a gimmick, since you have to wait to receive a disk for actual on-line access.

"Get Rich Click" . . .

On-line advertising has been much more accepting of guaranteed response than traditional advertising. YoyoDine is one of many businesses that made a performance guarantee. In their case, they ran a sweepstakes that required people to visit various sites. They guaranteed that as a sponsor of their "Get Rich Click" promotion, you'd receive at least 70,000 verified individual visitors to your website during the sweepstakes. If they didn't make those numbers, they promised to refund 50 cents per person less than 70,000.

Pay Only for Responses . . .

As of 1997, there was still more hype than business on-line. But in one year, from a standing start, Venture Communications (212/684-4800) claims to have generated two million actual leads for its advertisers on its website. And you pay only for the leads you actually get. Called *per-inquiry*, it's used mostly for situations in which you can afford to give away a free sample and then bill people. Many respondents don't pay because they just like free samples. However, at $5–10 a lead, per-inquiry might just work wonders for a national

---

Other Guaranteed Exposure

Traditional media (everyone before the Web!) don't normally guarantee how many people your ad will reach. But, in fact, TV often guarantees a minimum number of viewers. If ratings don't support them, they refund partial payment.

lawyers referral service, consulting firm, travel agent, and so on.

On-Line Consulting . . .

A&T Internet, a computer consulting firm (VAR), got their first huge client quickly. They make successful cold calls. They approach clients as businesspeople who can handle the computer technicalities. They offer a complete solution, from full hardware to website design. They find radio effective for raising their general visibility. They take a true consulting approach by turning down clients they don't think have the visibility or budget to be successful on-line.

On-Line Advertising Exchange . . .

Can you get other people to advertise for you on-line? Yes. On-line, anything is possible. As of 1997, about two-thirds of advertising revenues on-line were collected by just a dozen big sites such as browsers that everyone uses. Now services to combine smaller websites are starting up. For instance, Internet Link Exchange gives your small site one ad on the network of 50,000+ small sites for every two you put on your site. The extras are then sold to big advertisers who can get 50,000 placements in a single buy.

> **On-Line Growth**
>
> The number of users on-line is estimated to reach 150 million by the year 2000. The *Wall Street Journal* predicts that there will be one *billion* home pages by then! Whatever the true numbers, the potential is great, yet you can start one contact at a time.
>
>

On-Line Video Contact . . .

Brian Currier of Merrill Lynch loves to look prospects in the eye, so he bought video conferencing equipment. It worked a couple of times, but he couldn't find many people with equipment at the other end. It's now less expensive, though cruder, on the Internet. And people there like to play with technology, so they're open to contact.

Partnerships On-Line . . .

Trade Point, a nonprofit trade group, is selling information on-line in partnership with Dun & Bradstreet, Price Waterhouse, and similar companies. It's the free-enterprise theory of altruism. They're all hoping to benefit by exploiting the others' contacts and know-how.

Screen Saver Advertising . . .

A.L.T. Advertising and Promotion uses a screen saver to pitch its own services, and it also creates screen savers for its clients. Advertising on screen savers is a way of getting repeated exposure to your target audience direct on their computers.

Roundtable Sharing . . .

What's the hot topic in your area? Scott Jackson got his local chamber of commerce to sponsor a roundtable to share information about the Internet among local companies. Of course, he just happened to chair it! Great positioning for any consultant. Plus you get good stories to share even if someone doesn't become a client. The chamber also got publicity outside its member base.

On-Line Humor . . .

Carolyn Schler set up a website for the Schwartz Cohen CPA firm. *Net Guide* magazine rated it as "the sort of page Henny Youngman would have created if he were a CPA. There were links to business and finance pages, but we were more interested in links to Monty Python and Blue Dog Can Count." CPAs with a sense of humor, what an idea. Any clients who are on-line will tend to be more progressive and more interested in humor than those who aren't. This is the perfect personality for on-line. Many of the firm's clients now use E-mail to communicate with them, which impressed the partners. They calculate that clients downloading information is a $1,800 savings in the costs of sending out material alone, over traditional correspondence. Carolyn gets further publicity by speaking to the American Institute of Certified Public Accountants about on-line marketing. And she's even developed a practice advising other CPAs on how to do websites.

On-Line Access by Phone . . .

You can now make your website accessible to anyone with a Touch-Tone phone. One way is to have specific pages of your site set up to a fax-on-demand system. People first call for a menu of the website, then they can call back and have any document delivered to any fax machine. Other technology is also available, such as Web-on-call. This lets you keep in touch with the 80 percent of people not on-line.

> ### Content Is King
>
> "Content is where I expect much of the real money will be made on the Internet, just as it was in broadcasting . . . The Internet allows information to be distributed worldwide at basically zero marginal cost to the publisher."
>
> —Bill Gates,
> Microsoft Corp.

Partnership On-Line . . .

ConstructionNet is an on-line service for architects, engineers, contractors, and suppliers. They created a partnership with the Association of Builders and Contractors (ABC) to list all of its members free on the service. This gives ConstructionNet more resources for browsers to find, and naturally the ABC gives them free publicity.

Speed Sells . . .

Doyle Wilson may be the fastest home builder in Texas. At an average of 124 days from permit to completion, they save money too. They won a Baldrige Award for quality, so speed helps, not hurts. For more on their approach, see their website (www.doylewilson.com) which is another marketing and education tool.

On-Line Clipping Services . . .

The old-fashioned clipping service regularly cuts articles out of magazines and newspapers for clients. Now many clipping-type services are available on-line. You tell them what you are looking for, and they'll do a daily search for you and deliver it to your mailbox. You can look for items on your own company, clients, prospects, competitors, and general knowledge. Since so many rumors and outright falsities are being spread on-line, you want to make sure of what they are saying about your company so that you can respond promptly. One of the first on-line clipping services was e-Watch. Business Wire (800/227-0845) is one of the larger services in this area.

Better Research On-Line . . .

ADP consults with organizations on how to handle government regulations and paperwork. They position themselves as "the experts." They keep up on the newest regulations through on-line and other research. Then they notify clients and prospects, and generate more business for themselves.

Competitive On-Line Research . . .

Benn Konsynski, of Emory University, says one company visited a competitor's website a few weeks before a major trade show. The company found a preview of a major promotion to be kicked off at the show. They had time to change their pricing for the show so they wouldn't be upstaged.

Giveaways Aren't Upscale . . .

Electric Press was one of many small providers that started creating websites for other companies. They made 5,000 cold calls in the first six months and found less than 2 percent of companies interested. But in early 1994, few knew what the Web was. Giving away free sample pages didn't attract the type of upscale customers they needed. Electric specializes in websites with big databases that customers' customers can search to decide on a purchase. Once they got the first good customers, referrals followed.

Reading the Signs . . .

Most competitive information is subtle. For instance, one company spotted a competitor's want ad for software engineers in a Usenet newsgroup. Since the company had been focused on hard-

---

Finding More Search Tools

Good search tools are what make on-line research possible. The website www.search.com offers links to hundreds of search tools. As newer and better ones become available, they are included.

ware, the ad signaled a shift in corporate emphasis, which later emerged.

Website Surveys . . .

Ritchey Design designs bike components. They set up a website to gather customer reactions to a few questions that could be changed regularly. Getting reactions before manufacturing may save them $100,000 a year on development and design costs. They also educate consumers about the benefits of their designs which helps them with their dealers.

On-Line Partnering . . .

Virtual companies are easy to run on-line. You can extend your capacities by subbing out work to freelancers on-line. For instance, Real Estate On-Line was formed when one partner spotted a great realty ad site on-line created by the other. And Muffin-Head Productions (multimedia) formed after a wanted posting on-line.

Advertiser-Supported E-Mail . . .

Juno Online Services was among the first companies to offer consumers free E-mail service. Since E-mail is the most used on-line service, they got a big response and lots of PR: 50,000+ new users a week, even when not promoting. Consumers fill out a profile that allows Juno to select ads to display on-screen. Thus, advertisers subsidize the service, just as with most other media.

Can you flip costs around by getting employers to pay for legal services, tax help, shopping services, child care, or the like to create a new benefit for workers? It's often easier to make one big sale than 20 little ones. Juno also used partners such as Blockbuster and modem manufacturers to give away their service. Analogously, you might distribute free gift certificates for your good clients to give away—*if* you can convert enough samplers to paid clients.

On-Line Brainstorming . . .

Marketing Partners found it expensive to bring together buyers, clients, and others for brainstorming sessions in one place, so they tried a software program called Co-Motion Lite (Bittco Solutions, 800/265-2726). This allowed them to brainstorm over the Internet. In some ways it's better than an in-person brainstorming session because everyone can be typing in ideas at the same time, anonymity allows people to be crazier, and the program lets everyone rate various ideas and automatically ranks them for a final report. Within an hour they completed a very satisfactory session with a client and others.

BRAINSTORMING: A structured idea-generating process in which no discussion or criticism is allowed. It's fast free association; crazy ideas are encouraged, as is combining and adapting ideas.

Disks Marketing Disks . . .

If you're a service provider like Prentice Associates which helps people use computer disks to market themselves, you'll naturally use a computer disk to market your services. The company's brochure is designed to fit in a disk mailer along with a sample disk. One style Prentice uses can be adapted by anyone. A disk lets the company ask a series of questions that can be automatically scored. Your answers tell you whether or not the disk service Prentice offers could work for you.

The test-question format is a good one, whether you're selling plumbing services or high-tech consulting. It demonstrates your expertise by the quality of your questions, much like a work sample. *Forbes* magazine has used a similar disk from the Interactive Marketing Group to sell advertising.

Give Clients Links . . .

If you have a website, it costs you nothing to give your clients added value with links to your page, as consultant Dan Janal does. (And of course you'll have one on theirs.) It also gives you one more reason, other than selling, to contact them. Now take it one step further. Instead of having miscellaneous links that don't fit your page theme, the links can be attached to clients' testimonials. Haven't got testimonials from every customer? This is a reason to get them!

Intranet Marketing Support . . .

Henrichs Financial Group has set up its own private on-line system for the $80 million company. The system saves money in distributing documents and helps agents create custom proposals that sell. These systems are very much like updated bulletin boards that can be set up quite inexpensively.

Low-Cost Big Six . . .

Ernst & Young wants to keep its finger in with small, fast-growing entrepreneurs. The company has set up special consulting by Internet. For $6,000 a year, small firms can send questions to a private website. The questions are routed to appropriate experts, and E-mail responses are promised within two business days. Customers also have access to published material from the firm. Gartner Group and Giga Information have similar consulting on-line.

> ### Relationships Still Count
> "The consensus is strong that relationship marketing will thrive on the Net, thanks to its speed, low cost, and convenience."
> —*Direct* magazine

On-Line Boating Business . . .

Captain's Quest teaches seminars on becoming a professional boat captain. They also offer boat test-taking software and rent captains. Their capquest.com website has educational information, weather, Coast Guard data, and the like. It's a public service, but lots of business comes from it too.

On-Line Business Relationships . . .

Mike Bayer specializes in public relations for the legal industry using on-line methodology. In two years he provided services to 21 law firms in 11 states that he never met face-to-face. It was all done on-line with E-mail and his cyber-brochure. He's also hired a number of subcontractors unseen on-line, such as editors, list brokers, and researchers.

On-Line Personnel . . .

Transquest Technologies is an employment agency for high-tech clients. Their website doubled their business within three months. They did fancy effects and were rated the best job employment site on the Internet. This got them even more attention. It's also saved them thousands of dollars in monthly advertising expenses. Most of the candidates they want for high-tech jobs will be on-line if they're qualified!

Virtual Reality Realty . . .

Despite the great potential of the Internet for showing realty, it's slow happening. A company called eTours was the first company in the San Francisco area to put major commercial space on-line with photos and floor plans. It's also available on disk. Soon companies will let users take 3-D tours of offices and test how the offices would look with their own furniture in it.

Dental Success . . .

An upscale dentist put up a Web page. He began to attract people from a greater distance than his regular clientele. People who are on-line prefer to do business with others on-line. Just doing this Web page also helped his referrals. His upscale clients thought it was "cool" recommending a dentist with a Web page. He's getting about two patients a month and six additional referrals.

Personal Network Uses Old PCs . . .

Goode & Associates types dictation from hospitals. When they upgraded their computers, they had a bunch of old 386s left. So they offered them to their clients so that they could transmit transcripts by modem. They even installed the software and modems when necessary. Four smaller clients accepted, freeing up Goode's printers and saving $60+ a week in delivery costs to each account. Customers like the new service. Some larger customers also went on the new system using their own computers.

· · · *ACTION AGENDA* · · ·

"Failure is the path of least persistence."
—Anonymous

"Persistence is courage in action."
—Brian Tracy

On-line marketing is hot. But clogged phone lines and backlash to all the hype are also common. Is on-line a new, exciting marketing medium? Yes. Is it going to solve all your problems for free? No.

Like any other marketing idea or method mentioned in this book, the 44 examples in this chapter can help you build bridges to customers and prospects. But that requires work on your part. Persistence is courage in action. New behaviors are always uncomfortable. That's natural and healthy. But if you offer a useful service, you're not imposing on people if you let them know how you might help them. So take action and persist.

→ If you aren't on-line, get a basic account and surf around to get familiar with it.

→ If you've been meaning to do a website, look into the inexpensive software that will make one for you quickly. First-generation websites just sit there. Make sure to update useful information so that people will have a reason to come back. Second-generation websites use banners, frames, and other motion and interactive devices to get attention. Third-generation websites draw visitors through without their having to go back to the home page. Fourth-generation websites are under development now. They change for each user via custom databases. They've simplified the fancy effects. And they introduce new elements still in planning.

→ Who can you create links with? Ask everyone—most will say yes.

→ Who can you sell links or advertising space to? How about leads?

→ What forums and mailing lists should you be on? Can you start your own?

→ Get listed in the directories and then work to keep your entries at the top of the lists.

→ Set up custom search tools to go find you the type of material you look for.

→ Develop a good 10-word or shorter description of what you do to attach to your E-mail signature.

22

Service That Builds Relationships

"If we bend over backwards for our clients'
success, we can never fall on our faces."
—Michael May, Farmers New World Life

*R*emember that marketing is defined as anything you do to get *or* keep a customer. Even service providers who hate what they think of as marketing have to support the idea of giving great customer service. Successful companies in many industries have 90 percent repeat business. Since even average ones generally have 60 percent, providing great customer service is clearly the most important marketing you can do.

Unfortunately, the research shows that merely *satisfied* customers are not particularly loyal. Most studies show that to obtain referrals and good word of mouth, either customers have to feel a personal connection to you or you need to "thrill" them. For instance, a recent study found that 90 percent of customers said they were satisfied with their automobile, but only 30–40 percent actually repurchased that brand of car. AT&T found that 95 percent of customers were satisfied, but far more were defecting. It takes an emotional connection between customers and providers to create real loyalty.

Being a "friend" in the business who treats people as individuals is a powerful way to get and keep customers. Following are some ideas on how to build relationships.

+++

High Value in Customer Retention . . .

Employer Services provides payroll and employment-related services. They calculated that a 4 percent increase in their customer retention rate translated to a 21 percent improvement in net earnings. The REL Consultancy Group calculates that a 5 percent increase in retention can mean a 40 percent increase in banking profits and almost a 60 percent increase for insurance brokerage or laundry services in profits. Bain & Company found that a 5 percent increase in retention can increase profits 25–100 percent.

Better Bedside Manners . . .

A study in the *Journal of the American Medical Association* showed that doctors with better bedside manners are less likely to be sued by patients. Those in many of the more

---

Dr. Tattersall Provides a Timeless Lesson
by Tom Peters

The idea of . . . electronic [or any other] connections . . . is to forge close, lasting intimate relationships . . . with customers, even masses of customers, one at a time . . . Take the little case of M. H. N. Tattersall, an Australian physician. The *Wall Street Journal* describes an experiment he conducted on office procedures. After the visit of 48 patients, the doctor randomly split them into two categories. Half got follow-up letters, half didn't. Thirteen of the 24 who got letters later said they were "completely satisfied," the highest possible rating. Only four of the 24 nonrecipients made the same assessment. Think about that: A mere letter increased the number of fully satisfied customers by a factor of more than three.

What is a visit to a doctor? It's a complex event. Dr. Tattersall . . . brings years of scientific training and experience to bear on a diagnosis. Yet this one time twist, a follow-up letter, can completely change the patient's perception of the service rendered. Look at it another way. A doctor's consultation plus a letter is an entirely different service/product from a consultation without a letter . . .

I am suggesting that the technical part of "your" act is far from the whole story and that the worth of the nontechnical elements is often badly underestimated, or not even considered.

technical professions such as law, accounting, and medicine tend to intimidate their clients and may not take the time for little courtesies to build human relations. Doctors who had been sued were rated worse on how long they kept patients waiting, how much time they spent with patients, not treating people with respect, and not listening to their concerns and questions. This study also suggested that there was no difference between the technical quality of the care offered by doctors who were sued and not sued. It was the poor communication, misunderstanding, and lack of respect that seemed to cause the problems.

Salespeople Overestimate Relationships

When customers and salespeople both rated the quality of their relationships, salespeople greatly overestimated the relationship quality they had established. Do you?

MY CUSTOMERS LOVE ME

Big Customer Welcome . . .

One company goes all out to impress visiting customers or prospects. They do more than just post a board in the reception lobby. They make a big banner that says, "Welcome, Bob." All of their employees wear badges that say, "Welcome, Bob." And Bob has a badge that says, "I'm Bob." When he leaves, they give Bob the banner. He will remember his visit to this company more than anyplace else.

Showing You Care . . .

By knowing her clients well, one lawyer is able to build professional links. For instance, when she travels, she collects articles from airline magazines that might be of interest to her clients. She might send them only one article every few months, but it adds up to the fact that she is thinking about them and keeping in touch.

Thank-You Cards Get Noticed . . .

Venture Communications sends out a "Thank You For Your Business" card. While it's a standard card and not particularly original, it impresses me because I just don't get thank-you cards much. Do you send them? It also has their Rolodex card die-cut inside. And your Venture representative personalizes it with a note.

Promote Your Clients . . .

A big consulting company, MSA, sold to lots of banks. At an American Bankers convention they distributed buttons that said, "Thanks to Banks." Since nobody ever thanks banks, they were remembered and appreciated. They became known as the thanks-to-banks company, making them a preferred vendor. S E Rykoff is a big distributor of food to restaurants and institutions. For years, they've shown what a simple slogan on a dull truck can do. It says, "Enjoy Life: Eat Out More Often." The slogan supports their clients, so they get goodwill. And they do more business if people follow their "advice."

> **Acknowledge Customers**
>
> "People like to be recognized because they see themselves as important and worthwhile; a business that acknowledges this importance is a business that maintains customer esteem."
>
> —Schneider and Bowen, *Winning the Service Game*

Another area in which you can promote your client industry is letters to the editor defending them when they're criticized. Then send copies to people in the industry for greater visibility.

Recognize Clients . . .

Lonnie Hirsch, of the Practice Builder Association, says that recognizing a "client of the month" can build referrals, on average about 8 percent. Choose the client who has given you the most referrals that month, or other business ideas or support. Give a small, appropriate, award such as a certificate. If you invite the winner to lunch, take pictures of the client or of the event to post, with notices of it, around your office. Mention it to other clients, and let it be known that you are looking to recognize clients. Everyone likes recognition. Some of your clients will respond to this sort of program so that you'll get more referrals from them, as well as from the 12 people a year who you recognize.

Get Out in the Field . . .

Leon Steinberg of the Maslon Edelman law firm spends about half a day a week at one of his major clients' offices. He might give a presentation, attend management meetings, or whatever. By being on-site, he gets more contact and questions and shows how important the client is. He even gets to bill much of the time! Try it with a few of your biggest clients. Something good will almost always result.

Bayou Banking . . .

First Commerce Corp. figured that about 80 percent of its profits came from 20 percent of its customer base. Yet even this best 20 percent were giving the bank only 20 percent of their financial deposits and purchases. In order to build its relationship with these customers, First Commerce voluntarily moved accounts to pay more interest or lowered service charges. The bank has retained 94 percent of these most profitable clients.

> **TLC = TLC**
>
> It's a fortunate coincidence that TLC can stand for both Tender Loving Care and Think Like a Customer. If you put yourself in the customers' shoes, you're more likely to give them the kind of empathetic care they want.

Beg for Complaints . . .

Burke Customer Satisfaction consulting is among many to show that customers who have a problem that you take care of are *more* loyal than those who never had a problem with you. Complaints give you a chance to shine in handling them. Bribe people for complaints. It will pay off.

Changes Create Contact Opportunities . . .

When two designers merged their firms, it was a reason to send notices to their better past clients with fancy chocolate logos. They assured them that they, the principals, were still there and service would be better than ever. It reminded several dormant clients to call about new assignments.

One-to-One Marketing . . .

You can't build relationships if you don't know people! Follow Harvey Mackay's advice and gather information about their hobbies, interests, personal background, and family. A successful Midwest contractor established an "Executive Customer Focus" program that assigned specific accounts to employees. Each executive has the responsibility for establishing individual relationships with key customers and increasing contacts with them. As a consultant from FMI notes, these one-to-one approaches will give this contractor the edge.

Customer Advisory Boards . . .

A great way to get input from clients is to create a customer advisory board. If you are small, a board with big names can also be a promotional device suggesting your capabilities. IT&T Sheraton first put together boards with fans of the hotel, but they were so loyal that they didn't have enough suggestions on how to improve things. A board with some loyal customers, some weak accounts, and some prospects gave them the most value. They also found that members get stale after awhile, so they should be rotated off every two or three years.

Extra Work Pays . . .

Look for ways to impress people with your willingness to go the extra mile. A contractor wasn't ready to buy but mentioned that he was looking for information about a resort town in a neighboring state. The saleswoman for his supplies told him what she knew. Later she called the chamber of commerce in the town and asked them to send her brochures on the area. Then she wrote a note thanking the prospect for his time, and telling him that she had found the enclosed brochures and hoped he could use them for his next vacation. The following week the prospect was ready to buy. Helping him out despite the fact that he hadn't bought played a big role.

Educational Services . . .

Here are extras that some banks offer to their clients. Seminars or tutorials on on-line banking and reading financial statements; making "house calls"; serving on an informal board of advisers; and helping customer companies with small business information.

Frequent-User Rewards . . .

Ameritech is among many cellular phone companies that use frequent-caller rewards. The program has a strong appeal to customers, and people who sign up significantly increase usage and decrease defection. For restaurants, it's a frequent-eater club. For a beauty parlor, you get your card punched every time you have your hair done, and then earn a reward when your card is full. For a more professional service, a program like this might be introduced as just a fun perk in order to make it acceptable.

Glorifying the Client . . .

How can you show big clients you *really care*? To show their concentration on clients, GSD&M, an advertising agency, set up "war rooms" for each client's work. They were painted the client's colors, and the client's account strategy material was posted on the walls. A dedicated room pulls together research material and allows focused meetings. It also reminds employees who's the boss (the client!) and clients love having space dedicated to them.

A number of accountants have named parts of their offices for clients! Not only do clients love to see their names when they come in, but the people they refer feel more at home there as well. One agency estimated that referrals increased 10 percent from the people so honored.

Fun Builds Relationships . . .

A British Airways flight was delayed, and the crew decided to have a contest to pass the time. If you could guess the collective age of the cabin crew, you won a prize, with an additional prize for guessing the speaker's age. They told jokes and made the flight memorable. Southwest Air has gotten lots of publicity for this sort of thing. What are you doing to make your customers' experiences this memorable?

Your Clients Help Their Clients . . .

Boulder Designs helped architects and engineers with CAD systems. Once Boulder's clients were on-line with the systems, they wanted to exchange files for *their* clients. For liability reasons, architects need to keep paper copies of plans and designs, even though exchanging files with contractors and owners via computer is a lot more efficient. Boulder coordinated the clients' needs using Lotus Notes software and set up a special methodology for tracking E-mail and other communication for clients and architects. One client, architect Bauer Lewis, believes the new system has been crucial to its recent designs of Atlantic City casinos and Marriott Hotels. The system combined the efficiency of Internet electronic communication with the regulatory "paper" trail. Boulder got a copyrighted product to sell out of a customized service, and clients got a solution that improves their efficiency and communications with their own clients.

> ### Relationships and Service
>
> "The names of the marketing game in the 90s and beyond are relationships and service . . . [and] it takes time to nurture the customer relationships and render superlative service."
>
> —Jay Conrad Levinson, author of the *Guerrilla Marketing* books

Humor Would Have Helped . . .

This formally printed sign was posted on the door of a bank at Halloween:

> To Our Costumed Customers on Halloween,
> October 31, 1996:
> Because of the nature of banking, it is
> important that you remove your mask prior
> to entering the branch.
> Thank You, WestAmerica Bank

They made this sign a little too much like a formal legal notice. They should have made it cuter with nice hand-lettering, perhaps adding something like this: "There is candy for trick-or-treating in the lobby. But if you wear a mask into the bank, the trick may be on you!"

Listening Pays . . .

Motorola had been trying to do business with a Hungarian telecommunications company for years, but not cutting it. Finally, they decided to adapt an approach they called "Solution Selling" which is much like consultative selling, Spin Selling, Santa Claus marketing, and other techniques discussed in Chapter 4. Rather than push their line of products, they practiced listening to understand the true needs and frustrations of their customers. It took a year to find that the customer was more interested in service and relationship than simply technology. It changed their sales approach so that they were successful in landing a $100 million order for a phone system.

New-Age Pricing . . .

Suze Orman is a financial planner who specializes in retirement. She lets her clients tell her what her fee structure should be. She has a strong faith in people and God, and believes that "whatever my clients feel they want or can pay me" is what will work best in the long run. It is a "new-age" approach to pricing, but she's successful enough to be quoted in the *New York Times*, the *Wall Street Journal*, and *USA Today* and have a CNN show, seminars, and more.

Build Trust

"Trust—or the lack of it—is at the root of success or failure in relationships and in the bottom-line results of business, industry, education, and government."

—Stephen Covey

Official Thank-You Certificates . . .

Bullet Graphics Center does one better than sending thank-you notes to customers. It sends a fancy certificate that thanks them for being a supporter of their local small business community. It says, "In recognition of your commitment to promoting the success of small business, we salute your continued patronage within our business community, ensuring a stable environment for growth and prosperity." It has colorful seals and signatures that make it something that many people would put on the wall. If you're a smaller service company doing business with large corporations, certificates like these can be particularly appropriate, since corporations are often required to make an effort to use smaller vendors.

Personal Attention . . .

U.S. Air captain Marty Bell makes it a point to walk through the plane before takeoff. He greets passengers and asks them if there is anything they need. In the old days, it wasn't unusual for a child to be brought up to the front cabin and given a pair of wings. He carries on that sort of tradition. And once he gets on the intercom to welcome people, his message has a genuine, warm feeling, because he has talked to people, and knows where a lot of them come from. When they land, he gets out of the plane first and is there to greet you as you leave. This little extra effort to give things a personal touch is so memorable that he has been written about on several occasions.

> ### Do Customers Love You?
>
> "Customer satisfaction does NOT lead to repeat business! There must be an emotional bond—almost a love vs. hate. That predicts repeat business."
>
> —Robert Peterson, University of Texas

Price Is Not Everything . . .

Pacific New Media lost a printing job from a regular client because they were not the low bidder. However, they kept sending the client their newsletter. Eventually the client came back with a large, complex job for which quality was essential. Now Pacific has again become the company's exclusive printer.

Relationship-Building Gifts . . .

When things get slow for this insurance agent, he buys bags of fruit and drops by his best clients. He thanks them for their business and leaves some fruit. It peps him up to talk to happy customers, and sooner or later one of them buys a new policy or gives him a hot referral.

Flowers would work too. Who could you visit during your next lull?

Serve _Fewer_ Clients Better . . .

Some manufacturers use an approach called Account Specific Marketing (ASM) with their retailers. It's a type of one-to-one marketing (Peppers and Rogers). In ASM, you behave differently with every customer. That's what personal service should be all about in your business. A recent study by the University of Maryland and the National Account Management Association confirms this in an indirect fashion. Salespeople with *fewer* accounts do better than those with more accounts. Several items in this book establish that most clients have more business to give you. Focusing your efforts on 20–100 prospects and customers lets you build the relationships, give them better service, expand the business, get referrals, and so forth. Chasing after everyone makes you ineffective for all.

Share Information and Awards . . .

Calfo/Aron sends clients framed copies of any design awards they win for that client's work. They also let clients know about their work being used in self-promotion brochures or portfolios. Clients are flattered to be submitted for awards or used as samples of C/A's "best" work. Another thing C/A does is explain new technology available for jobs using a benefits approach. For example, "The new XY-2000 we use (boring feature) lets us improve quality for your brochure (advantage) which helps you sell clients better because they can picture the results you provide (benefit)."

Show Their Progress . . .

People like to see evidence of their own progress. Graphs of clients' financial positions over time are used by bankers, accountants, stockbrokers, financial planners, insurance agents, and others. When clients see a graph showing growth in their positions, they trust you even more. Even a lawyer can graph the progress of a case. Likewise, a landscaper, an M.D., a nutritionist, an architect, a personal coach, or anyone whose services take time or repeat over years.

The Personal Touch

In one nursing home, all the letters saying how wonderful the facility was came from families served by the same nurse. She always took the time to greet each relative by name and tell them how their loved one had done between visits. She became the model for a new training program, and this nursing home had a waiting list while others had unused capacity.

Singles Boost Dry Cleaner . . .

Uptown Valet, a dry cleaner, started posting pictures of its customers on the wall. People who use dry cleaners regularly tend to be the same types of busy professionals. Singles started asking about people they spotted, so Uptown started an informal singles connection service. It boosted business. Printers often post business cards of customers. So do some restaurants. It provides your customers with more exposure, shows you have lots of customers, and costs you nothing but wall space.

Turning Down Business Sells . . .

Years ago, Arrow Messenger Service turned down a half-million-dollar contract for the Chicago work of a national delivery service because they knew they couldn't handle it. A few years later they used that story, and a reference from the firm they'd turned down, to get an even bigger contract that they were ready for. When you're honest and polite, and you keep in touch, turning away business can build your credibility and relationships.

Use Customers' Names . . .

Barista Brava coffee shops are one of a number of businesses that encourage their "bartenders" to remember customers' drinks. Their record holder supposedly knew the drinks of 26 consecutive customers without having to ask during a morning rush. Trying to remember customers' names or orders is a strong form of relationship marketing. It makes each customer feel special, and it gets them interested in seeing if you can remember, so they're more engaged even if you fail.

Building Better Relationships . . .

One salesperson increased his business when he started thinking of everyone in the client company as customers rather than just the decision maker. It improved interactions at all levels and made future sales easier. Your firm should encourage other people besides salespeople (secretaries, technical staff, top management, etc.) to build relationships with clients.

You Need More Than Customer Satisfaction . . .

The point is made in several of these items that if you measure customer satisfaction, you are way ahead of most people. But customer satisfaction isn't enough. For instance, a recent study found that 90 percent of customers said they were satisfied with their automobiles but only 30–40 percent actually repurchased that brand of car. AT&T found the same thing with their long distance service. Ninety-five percent of customers were satisfied, but far more were defecting. It takes a personal connection between customers and providers to create real loyalty.

Restaurant Experiences . . .

Consumer surveys show that patrons like restaurants for how they are treated, for being recognized as individuals, and for the overall dining experience. Food and price rate rather low in importance. The Cha-Cha-Cha Caribbean-style restaurants have not only colorful and spicy dishes but also loud and lively atmospheres. The owners consider it a "theatrical performance in which you must have the timing down perfectly." Combined with personal attention to patrons, word-of-mouth referrals keep business booming.

· · · ACTION AGENDA · · ·

". . . to become what we are capable of becoming is the only end of life."
—Benedict Spinoza

There is no room for excuses in the customer service area. Most service providers claim they get most of their business from referrals. But great quality and service will no longer set you apart from the competition. As Ken Blanchard, Tom Peters, and others say, they are just the cost of doing business today. Don't neglect building relationships with customers and prospects. Then reap the results from some of the 35 items here.

→ Buy or print note cards and send out thank-you cards to your customers and prospects regularly. Consider a more formal certificate or award program.

→ Visit customers in the field on a regular basis.

→ Apply the 80/20 rule and pay more attention to getting more business from the key 20 percent of your customers. Should you drop your worst clients to be able to serve the rest better?

→ Ask customers for their input before you develop a new service.

→ Create a customer advisory board if you don't have one. Revive yours if you do.

→ Would a "frequent-user" program fit your business?

→ If you sell business-to-business, can you help your customers serve their customers better?

23

Service That Sells

"If you're looking up at me (the boss), you've got your ass pointed at the customer."

—Jack Welch, GE

Not all customer service will be aimed at building relationships as in the last chapter. It is possible for your great service to be a general standard and for your relationship to be largely an image in the customers' minds.

You have probably heard that it costs five or six times more to get a new customer than to keep an old one. I prefer the estimate suggested by Arthur Andersen's partner in charge of customer satisfaction: getting a new customer can cost *10 to 15* times more than retaining an existing customer. Whatever the exact number, I'm sure that if you work out your own economics, you'll find it very worthwhile to try to keep and thrill your existing customers versus reaching out to get new ones who may or may not be loyal.

Here are some examples of "bigger" service initiatives.

+++

Comarketing Partnerships . . .

Why do airlines cut partnership deals with each other? Because they can expand their range of services, exchange prospect lists, and offer customers more convenience. The partnership between United and Lufthansa is just one example. They can add destinations for their clients and go after new prospects whom they couldn't serve before.

What other services would work with yours? Gym and diet consulting? Beautician and plastic surgery? Driveway resurfacing and gardening? Roofing and painting? The possibilities are endless.

Pride of Service . . .

Five stars is the top designation any hotel can win from Mobile and other rating services. There are only a few five-star hotels in the country. At a new resort near Palm Springs, the smart boss gave all the employees pins with five stars on them. It built pride and an image to live up to. They said you can't be a "three-star" person seeing 200 five-star pins on your coworkers every day.

"Kleenex" Service Still Rare . . .

Skiers don't spit in their goggles to keep them unfogged as skin divers do. So, why is there only one ski resort that gives you Kleenex to clean your goggles as you're going up the lift? Tom Peters is an inquiring mind who wants to know. Perhaps the lack is part of the masochistic pleasure built into the skiing experience!

Service Guarantees . . .

CPA Troy Waugh helps other CPAs with their marketing. He guarantees his work and believes that it makes it worth clients' while to switch providers. Older professionals tend to hate the idea of guarantees. But a guarantee doesn't mean people can get all their money back for years of work. You use it at the beginning to get them to try you. It makes you look strong.

Guarantees Sell . . .

When Delta Dental Plan introduced its money-back guarantee for excellent service, it caused a commotion. After five years of experience with the program, Delta attributes 20 percent of new subscribers to the guarantee. Revenues have about doubled during the period it's been in place. Their legal department hated the idea, but it reassures customers. It also tells employees what things are important to take care of. And it has not been abused.

> **Guarantees Risk Little**
>
> If clients are so unhappy that they want their money back, you don't want them around complaining anyway. Far better they tell others about your guarantee than about their unhappiness.
>
>

Perfect Pest Performance . . .

What can you do perfectly? "Bugs" Burger's story is a classic you may have heard. He stormed out of the Florida Pest Control Association years ago because they laughed at his idea to provide perfect service. He charged up to four times more than average and absolutely guaranteed no infestations. If a guest in a restaurant or hotel he served saw a bug, he picked up the tab for the meal and then sent the guest a gift certificate. He used his fees to train workers right. He took unemployed people off the street and created pride. His employee turnover went way down.

Guarantees Work . . .

Strong guarantees work for more than pest control services. Coffield Ungaretti & Harris is a major law firm that advertised a satisfaction guarantee in the *Wall Street Journal*. They attribute much of their 40 percent growth recently to it.

Resell Customers . . .

Jennifer Flint of IHS calls customers a few months into their service contracts and asks them if they would do it again. Why not try it with your customers? If they say no, you have time to do something about it. If they say yes, maybe you can sell an extension early. You don't have service contracts? How about retainer arrangements? Or any longer job in construction, law, etc.

Add-On Services . . .

A housecleaning service offers to do laundry and dishes while they're there. Another service they could offer is to put something in the oven so that dinner would be well started too.

Speed Sells . . .

Northwestern National Insurance revamped their procedures so that price quotes could be produced immediately on a laptop. They cut costs and increased their success rate by 50 percent because of the fast quotes. The longer you take to get back to people, the more chance they'll go somewhere else.

> **A Speedy Edge**
>
> Many experts have repeatedly pointed out that faster service is better service. Yet, it takes months to get an appointment at Kaiser hospitals. So far, speed is more lip service than real service at most companies!

Create More Locations . . .

Glendale Federal Bank is testing mini-branches in Kinko's copy shops. It's a good location to reach businesses, compared to supermarkets for consumers. Many services could put up information racks of literature in stores.

Leasing for Loyalty . . .

If you combine your service with products, as many computer consultants (VARS) do, offering the additional service of helping arrange leases can make it easier to sell the rest of your package. Visionary Design Systems and PC Connections both plug leasing strongly to their clients. Likewise, Trellis Network Services says that because leasing makes buying easier, it often generates larger sales. And as the one arranging the deal, it also links *you* more closely to the client over the term of the lease. On the other hand, if you sell leasing services, you can arrange for others to sell your services to their clients who need it.

On-Time-or-Free Guarantee . . .

Express Press has always advertised that every job is on time or it's free. They do an average of 4,000 jobs before they miss one, so the cost is trivial, but the customer reassurance is great. Yet another argument for an impressive guarantee.

Service That Sells . . .

Maybe you're sick of hearing how good Nordstrom's customer service is. But as long as Nordstrom's keeps coming up with new stories, it'll keep getting publicity and word-of-mouth referrals. Sending birthday cards to you is old hat. But how about sending cards to your kids? And on the product side, there's sending notices when it's time to have your kids' feet measured for new shoes. And then there's the story of ordering it for you from the competition.

What kind of stories are customers telling about you?

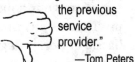

> **Service Is Personal**
>
> "It seems fair to conclude from research that 70 percent of customers who defected did so because they didn't like the human side of doing business with the previous service provider."
>
> —Tom Peters

Extra Service . . .

The Hawaii Prince Hotel greets new registrants with a hot, moist, steamed washcloth. It's a great extra, and it gets them considerable word of mouth and publicity as well when they have speakers or writers who stay with them and then tell the story.

Give Extras for Win-Win . . .

Speaking at large associations can be very profitable, and generates lots of business leads. Bruce Wilkinson offers his association clients extras to close the deal and publicize his sessions. He offers free consulting before and after his talk for several hours. This extra increases his referrals to other associations. And the contact with members before his talk generates word of mouth to fill his sessions. It also gives him a chance to show off his consulting skills where people would normally see him only as a platform speaker.

Restaurant Faxes . . .

Champs-Elysees, a restaurant in Sausalito, faxes the day's specials to customers in the morning, and then takes phone or fax orders for delivery or pickup later.

Now that they have a website, people can also check it to see what's on the menu.

Could you deliver or make house calls?

Better Graphics Service . . .

J. Hunt and Fultx, a graphics firm, has a large credit card company client. They voluntarily created an on-line database of the logos of hotels and restaurants that accept the card. To create ads, any of the businesses can grab its digitized logo from the database. Since other firms don't offer this service, it gives H&F an edge.

Moving Made Easy . . .

How can you take a generic service and make it special? An L.A. moving and storage firm delivers storage containers to your house. After you load up, they pick them up. It saves customers a lot of time, the hassle of borrowing trucks, and so forth. Similarly, there are mechanics and massage therapists who make house and office calls.

How can you make yourself more convenient for clients?

> **What Can They Talk About?**
>
> What do you do that is so extraordinary that clients will tell stories about your great service as they do about Nordstrom department stores? Isn't it time to plan something?

Extra Service . . .

A woman who attended one of my seminars specializes in helping people move into their new homes. She unpacks for them and leaves flowers. As a bonus, she stocks their refrigerators for them. That provides great service that people talk about and remember.

In similar fashion, a real estate agent could arrange with a local restaurant to give a special two-for-one coupon for newcomers the first night they are in town. Any restaurant could benefit from real estate people giving away these certificates to thrill their clients with. (Restaurants normally have to pay third parties to give away coupons.)

A Disneyland Hiring Tip . . .

If you want people who will be better at customer service and handling walk-ins and inquiries, take this tip from Disneyland. If they don't smile in their interview, don't hire them. Disneyland figures that Disney training is tops—but they need to start with happy, friendly people who are outgoing. You should do the same if friendly staff are important to you.

Another Paid Guarantee . . .

A senior living community not only guaranteed service quality, but also had a fee schedule for lapses. Ten dollars for a missed phone message, $15 for a poor meal, and one month free rent for failure to deliver medication. It provides ongoing feedback to keep their system efficient and great word of mouth, including publicity from Tom Peters.

Banking, Not Used Cars . . .

Bankers are among many professionals uncomfortable with the new world they're expected to sell in. And like many other people who don't like selling, they often do it the worst way. Sales efforts at some banks are similar to the bad days of the auto industry, says Scott Galloway of Profit Market Research and Consulting. Profit sent undercover shoppers into 50 of the country's largest banks. They presented themselves as inexperienced investors who wanted a safe alternative to low-yielding certificate of deposits (CDs). Many bank sales reps pitched investments without regard for the customers' goals. In order to counter this sort of trend, Bank of America has set up a program that profiles a customer based on age, assets, goals, and so forth. Reps make their suggestions based on this profile. If a B or A rep sells a product not suggested by the profile, it is spotted by a quality-control manager. A manager then calls the investor and discusses why it might be inappropriate. If it is, the bank undoes the transaction to better suit the customer or cancel it. This is an example of taking care of customers rather than just selling to them.

A Little Mistake? . . .

One utility company discovered that it was receiving two million extra calls a year because its bills did not have a due date on them. Could some little item in your paperwork be causing customers consistent problems that then cost you time?

Better Complaint Resolution . . .

If customers have a problem that is resolved, they can be even more loyal than customers with nothing to complain about. But how you resolve the problem makes a difference. A consulting firm, Technical Assistance Research Programs, finds that 68 percent of customers remain loyal if it took only one contact with your company to fix a problem. But only 33 percent do if it takes three or more contacts. Take this even further and try to have the first person who talks to customers regarding a complaint handle the situation, rather than annoying them by forwarding their calls around.

> **Thanks for Complaints**
>
> Never make excuses. When the first thing you say in response to a complaint is "Thank you for bringing that to my attention," customers relax and speak more frankly. Unfortunately, most companies and employees don't receive complaints well.

Better Prospecting and Service . . .

Adams National Bank makes "house calls" to possible business borrowers. That's unusual enough (although getting more common as competition increases). Adams goes one further and processes your credit on a laptop on the spot! Now, that's service.

Better Taxi Service . . .

Shorty Jones won a Taxicab Driver of the Year Award for his great service. He has a cell phone that passengers can use and takes five major credit cards. He also carries booster cables and a slim jim for starting your car or breaking into it if you locked your keys in it.

Phone-In Cabs for Service . . .

Customer service consultant Keith Bailey provides another reason for a taxi driver to offer passengers a cellular phone in the cab. When the Seattle driver didn't know where an address was, he gave Keith the phone to call for directions.

What could you do to make it easier for customers? How about lending them a pager so they can shop in the mall while they wait for their dinner table, or their oil to be changed? Maybe just giving them your home phone number for emergencies? You decide.

Look for Small Jobs

Customers have to buy a service to experience it. Look for small jobs to prove yourself. That's one way to build relationships while customers feel safe.

Better Waiting Room Service . . .

One car repair company posts a movie schedule of the videotapes that they play in their waiting room. Some customers schedule their visits around what's playing! They also have a popcorn popper next to the VCR.

Why don't more doctors' and dentists' offices play videos while people wait? You might even be able to coordinate with a local video store to stock rental copies of the movies you're showing so your customers could see the whole thing later that day and then return it to the video store.

Customer-Convenient Shifts . . .

Hongkong Bank of Canada runs shifts 24 hours a day, so customers can call in anytime from China, or the world. So does Boatmen's Bancshares in St. Louis, without overseas business. Can you compete?

Customers Judge You on Little Things . . .

Scandinavian Air's Jan Carlzon (*Moments of Truth*) was famous for pointing out that if there are coffee stains on your airplane trays, customers figure you don't maintain your engines well. Seminar leader Lou Heckler looks behind the bathroom door of his hotel room. If it's clean there, then he eats in the restaurant. It's not totally rational, but customers make judgments about the tangibles when buying things they can't judge. And this does apply to you! If you're a lawyer, customers judge you by how fast you return their calls. If you're a car mechanic, by whether or not you wipe the grease off of the car and leave a paper mat inside. Make sure you do the little, obvious things, such as cleaning up your waiting room, or getting your receptionist to use people's names.

Database Service . . .

Until Garland Heating and Air Conditioning installed a good database, when customers called with problems, the company couldn't respond quickly. In order to give good customer service, you should be able to access the right file in seconds, so that callers know you're up to speed. Garland now combines this with pagers for service people to produce very fast response time.

Delivery Plus Storage . . .

To find new services to offer, understand your customers' needs. For instance, Associated Distribution Logistics uses small messenger services around the country to store critical parts inventory for IBM and Xerox. Then when a technician is missing something, he or she can have it delivered locally, saving a trip back to the office, and reducing parts inventory storage.

Delivery Sales . . .

Snap-On, Mac Tools, and others sell out of trucks they drive to service stations and car repair shops. The Bookmobile delivers books—that's a service. Can you take eye exams, dental exams, or even legal checkups to senior centers, shopping centers, schools, or business parks? The IRS makes house calls—why not an accountant? Be creative. Set up temporary shop with a business somewhere that wants to cooperate in the publicity for both of you.

> **Wow Customers**
>
> "In whatever you do . . . make sure there is a 'wow factor,' something that will grab people's attention and make them notice that you've sweated the details."
>
> —Carl Sewell, *Customers for Life*
>
>

Entertain the Kids . . .

If you deal with families, it can be very worthwhile to have a playroom for the children so the parents won't be distracted from their work with you. For instance, in one bank waiting room, there is a table with a Lego plate top and a net in the center with more Legos. Any children who like to build can sit and play there while their parents are transacting business.

Evolving Your Services . . .

Smith Haughey started in insurance legal defense work but has evolved into much more. For instance, they've developed computer expertise in handling paperwork that can be marketed independently. Because many of the firm's clients are involved in sensitive litigation, they also need crisis communication help. So, Smith Haughey contracts with a public relations specialist in this area. And, of course, favorable publicity doesn't hurt settlement and trial outcomes either! In a bigger case, the Minneapolis offices of Shandwick USA, a large national PR firm, and Dorsey & Whitney, a large law firm, have a crisis management group with its own 800 number to both firms. They jointly refer and do audits for PR and legal exposures. It's a strong source of new business for both. Worth rolling out.

Fast, Extra Service . . .

A local VCR repair shop did a job in two hours, instead of two weeks. They took the unit apart in front of the customer and showed her what was broken and what would be replaced, which reassured her that the work was justified. She picked it up in a couple of hours, and it had been cleaned as well. Not everyone wants to know what goes on inside every car, VCR, or television, but consumers are often suspicious that you're just "making things up" once you have their equipment in your power. Cleaning is an example of throwing in an extra that doesn't cost you much while you're working on a job anyway and enhances the perception of service value.

Go the Extra Mile . . .

When a check to one of its clients bounces, one bank does "collection services over and above the call of duty." Bank reps not only report that a check is bouncing from one of your customers, but they also call the

...k on which the check was drawn to find out the sta-
... of the account, and advise you what to do.

Where can *you* go the extra mile for customers?

Heavy-Duty Speed . . .

Farnell Components is the European distribution hub of
an electronics parts company. Its workers must answer
99 percent of calls before the caller hears it ring, and 100
percent by two rings. They must ship 99 percent of all
orders the same day the order comes in. These tough
goals are linked to bonuses.

Impressing the Neighborhood . . .

For jobs such as street work that disrupt local neighborhoods, one contractor created a printed sheet with information on the job, start and finish dates
of the project, and how they were avoiding disruptions for the neighborhood.
Also give people a number to contact for
questions and problems. The media will
also find this information useful.

> **SOAR to Success**
>
> Use the SOAR formula to
> improve your customer service:
>
> **S**olicit customers' ideas and
> suggestions.
>
> **O**pen the communication
> channels.
>
> **A**ct on what you hear, good
> and bad.
>
> **R**eward employees who
> gather customer comments.

Insurance Service . . .

An auto insurance company is able to
use technology, such as cellular phones
and computers, to dispatch adjusters
within hours of an accident. They have
authority to write checks up to $3,000
on the spot. Don't you wish your insurance company did?
Can you cut bureaucracy for your clients?

More Service Guarantees . . .

IT&T Hartford Insurance has a personalized program for
customers. Each rep finds out what a customer wants,
and delivers a guarantee. For example, once they have
agreed to get a policy done in a certain time, if they fail
to meet the deadline, they pay $50 to a charity of the
customer's choice. It's a strong-sounding guarantee, but
the company can take a tax deduction on any donations
when they fail, so that it costs them considerably less
than face value!

Nontaxing Guarantee . . .

The Eric Thomas Group accounting firm has been able to win business from clients of Big 6 giants. One way is a 10-day guaranteed turnaround on any tax return or they pay $50 a day. They've had to pay out only once, but clients love the deadline promise.

Offer Extended Hours . . .

Many professional service providers keep "bankers' hours." It's the easiest thing in the world to offer early, late, or weekend hours as a chiropractor, doctor, lawyer, and so on. The Bank of Boulder, for instance, offers customers extended hours of 6 A.M. to 11 P.M. for drive-up windows. About 16 percent of new customers reported that they chose the bank because of its extended hours, even though many of them don't use the service often.

Premium Service and Prices . . .

Tom Peters talks about Demar Plumbing. They grew from $200,000 a year to $3 million+ by *not* being like other plumbers. They offer 24-hour service on a same-day basis. They schedule appointments closely, not "afternoon" or "morning." They train their people and offer bonuses of up to 35 percent based on customer satisfaction ratings. Their trucks are neat, their uniforms clean. They don't just act like "plumbers." You shouldn't either.

Repair Service . . .

Little courtesies can mean a lot to customers. Childress Buick/Kia repair service makes sure that car radios programmed electronically don't lose their stations when mechanics disconnect batteries. They plug in a smaller battery that holds the station programming.

Ask your employees and customers for ideas that could make your office or service more comfortable.

Service Recovery . . .

You think you have it hard: UPS competes with FedEx on one side and the post office and similar businesses undercutting them on price on the other. And they do it with

...ster drivers. They missed a pickup ... us one time. When we called the next ...ay to complain, they voluntarily got our package on a same-day commercial flight so that it arrived about when it should have.

You may not be able to fix a problem, but can you make it up to people in a dramatic way?

Super Service Recovery . . .

American Airlines damaged a brand-new piece of luggage that couldn't be repaired. Their damage claims department wrote a check for $50 *more* than the bag cost to make up for the trouble. And then they called to let the passenger know that there was a luggage sale at Macy's. That's the extra human touch that is worthy of attention.

Service Thrills . . .

The Food and Drug Law Institute used to have a decentralized system that often took four to six weeks to fill an order. After setting up a centralized service department, they cut turnaround time to 48 hours. Customers were thrilled. The emphasis on delivering better service caused a number of other changes as well, such as cross-training reps so that different people could fill in for one another. They say it looked obvious after the fact. They don't understand why they never thought of it earlier. Now you've thought of it.

Speedy Service = 35 Days? . . .

Plane engines take a while to service. Customers of Greenwich Caledonian in Britain were impressed when the company cut service time in half, from 70 to 35 days. You should be able to do better. But if you promise speed, you'd better deliver!

Key Service People

Think about who your customers interact with the most in your business. Could it be the people who answer the phone or greet them at the door? The bank teller is more important to customer service than the vice president who never talks to customers. Are your greeters rewarded for remembering names, the first key to customer appreciation?

Better Complaint Handling

"For any customer complaint, first we listen. Without interrupting. After all, if we handle it right, we can turn that dissatisfied customer into a satisfied customer for life."

—Harvey Mackay,
Swim with the Sharks . . .

Super Service Thrills Them . . .

Diana Bonazza won "Employee of the Year" for her chain of hotels because she'd do anything to meet guests' needs. For instance, when one guest got dirty falling off of a horse, after the hotel laundry was closed, she took the outfit home and washed it in time for his checkout the next day at 7 A.M. You have to look for those opportunities to thrill clients. You'll never know when they come up.

Train for Great Service . . .

If you want superior service, you need to invest in superior training. Duh! Too many businesses just give it lip service and leave it at that. Dierbergs Markets' new employees get a month of training before being let loose alone on customers. Beyond the grocery store, more traditional service businesses such as SSM Health Care and Boatmen's Bancshares are doing the same thing!

What Do Customers Need on April 15? . . .

A local post office box and mailing center has been bidding to become a postal substation because it will bring

---

Customer Recovery
by Ken Blanchard

One of the best sources for service stories is all-out recovery. Recovery means if you make a mistake with a customer, you do *whatever* is needed to fix the problem and create or win back a devoted customer.

Let me give you an example of the power of customer service recovery. A hotel in southern California had a history of poor guest comment ratings. A foreign owner took over the hotel. The new owner felt the poor guest comments were the result of a worn-out and battered physical plant. They put millions of dollars into refurbishing the hotel. The general manager brought all the hotel workers together and told them: "It's going to be tough sledding around here the next nine to twelve months. The noise and inconvenience may not be popular with our guests. Do whatever it takes to recover from any inconvenience caused by our refurbishing. If you want to send someone a bottle of wine, do so. If you want to hire a babysitter for them, do it. Do whatever it takes to recover from this bad situation."

The hotel entered their remodeling phase. Management was amazed that guest comment ratings were now the highest ever in the history of the hotel. Guests' memories of their experience with the hotel were formed by the customer-oriented staff that was willing to admit when things went wrong and recover as well as they could.

them more business. But in the meantime, when April 15 rolls around, they stay open until 11:30 P.M. They sell postage on their own postage meter, and then at 11:30 P.M., they run your tax returns to the one post office in the county that is still open. Thus, they offer all of the service of a post office and the added convenience of a local site.

What Do Your Clients Need? . . .

Lori Hechler, a speaker in Florida, lauds a laundromat in Fort Myers that gives you a continental breakfast if you drop off clothes by 9 A.M. Perfect for the commuter. They also do dry cleaning, which is perfect synergy.

Why Not Ask? . . .

Sales speaker/writer Jeffrey Gitomer has stayed at 500 hotels over the last three years. The Broadview Hotel in Wichita was the only one to call him *before* he arrived and ask if there was anything special he needed. Few people ask for anything, but it sets a real service tone from the start. For hotels that don't call, here are the most asked-for items:

- Iron and board
- Special food
- Electronic hookups
- Newspapers
- Refrigerator, juice, soda
- Places to eat
- Places to have fun

What Customers Want

From a survey of customers of professional service providers here are things clients wanted:

- An account executive who is trustworthy
- A friend or business partner
- Someone who brings me business
- Someone who brings me profitable ideas
- Someone who builds my reputation

· · · ACTION AGENDA · · ·

"It's time to fish or cut bait."
—Southern folk saying

"Fish or cut bait" is often used as if it meant "do it or quit." But it literally means do *something* to help the fishing. You undoubtedly believe in the importance of customer service. But are you demonstrating that in your behavior? Isn't now a good time to try something new from the 55 examples here?

→ Can you improve the speed of certain services?

→ Can you strongly guarantee your service? How about money back if not satisfied?

→ Can you add extra services that clients need?

→ How can you train your employees to improve phone answering and service?

→ Can you implement a policy that employees *can't say "no"* to a customer without permission?

→ Should you clean up any little things customers may be judging you on?

24

Networking

"Relationships determine success."
—Philip B. Crosby, *Quality Is Free*

*A*s the "Godfather" said, all business is personal. Most of us like to do business with people we've met. If they share our interests and are in our social circles, even better. Then they will want to serve us better, because we know who they are and "where they live"!

As you've read this book, you've probably realized that the distinctions among service, selling, networking, and even friendships, are hard to make. I particularly encourage you to use networking to balance your life. I've coined the term "leisure networking" to emphasize that your best contacts come in natural and enjoyable environments. Schedule more leisure for yourself where you'll meet people who share your interests. Whether it's church, wine tasting, sports, or bridge, the business relationships possible can reinforce you for giving higher priority to your own life balance. So, get out there and network—it's good for you!

+++

Golf Marketing . . .

Everyone says lots of business gets done on the golf course (or similar settings), but who, really, is getting it done? Golf Event Management holds seminars to train executives and meeting planners how to best use their time on the golf course for marketing. Prudential Reinsurance is one of the many companies that have used this service. One tip trainees learn is to discuss business only on holes 5 through 15 so that people have a chance to get to know each other early, and later can concentrate on the last few holes that are more important for scores.

Fun Advice . . .

The stereotype is that bartenders give advice. So, the All Seasons Cafe in Calistoga, California, enlists guest bartenders such as lawyers, accountants, and reps from the Small Business Association to *really* give advice from behind the bar. Everyone has fun, and new connections are made.

Bonding on the Gun Range . . .

Russ Krull rents and sells heavy construction equipment. He invited 23 coworkers and clients to the Ilion Fish & Game Club for target shooting. He says, "As soon as people were invited, we got additional business we might not have gotten." You might call it blue-collar networking at the gun club instead of the country club—the same social bonding and business building goes on. Krull says he'd tried open houses, customer appreciation days, and safety seminars but couldn't get the principals they wanted to come out. They tended instead to get employees who were happy to get a free meal and a half a day off. "To catch bigger fish, you have to use bigger bait. Every time people see the gun [they receive on graduation], they are going to be reminded of the outing," Krull said. Jean Donnelly of Coopers & Lybrand took three coworkers, six clients, and two prospects for three days at Ilion. He said he's had requests from his clients to submit business for new lines of work as a result.

Leisure Networking . . .

Examples abound of natural "sales" contacts being made because the seller shares an interest with a prospect. Lawyer Ralph Francis got one of his biggest clients because they met while mountain biking and Ralph understood the client's mountain bike product. Enjoy leisure more, and you'll meet more people.

Networking for Survival . . .

Elish and Company, a custom cabinet-maker, spent so much on their expansion that they couldn't afford to advertise. They filled their pipeline by sending employees to meetings of local builders' groups. Their goal for each employee was to talk to five possible customers, handing out brochures and business cards. It worked, and the company not only survived but expanded.

> "Your business success is proportional to (1) the thickness of your Rolodex, (2) the rate of Rolodex expansion, and (3) the time devoted to Rolodex maintenance!"
>
> —Tom Peters

Go Where Your Clients Are . . .

Rick Allen likes to climb cliffs with his bare hands. And when he can't get out, he finds a gym with rocks on the wall. He overdoes it at his "old" age and tears up muscles and tendons. When he went to a physical therapist, she asked how he did this to himself! Rick said, "Come and see," and got her to the gym. She started climbing and got lots of other new clients and referrals. (Would it be fair for her to just stand on the ground and egg the climbers on until they hurt themselves and needed her services?)

Where do your clients hang out? Start asking them.

Association Marketing . . .

Equitable, Prudential, and many other insurance companies do billions in partnering to sell insurance. But few single agents use association tie-ins strongly in selling individual and add-on policies. Anyone can use associations for help by simply becoming the only supplier in your area who regularly attends local chapter meetings. Then you'll be the expert to call.

Go to Seminars . . .

When you see a seminar on something you sell, such as marketing or legal advice, attend. The other people there are good prospects for you. Many people have made an informal connection with someone sitting next to them and ended up doing business together.

Start a Nonprofit Group . . .

If you find that giving away free consulting samples brings you more work, you can start your own part-time nonprofit group. (Check the Nolo Press books in the library on how to do it.) You can draw a salary, but not make a profit. It makes your efforts more "official." And non-profit mailing rates are very low. It worked so well for the Association of Individual Investors that they set up chapters around the country.

The Basic Handshake . . .

Mike Stevens markets printing big-time. He believes that teaching employees to shake hands is worth the embarrassment. Sometimes men and women are awkward about handshaking etiquette. The basic rules are: firm but not hard, make eye contact and smile, pump two or three times about two inches straight up and down. Higher status offers first. (In earlier days, women offered first, so if men hesitate, women can make the first move to put them at ease.)

Looking for Someone?

When you're at a large event and want to find a particular kind of person, ask. Ask the people at the front door, ask the president of the group, ask the speaker. It gives you something to talk with them about, and you can use their referrals as an introduction to the people you're looking for.

Send Books . . .

One accountant loves to read and goes to lots of bookstores. He has segmented his referral sources into A, B, and C. The dozen As are lawyers and bankers who refer to him regularly. He knows their interests well and keeps in touch. One way is to send them books on topics they each like. He puts a sticker in the books saying they are thanks-yous from him. The *B*s get less material. The *C*s are potential sources. Two or three times a year, he sends the same book to his complete list of 50+ contacts. (He buys the title at a discount from the publisher.) Referral business is up almost 20 percent in six months. He is now experimenting with audiotapes. Those will be appreciated by most people who commute by car.

Business Card Notes . . .

Mary Lea Balsley is a consultant and speaker. Her business card is very fancy. It's two colors but looks like four because it has a picture of fire done in screens of red and black. It's folded to make four panels, so it has lots of room for information inside. And on the back is space for notes. It says, "Met at _____. Date _____. What you'll do: _____ . What they'll do: _____. How you'll contact them: _____. When you'll have completed action: _____ . When you need to next contact: _____." Plus there's a reminder that "business is relationships." Providing an official space to take notes on a card is a good reminder for people to follow through.

Custom Cards . . .

Bob Podd, a software marketing consultant, had his card specially imprinted with a convention name and date so people attending would remember where they got it. His company name also makes the point: Software Results, Inc.

Trivia Marketing . . .

Using trivia is effective, in person and in advertising. It attracts attention when you meet people personally and offer them an interesting tidbit to take home or pass on to others. In your advertising or other communications material, it can also lend itself to eye-catching graphics. For instance, in one

> **Dealing with an "Old Boy" Network**
>
> "When you want to be accepted in other people's worlds, you need to show that you're trying to fit in. Show your interest and give it time."
> —Ken Blanchard

day, Americans use 550,000 pounds of toothpaste, or almost 2.5 million tubes. One award-winning campaign pictured one giant tube holding all of those pounds. A dentist can use this bit of trivia. What can you use?

Mastermind Support Group . . .

An accountant and a lawyer each got assigned the business development role at their firms. They knew little about marketing and weren't comfortable selling. When they discovered that they were in similar boats, they started getting together regularly every Friday night. They planned individual calls for the following week and critiqued the previous week. They even sometimes taped sales calls, with permission, for review. It was the blind leading the blind, but they got better fast. Active help, public commitment, and support work wonders. The two professionals also became friends and good referral sources for each other. If they'd taken it one step further, they could have made cold calls for each other on the phone to set appointments. There's less feeling of rejection that way!

Live Networking Referrals . . .

When a current client introduces you to a prospect at a meeting, Richard Weylman says to make it a point to walk away after a few minutes to give them a chance to talk about you! Your client will plug you to the prospect in confidence. Then you can come back and move ahead.

Niche Networking . . .

One CPA in Atlanta had a commercial roofing firm as a client. This gave him the experience and the reference to get another. Only eight big roofing firms fit his target market, but he is doing a lot of business with several of them. By the time he's finished working with as many as he can, he'll have developed other referrals to other areas of construction. Carefully moving through a niche, and then from one niche to related niches, can build a lifetime business.

Trade Show Exposure . . .

A national commercial lender kept visible at the trade shows of big industries it served. Whether it's serving on panels, or just visiting prospects at their booths or in the aisles, they take you much more seriously when you know about their worlds.

Plan for Relationship Building . . .

When you meet someone through networking, have items you can follow up with that aren't sales materials. Lew Chumich keeps files of clippings, articles, and fact sheets that different types of prospects may appreciate. That way, he always has "personal" material to send later. Good cartoons and other humorous items can also help make up for your serious demeanor or subject!

Better Networking Groups . . .

Most groups that have networking events don't run them as effectively as they can. A group of chambers has one yearly joint mingler. They put different colored stickers on members' badges along with a number (always have name badges). Then after free mingling, you sit at tables with your color stickers, introduce yourselves, and suggest leads for each other. Then you switch to a table with your number and do the same. It's much more efficient than just mingling all evening.

Networking Tasks . . .

Linda County runs events that use the mingling period more effectively. She gives everyone a sheet to fill out that requires getting to know others in attendance. You have to find someone who wants to start a business, someone in business for five years or more, someone you'll get together with later, and so on. You have to write everything down with your name and submit it for a raffle. (Businesses that participate donate the raffle prizes for publicity.) Other information people can collect includes

Make a List

Make a list of both the types of people you'd like to network with and the types of people you can help. Join groups that bring you into contact with both types.

asking someone what kind of business or individual is that person's ideal prospect. People become goal-oriented about gathering information that is useful to building relationships instead of just small talk. And remember, you should be doing this without a "game."

Block Parties . . .

As practice for a client party, have a block party with other local businesses a few weeks before. This exposes you to area businesses that can become referral sources, and to some of their clients. One professional got two new clients at one when she was new to her office.

Network for Your Clients . . .

Many real estate agents who farm a neighborhood know a good many of the people in it. If you're one who doesn't, when you sell a house, why not go around to the neighbors of the newcomer ahead of time, lining up possible contacts for them. Not only are you thrilling the new mover, but you're also giving yourself a subtle plug when you introduce the newcomers, and helping yourself to farm the area. Almost any other professional could use this strategy in a more general sense. When you get new clients, you could make a few networking calls on their behalf. It's also an excuse for you to call strangers.

Political Database Example . . .

Bill Clinton started keeping a database when he was in college. By 1980, it had built up to 10,000 names. And, of course, it's grown since then. Once it could be put on a computer, he was able to keep systematic track of people who would be worth knowing, along with his contacts and interactions with them. For each of his campaigns, he then generated a stream of letters and phone calls to keep in touch. Harvey Mackay did much the same thing to promote his book *Swim with the*

Give First

When you're talking to strangers, think how you could help them immediately. For instance, ask them what would be a good referral for them. They'll see you differently, and they'll probably ask you the same question!

WHAT KIND OF REFERRALS WOULD YOU LIKE TO HAVE?

Sharks . . . If you'll build and keep a database for more than 30 years, you'll be successful too.

When Prospects Speak, Take Action . . .

The Construction Superconference generally has a panel of huge construction companies telling lawyers in the audience how to do business with them. From an audience of hundreds, no more than two or three follow up and contact the speakers the way they suggest! If your prospects are successful, they're probably speaking somewhere. Meet them there, and listen to their advice.

> ### Be a Better Listener
> Good networking takes good listening. Try these techniques:
> * Lean slightly toward the speaker
> * Pay close attention; don't be preparing for your turn to talk
> * Nod and say, "uh-huh" occasionally
> * Agree when you can; don't say, "yes, but . . . "

Be a Support Center . . .

If you're a service that helps small businesses, why not become a "resource center." Collect videos, audios, books, and articles on different aspects of starting a business. Let clients and prospects come to your office to check them out. Get other professionals involved as resources. You can also run monthly roundtables to share information. It works. You'll get acquainted, get word of mouth, and get new clients.

Car Wash Cleans Up at Mixer . . .

Hosting a chamber of commerce mixer helps your networking but has a cost. How can you get more out of it? The Grand Prix Car Wash in San Pablo, California, always washes the cars of chamber of commerce members when they host a mixer. It's low cost for them, and it increases attendance. And I know that people remember, because Simon Ellis, the president of the chamber, told me about it.

You could have staff give free estimates, produce educational seminars, answer personal questions, or _____?

Women's Networking Groups . . .

Jeannie's housecleaning service has success getting business from meetings of women's groups that the owner attends. Even when both members of a couple work, the woman tends to "be responsible" for taking care of housekeeping. The owner also uses flyers and occasional door-to-door work to market her services when she is in a neighborhood and has time.

Complete Networking Sells . . .

In analyzing lost sales, Larry Boardman found that individuals other than the people they were negotiating with were making the decisions to purchase from their competitors. His reps were selling at the top but not always networking throughout the organization. You need to communicate your value and solicit feedback from everyone involved in the process in order to close deals. You also get more information this way. His company now requires salespeople to outline how clients made purchase decisions—every step of the process and every person involved. The process of collecting this information alone has helped them network effectively within companies.

Create a Group . . .

Donna Parolini started a consulting business to auto parts companies to help them develop business plans and strategies. One of her contacts suggested that she start a group for auto suppliers. Each participating company now pays her $5,000 a year. The group meets every six or eight weeks and brainstorms solutions for dealing with automobile companies. Parolini runs the West Michigan Automotive Supplier Council and sets the rules to keep it from being anticompetitive. It ends up being a networking, mastermind, brainstorming, and consulting group. Creating a group can both be profitable in itself and build other consulting business.

Help Others and Your Networking . . .

If you have a nice conference room in your office or building, you can lend it out to nonprofits such as the United Way, as well as to your clients. Many people don't have good places to meet. If you're well located, you can help others at no cost to yourself. It could even be a tax deduction with the nonprofits. But your real goal is to build referrals and meet occasional movers and shakers who contribute time to worthy causes.

Hiring Help . . .

If one of your targets is high-income groups, the best way to reach them is to socialize at charity events, private school fund-raisers, and the like. One high-income professional hired a "sales rep." He was able to find someone who both had sales skills and was a socialite in her own right who, because of a recent divorce, needed extra income. He paid her $1,000 a month plus bonuses based on profitability from new patients. The rep handled it more like a referral situation than a sales position. By bringing in her friends and other people she met, she produced 14 new cases a month for the first six months, and got a lot of publicity for the practitioner because he served as sponsor for many of the charity events that she frequented.

Indirect Networking . . .

Julie Allecta, a lawyer, goes to meetings of groups that produce business for her clients and prospects. When these contacts mention her name to prospects, it has more impact because prospects perceive her as able to influence people who can do business with them.

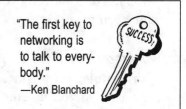

"The first key to networking is to talk to everybody."
—Ken Blanchard

Keep in Touch, Both Places . . .

The theme of this book is to build relationships, which means you have to create contact. Calling old clients to check in gives you a chance to connect with a new person when the old buyer has moved on. One photographer always asks where the old contact has gone: they become potential advocates for you in the new company. One copywriter for software has gotten lots of new business this way. In a fast-moving industry, such as Silicon Valley, sometimes this is all you have to do to get new clients!

Make Your Own Badge . . .

For networking events many people make a custom badge. This helps set you apart and is a good conversation starter. It also gets your messages across the way you want it to. The simplest way to make the custom badge is to enlarge your business card on a copy machine to fit the plastic holder that you get at most conventions and trade shows. Use your creativity for a fancier one.

Networking at Toastmasters . . .

One professional sent a staff member to the local Toastmasters meeting to practice speaking (highly recommended, incidentally). Over the weeks, he met three people with whom he followed up and had lunch and who became clients. Another person who went on his own told the group his consulting areas. They made an effort to give him leads.

> **Introduce Yourself Better**
>
> When you meet someone, don't just give your "name, rank, and serial number." Develop something to say quickly about yourself that shows your uniqueness so people will want to talk more with you.

Networking by Volunteering . . .

Many people say they find volunteering to work for their industry group boring. But it's a good way to get known to a wide circle of prospects, while painting yourself in a positive light. Fair pay for boring work.

Networking Card Sort . . .

Write notes on business cards when you get them at a meeting so you'll remember details about that person. One professional then sorts them into good prospects versus others. The prospects get a follow-up call and the others only a stock letter or newsletter. She saves time by spending her energy on her best leads.

Networking for Your Clients . . .

If your bank isn't helping you network with its other customers, get another bank. That's one of the criteria that Janis LeBude uses in selecting a bank. She also helps her vendors network with each other. Of course, the same goes for lawyers, accountants, bookkeepers, and so forth.

Networking Math: 10 Percent = 100 Percent . . .

A Stanford study by Joel Podolny and James Baron showed that small increases in the size of your network can double your odds of success. If your existing network is not producing much in the way of referrals, try to add 10 percent in high-quality contacts. They can double your results.

Networking Through Church . . .

Gary Perkins was new in town. When he settled in at a new church, he naturally told everyone about his computer consulting business. The church needed to have its computers networked, so he helped out. Afterward, one of the board members introduced him to one of his clients, which resulted in a job and the start of his new referral network.

Networking Through School . . .

One professional kept involved in local alumni relations from her college. It was part of her social life and brought in a lot of business. If you attended college in another area, there are probably lots of other grads in your current area you could network with, if there's not a formal group already. Other people do the same with their high school alums. I even know people who are involved in their grammar school affairs 35 years later! Relationships can be built on any reasonable basis of similarity or attraction.

> **Be a Giver**
>
> If you're an expert, people will ask you for free advice. Decide how much you can afford to give, and then do it cheerfully.

Old Alums Are Not Forgotten . . .

Allen Hitchcock sends out football schedules to local alums of his university—a national football power. They reinforce the tie between him and prospects, serve as a handy reminder, and keep his name in front of people for the whole season.

Networking with "Your People" . . .

We all like to do business with people who are like us. A Japanese-American insurance agent targeted most of his mail solicitations at people with Japanese names. A Filipino accountant advertised in ethnic papers, participated in related groups, and built a half-million-dollar practice. Almost anyone is part of an ethnic, religious, or hobby group.

Newsletter Networking . . .

Many companies use a newsletter to keep in touch. (Newsletters are covered in Chapter 14.) Remember that gathering material for your newsletter (or a magazine article) is also a reason to keep in contact or meet new people. Calling people as a "reporter" is almost always an acceptable reason to be in touch.

Prospects Like to Meet You . . .

Marketing is more than selling a service. You're also selling yourself. And when you're looking for a new job, you *are* the product. In one survey by Drake Beam Morin, 62 percent of new jobs came from networking and personal contacts. Next closest was a search firm at 14 percent. Your clients want to find you directly too.

Volunteer Work . . .

Volunteering at the right organizations can build your network. For instance, one consultant who volunteered at the Pittsburgh Ballet said, "It's a wonderful place to make contacts." Choose organizations that your successful prospects would support or enjoy.

Find Clippings for Clients . . .

If you only contact people when you want something, it doesn't make for much of a relationship. Kit Grant, a consultant and speaker, clips articles that his clients might like. He faxes the articles to them with a quick note. These nonselling contacts build relationships. Clients and prospects are flattered when you remember them with something relevant to their business or personal life.

Bill Blades, another consultant and speaker, was being considered as the keynote speaker for a trade association meeting. He happened to see an article about the best restaurants in the town where the meeting was to be held and sent it to the trade association with a note that said, "You might want to include this in your registration packet for attendees." He got the job. Bill had been one of three speakers under consideration. The executive director of the association told Bill, "I was kind of leaning your way, but your sending me that fresh article showed you were thinking about me. I really appreciated that."

Exercise Marketing . . .

While a chiropractor worked out at the gym, he noticed that weight lifters often ground heir teeth when lifting heavy weights. He found an article on the problems associated with jaw clenching and posted it at his gym with a note that people give him a call if they had this problem. People he helped told other weight lifters, and he quickly became the local expert on the jaw-clenching problem.

· · · ACTION AGENDA · · ·

"A good beginning makes a good
   ending."
                              —English proverb

You'll be well begun if you make networking a conscious part of your marketing. Use some of the 49 items in this chapter. If you don't schedule it, you won't do it—so, do.

➜ Make a list of groups that might be useful to attend.
➜ What leisure groups would you enjoy networking with?
➜ Ask your best clients what groups they belong to or support and perhaps attend meetings with them. When they act as your host it gives you a walking referral.
➜ Collect material you can send people to keep in touch. That means knowing something about their interests.

→ Send this book out to your entire holiday list to make a really big impression (unabashed plug)—I can get it for you wholesale!

→ Can you host an event or party soon?

→ Where could you take important prospects and clients that would really impress them?

→ Set up a database of your contacts, and keep better track of when you're in touch with them.

25

Earning Referrals
The Ultimate Marketing Tool

"Business is built on the loyal customer, one who comes back and brings a friend."
—W. Edwards Deming

*R*eferrals are the best form of marketing to new prospects. You will do business with far more referred prospects than any other kind.

If people with no self-interest involved say something nice about you, it has high credibility. Customer referrals may be the best type because customers can speak of their own experiences, but productive referrals can come from many other sources as well. Your own employees, your friends, past workmates, people who live near you, suppliers, professionals, and even competitors are all good sources of referrals. Also remember that written testimonials are a kind of referral too.

There are things you can do to stimulate referrals. Yet, most people rely on the "prayer" method: they just hope someone will refer them! You can do better by following some of these examples.

+ + +

On-Line Referral Lesson . . .

Exchange Network Services started as a free computer bulletin board service in a home bedroom. At age 14, Michael Krause became an Internet access provider. Eighty percent of his first 5,000 subscribers came from referrals. As young Michael says, "If you talk to your customers carefully and explain everything in language they can understand, then they tell their friends." If customers can't understand over the phone, Michael's solution is to "get in my car and drive out to their house." (Easy for him to say now that he's over 16!) Great service and house calls. Now, why don't more companies think of that?!

Deadly Marketing . . .

Here's a real specialty—I'm tempted to say, "a dying niche market." It's cleaning up after murders and suicides. Crime Scene Cleaners has a name that advertises for it. They only get about one job a month during normal parts of the year, but during holidays it can go to two per week. They need strong contacts with local police and coroner's offices, and other janitorial services that don't want to handle the gruesome details. They are also themselves an unusual referral source for counselors: they bring along a binder of therapy referrals to help the living when they clean up.

Word of Mouth Preferred . . .

Almost all service providers say they get most of their business from word of mouth, and almost all consumers say they prefer to either know a service provider personally or get a referral. One survey of financial planners found that 80 percent of consumers ask friends and coworkers when looking for a personal financial adviser, but it doesn't say whether the people who advise them got their information from mail, media, or other outlets—such as articles you've written. Most everything you do that makes people aware of you will increase your word of mouth too.

Easy Cross-Referring . . .

It's natural for one professional to refer clients to another: a doctor to a dentist, a lawyer to an accountant, and so forth. One way to encourage professional referrals simply is to arrange for other service providers to put a P.S. at the end of any letter they send out, or at the bottom of their bills, newsletters, or other mailers. The P.S. simply says:

> If you need the services of an excellent
> _____, I'd like to recommend my friend,
> _____. He/she has room for a few new
> clients, and has given my clients first choice to
> fill those spots. He/she is also offering a special
> _____. If you need this service, please
> give him/her a call at _____.

One professional used this strategy regularly with colleagues and averaged four new referrals a month at essentially no cost.

Positioning Creates Publicity and Referrals . . .

Ecoprint has increased its customer base 50 percent over three years without any sales effort. One hundred percent of new customers come from referrals and publicity. The whole process started with a super emphasis on environmental concerns. The company got national and local publicity for doing everything to recycle, reduce pollutants, and so forth. Customers feel good having their printing done at Ecoprint. That keeps them loyal and referring.

Thrilling Customers . . .

Nordstrom's isn't the only company that delivers great service in order to create positive stories about themselves. An Illinois auto repair shop didn't finish a customer's car in time for a three-month vacation in Florida. They loaned the customer a car and then had an employee drive the customer's car down to Florida when the work was done! The customer was bowled over, and a good employee got an unusual perk.

You Always Get Word of Mouth

Wayne Dyer points out that you get word of mouth from *every* customer.

You just don't know whether it's good or bad!

When do you have a chance to go above and beyond "good" service?

Referring to Yourself . . .

Ministers and justices of the peace are good referral sources for financial planners, insurance agents, and the like. Donald Regier is a minister *and* a financial planner, so he can provide his own referrals. He marries 100 people a year as a justice of the peace. When he sends a follow-up note to congratulate them, he arranges many appointments to go over their financial needs.

High-Powered Referrals . . .

When an insurance agent says you need insurance for estate planning purposes, you may figure the agent is only trying to sell more coverage. So, insurance agent Gene Pope works as a team with estate planners, attorneys, trust officers, and other professionals. When they say more insurance is needed, it's objective.

Who could you cross-refer with?

Leads Clubs . . .

One way to find a group of people who have an interest in your success is to start or join a leads club or tips group. The basic rule is that everyone has to bring a lead every week. To avoid conflict, only one person in each type of business can join. The requirements for the leads vary from general information to a specific lead for a specific person with an appointment set up on a preliminary basis. If you don't bring leads consistently, you're out of the group to make room for somebody who will be more productive.

Typically, people such as real estate agents, loan brokers, and bankers do business with each other within the group and are good sources of mutual referrals. The more everyone needs your service, such as insurance,

---

Upscale Referrals

"The affluent respondents whom I have interviewed report that interpersonal endorsements (word-of-mouth) were the most influential in their decisions to patronize a variety of service providers."

—Thomas J. Stanley,
Networking with the Affluent and their Advisors

the more luck you'll have with a group like this. They can be as small as five people if you're all go-getters, working hard for each other. More commonly, they number around 20 or 25 people, which gives you about a minute to introduce yourself, remind people what is a good lead for you, and give your lead each week.

Running a Leads Group . . .

How you run a leads group makes a difference. For instance, the Solano Executives Association uses a form for you to write your name and fill out your official lead. It can then be passed to people who are interested in it. You should also call people anytime before the regular group meeting to give them a hot lead (which you get credit for if you don't have another lead). You also want to push for leads that are specific to members, rather than just information about a new business opening or the like. And you want to help build relationships over time. Only a few groups have a social outing every quarter to facilitate this.

"Government" Referrals . . .

Small Business Development Centers (SBDCs), SCORE, and local colleges all have free resource centers for small businesses. One woman consults for them at a low rate, but it keeps her busy. It also gets her name in the paper every week for the free consulting sessions sponsored by the SBDC at a local chamber of commerce. And you don't have to work cheap to get referrals. Many people give referrals to experts who've made the effort to get acquainted.

> **Objective Views**
>
> "Satisfied customers are an organization's most successful salespeople, because they do not stand to benefit financially from recommending the organization to others."
>
> —Eberhard Scheuing, *Creating Customers for Life*

Managed Care Help . . .

Peer support groups can work wonders. One professional in the health industry organized a monthly discussion among medical people on how to deal with managed care issues. Some of the participants were against HMOs and managed care providers; others worked fine through managed care systems. The person organizing and moderating the sessions ended up getting many referrals from the M.D.s and others in the group, so he extended it even further. He wrote a letter explaining the situation to other potential medical contributors, inviting them to come to the meetings. He held the group size to 15 practitioners per meeting. The organizer has gotten at least 45 referrals from the group, and even some from people who didn't attend, just because of his increased visibility.

Hiring for Contacts . . .

Hiring right can build your image *and* help your marketing. Armstrong Ambulance is the Cadillac in its market. One of the things that helped the company turn the quality corner, and get city contracts, was to hire moonlighting firefighters. Firefighters have lots of time off plus paramedic training and local connections. It's surprising what people will do for you sometimes if you hire them (or their kids). And it often doesn't cost you much.

> HELP
> WANTED
> PEOPLE WITH
> TRAINING
> AND
> CONTACTS

How to Ask for Referrals . . .

Many professionals don't want to ask for referrals because they think it looks as if they don't have enough work. Even worse, when clients ask most professionals how things are, they say, "Really busy; I'm behind." Chris Frederiksen says that's not smart. He trains his people to say, "Business is great, but we're always looking for quality referrals to more people like you."

Ask Everyone for Referrals . . .

After radio interviews, the host's assistant asks guests for the names of other stations on which they've done interviews, so that she can call and try to arrange for the host to be interviewed there. A clever role reversal. And a good example of how you can ask anyone for referrals. The worst they can say is no!

More on Asking for Referrals . . .

Hyatt Hotel's Gold Passport Club included a standard letter when they sent customers their new cards. It said

in part: Your enjoyment and use of Hyatt on so
occasions means that you know how valuable n
06bership benefits are. Because of this, we'd like to
you the opportunity to recommend a passport memb
ship to a friend or business associate. We've included
postage-paid application and a one-time trial card so tha
they can try the membership firsthand.

This approach makes it easy for people to pass on information and a freebie. It would be worth doing this in an
entire letter a little more completely.
You could use the same idea with any
big user of your services to encourage
referrals.

Start Small, Work Up . . .

Mike Perrone, president of Fields
Financial Services, says, "There's only
one way to get in to see big banks or big
insurance companies, and that's to
please the little ones first." No big company wants to work with a consultant or
service provider without a track record.
By working with smaller people in their industry, you'll
develop better referrals and connections into the big
ones. This also proves that you're in it for the long run
and you'll be around later when your big customers need
you. Of course, if your services help make your small
customers big, that's a great marketing story.

> ### Why People Refer
>
> Aside from the given that
> people have to like what you
> do:
>
> - Some people are more
>   "referral types"; they enjoy
>   helping others.
> - Some people expect referrals
>   in return.
> - Others wait for you to give
>   them a referral first.

Your New Marketing Partners . . .

Joseph Coffman markets group medical coverage to business members of three local chambers of commerce.
Each mailing has a letter of endorsement from the chamber director. The chambers also refer businesses to him
directly. To qualify for the coverage, people must belong
to the chamber, so it's a benefit the group offers (and
the chamber may get a commission). And the third-party
endorsement is great for the insurance provider.

What else could be offered through groups? Your imagination is the only limit: discounts, affinity charge

cards, sponsored maps, banking packages, software. Start with groups you know well, since they're putting their reputation behind you. Then join and get to know new ones.

Anchors Aweigh Referrals . . .

Ask everyone for referrals. Chief Martinez, a Navy recruiter, called for my then 18-year-old son. When I said he wasn't available, he asked if there was a way to reach him. When I said that he was probably not interested, he asked if I knew anyone else he should be talking to who could be interested.

If you keep asking, you're more likely to receive.

Complaints Produce Referrals . . .

Many studies show that people who complain are more interested in working with you than are noncomplainers. One professional wrote a brief letter specifically asking for ways that he could improve his practice. He was explicit in saying that he wasn't looking for compliments, but rather for things that might be wrong, or things that could be improved. Every client who returned a questionnaire was followed up by phone immediately if there was a problem that could be dealt with, or just to be thanked, if not. In the six-month period after the letter and brief questionnaire went out, 44 referrals were generated from this group.

The simplest questionnaire I like, which also can be a great source of testimonials for brochures and other literature, is:

1. What do you like about the way we do things?
2. What do you dislike about the way do things?
3. Is there anything else you can tell me to help me improve things for you?

You may also want to include specific items about your staff or other narrower topics.

Recovering from an Error

"When you make a mistake, don't defend it. Never argue with unhappy customers. Start by assuming they're right."

—Ken Blanchard

Professional Gift Certificates . . .

Many service providers offer a free introductory session. This is so commonplace that it's not much of a thrill. One clever professional created a $75 gift certificate redeemable for two or three specific services, which amounted to free evaluation sessions of a client's situation. Printing it up as an official gift certificate, with fancy borders, gave it a lot more perceived value than a coupon or general offer. He mailed 500 to people near his office. He hand-addressed and stamped the envelopes—which made them look personal rather than like junk mail. He also gave gift certificates to his current clients to pass along. The mailing of 500 brought eight people in. The referrals from current clients brought in 12, a good return on the investment.

Niche Market to Deaf People . . .

A professional had an audiologist as a client. The audiologist wanted to send a deaf client of his to him and said that, as long as he was considerate of the client's hearing loss, there would be no problem. But he added that if his colleague wanted lots of business, he should install a telecommunications device for the deaf (TDD). This is a keyboard-operated telephone that costs about $150. He also recommended hiring someone half-a-day a week who could interpret for deaf people. Focusing on this group eventually required two days a week of these services, and the group became his fastest growing profit center. Merrill Lynch and others also have marketing campaigns aimed directly at people who are hard of hearing.

Look for referrals from audiologists and speech pathologists. Give them your flyers with your TDD number on them.

Doughnut Delivery . . .

The wife of the owner of a collision repair shop delivers boxes of doughnuts to insurance agents' offices. On Valentine's Day she takes cookies. She includes an information sheet on the shop, which notes the fact that they have 20 loaner cars for customers. Another shop delivers doughnuts to the teachers' lounge at a nearby school, with its business card taped to the lid of the box. Guess who gets the teachers' business?

Provide Training for Products . . .

People should spend several times the cost of a software program to set up and train on it, especially as software costs come down. One accountant was approached by a software company to be listed as an authorized consultant for buyers. It cost him little and brought him six new clients in a few months. Whose products could you support?

Client Parties Create Referrals . . .

Chris Frederiksen, an accountant who knows marketing, likes to have two parties a year. The main one is for clients on March 15. Since that's the middle of heavy tax season for most accountants, clients are impressed that he's so on top of things. Clients are encouraged to bring guests. Some sign up on the spot because their accountants are so busy they won't return calls. (Chris encourages regular clients to take extensions, which leaves him time to pick up last-minute clients like this.)

Bring-a-Friend Seminars . . .

Paul Herreras, of the Practice Builder Association, suggests a twist on how to get people to seminars. Make it a bring-a-friend talk. Give all of the clients you invite a couple of flyers, and suggest that they bring a friend. By getting people involved, they'll be more likely to attend. Friends will be more likely to come because someone they know invited them. This is a nice way to get more people to the seminar and, at the same time, make it informal, filled with people you've personally invited.

Why People Don't Refer

Some clients who like you still don't make referrals because:

- They're afraid that if there's a problem they'll be blamed (you can offer a guarantee to reassure them).
- They think you already have all the work you want.
- They never thought of referring.

Referral Bribes . . .

The Ski New Hampshire association got an excellent 7 percent response to its mailing to past skiers offering free lift tickets if they referred someone who bought a special season package. Bribes can work!

Special Offers . . .

Great plastic surgery doesn't always lead to referrals, since your best customers may not want to admit they use you! One plastic surgeon moved to a new area and found an esthetician (facial special-ist) who was willing to work with him. She rounded up five of her clients for a half-price facial laser "resurfacing." He rented a laser machine for the morning. Clients were sworn to secrecy about the price while promising to give referrals.

Aggressive Referral Seeking . . .

In their book *Marketing Without Adver-tising*, Phillips and Rasberry mention asking satisfied clients to look in their Rolodexes for people to refer you to. I've since heard of several people who did this in one way or another. It seems very aggressive, but if the client is happy with you, it jogs the client's memory, gives you the correct spelling and phone number for the referral, and gets you five times more names to follow up on. Use a "party plan" approach to have referral parties at which you all write letters for each other, or make phone calls.

> ### Training Staff
>
> Here are some ways to make your office more friendly to clients, thus building relation-ships for referrals:
>
> - Staff name tags will make customers more comfortable.
> - Have staff greet people by name and introduce themselves.
> - Reward staff for positive letters or comments from clients, or for referrals.

THROUGH THESE PORTALS PASS THE MOST IMPORTANT PEOPLE: OUR CUSTOMERS.

Better Referrals . . .

Here's a statistic on how to improve the quality of your referral leads. About 60 percent of leads that are given through positive referrals will do business with you if you're persistent. But about 90 percent of referral leads will do business with you if a third party actually sets up the appointment for you. Part of this is because the third party will screen a few people out who don't actually want to talk to you. The other part is that they'll be stronger, more immediate referrals.

Contractual Referrals . . .

Speaker/consultant Bob Bloch has a clause in his contract with clients that says that if they are dissatisfied, the full fee will be refunded. But if they are satisfied, they must write five letters of recommendation to five people like themselves as part of the fee. In seven years of using this system, he's never had a refund. He gets the names, addresses, and phone numbers of the referrals and he eventually sells to 85 percent of them.

Create Agents for Your Services . . .

If you sell photography, graphics, or other services that can be displayed, you can enlist a few fans as "agents." Some clients will respond well to a commission or discount for displaying your work. Then, when people ask them about you, they call immediately with the lead. It won't fit for most clients, but some will even hint at it. I've used it as an editor, as have designers. For psychologists it's a no-no.

> **Professional Referrals**
>
> Many professionals could help their clients with referrals. For instance, one printer referred a client to a photographer and worked with him to get exposures that would print better for their mutual client. The client was so thrilled that he talked up the printer to everyone. Who could you exchange referrals with and cooperate more with in order to help your mutual clients?

Cross-Training Referrals . . .

One new chiropractor used a personal trainer and finally thought to ask him about referrals. After making arrangements to cross-refer to each other, they built a great working relationship. She received 21 patients in three months from the trainer and, of course, reciprocated with her clients. Once you've gotten referrals from people you know, you can move on to other people in that category to extend your reach.

Getting Immediate Telephone Referrals . . .

Here's the way one professional recommends pursuing referrals once someone has agreed to give you some:

"If they were here, you'd introduce us, wouldn't you?"

"Yes, of course."

"Then would you take a minute to pick up the phone and introduce us now? It will also give you a chance to say hello to them." (This works leaving a message too. When you call back yourself, they know who you are and are expecting the call.)

Give Away Extras . . .

An accountant sent out 300 tax organizers on January 1 to his clients. His referral touch is that he sent each client an extra one to pass on to possible referrals. He got 30 new clients from the effort!

Give Clients Something to Talk About . . .

To generate word of mouth you have to give clients and prospects something to talk about. Ketchum Advertising, in Pittsburgh, went all out on their office decorations. They have everything from a wooded, stream-like setting, to clever graffiti in the stairwell, to giant chairs. It demonstrates their creativity, it stimulates their creativity, and it entertains clients. And, of course, it gets publicity and word of mouth.

Hosting Referrers . . .

Ben Coleman, of Restland Funeral Home, started hosting ministers' breakfasts. They've become so successful in building relationships and referrals that Restland has allocated one person to do nothing but work on relationship building with local clergy of all denominations.

Develop Your Systems

In order to help yourself follow through on referral leads immediately, develop a form letter that you can send by simply inserting the name that someone gives you. Developing and using these letters more than doubled referrals for one professional.

Dear ———
your friend,
————,
Suggested
I contact
you....

Make Referring Easy . . .

Make it easy for people to give you referrals. Develop a choice of form letters for them to send so they can simply copy or adapt them.

More Quality Referrals . . .

Everyone says to ask prospects for referrals right after they have purchased. But David Dunn in England suggests asking for referrals from prospects who have *not* bought. As long as you had a rapport with them, they may still be comfortable giving you referrals. They may even feel guilty about not buying, and they can handle that guilt by helping you find others who'll buy.

Nonsales Staff . . .

Greeneville Printing Services gives every employee his or her own business cards to distribute in social situations. When customers bring in a card, they're given a 10 percent discount, and the employee receives one hour off per sale.

Personal Promotional Parties . . .

If you have a friend or mentor who wants you to succeed but isn't sure how to refer you or help you, consultant Bernard Zick suggests having the friend throw a party for you. Have a theme such as Groundhog Day, or something else that's a good excuse for a party. The guests don't know it, but you're the star. Its real goal is to invite people to meet you. Your contact then selects the people, briefs you on some of them, and makes a point of introducing you.

Mix Prospects with Happy Customers . . .

A travel agent had a creative welcome-back party which creates further goodwill with customers. Plus she invites prospects to her events. After a Tahiti cruise, she sent out zip-lock invitation bags filled with sand, shells, and a drop of blue food coloring with instructions to add water to "reconstitute Tahiti." Cute. By mixing your happy customers with prospects, they'll sell for you too.

Letter Creates Referrals . . .

J. Abraham is an expensive marketing consultant. One of the things he recommends is a letter to existing clients along these lines:

> I appreciate your business. Our relationship has been an excellent one for me, and I've found that my best new clients come from referrals from old clients.
>
> I'm writing just to let you know that my practice is getting full, and I'll only be able to accept a few new patients in the near future.
>
> Before I accept any new people from the outside, I wanted to let you know that if you want to refer any of your friends, family, or associates, I'll be pleased to give them first priority. I only ask that you let me know soon.
>
> Please give me a call or drop me a note and register your friend's name so that I'll know how many spaces to save for you.

One practitioner sent the letter out to all patients, and then followed with a phone call to a few frequent referrers. The result was 22 referrals in 30 days.

Do Lunch
Occasionally, invite a referral source to your office for an informal lunch. Call the person's assistant beforehand and ask about his or her favorite foods. They'll enjoy lunch and be impressed at your thoughtfulness.

Cultivating Referral Sources . . .

Edit Ink provides manuscript editing for authors. One way they solicit new business is to mail to book publishers listed in directories. They offer a 15 percent referral fee and include a sample letter that publishers can send to rejected authors. The letter recommends that authors get editing help and gives Edit's contact information. They also call themselves "book doctors" which has a certain official sound to it.

Referral Coupons . . .

Coupons can work for more than groceries. One professional encourages more referrals by offering discount coupons for her clients to give to their friends.

Referral Reminder Trick . . .

Terry Lewis carries five paper clips in his pocket every day. Every time he feels one, he asks the next person he sees for three referrals. When he gets them, he throws out that paper clip. At the end of most days, he has 15 new prospects to call. It sounds silly, but it works. It may even disarm a tough source to tell the person you're asking why you have a paper clip in your hand. If people get a kick out of it, they'll loosen up and give you more names.

> **Sample Thank-You Note**
>
> "Referrals like yours are the nicest compliment we can receive. We appreciate your confidence in us. Through referrals by good clients like you, we have created a positive work environment. A 'thank you' hardly seems enough for your trust and consideration. Thank you again for your confidence."
>
> —Jim Rhode, *10 Secrets of Marketing Success*

Referral Sources List . . .

Here are the referral sources one accounting firm targets: its own staff, computer salespeople, personnel agencies, other CPAs, bookkeepers, office equipment salespeople, bankers, lawyers, community leaders, old clients, and new clients. The firm tries to keep in touch with and give referrals to all these sources. You should have your own master list too.

Don't Forget Referral Thank-Yous . . .

Janet Thompson, a marketing consultant, actively asks for referrals. She tries to reciprocate and always sends thank-you notes. If a referral works out well, she'll send a box of chocolate truffles. That's not a "trifle!"

Referrals from Hotels . . .

Visitors to your town often need emergency service, whether it's for contact lenses, health concerns, legal advice, accounting, reproduction of documents, or the like. If you think your services are needed, contact local concierges at hotels, and get on their lists of preferred providers. You need a one-sheet or resume with your picture and some of your credentials as a handy reference for hotels to give out. By making personal contact, one optometrist became the first source who hotel staff recommended to guests who had broken their glasses or lost contact lenses. He also began to get business from the hotel's employees. Over a six-month period he got six referral patients per month from the hotel, and 22 employees who became ongoing patients.

Gifts Create More Referrals Than Prayers . . .

One professional gives clients special $100 discount cards to give out to their friends. This makes giving a referral a present for them to share. He figures it increases referrals by 10 percent. It could be far more if your current referral efforts are based only on the "prayer" method.

> ### Success
>
> You are a success if you're someone who . . .
>
> "gained the respect of intelligent men and the love of children . . . who looked for the best in others and gave the best he had."
>
> —Robert Louis Stevenson

Referrals Pay 100 Percent . . .

Someone with no speaking experience wanted to reach great prospects in a hurry. He propositioned Tony Robbins (a big motivational speaker) to put him on his program. He offered to pay Robbins 100 percent of the income for six months that he derived from any clients obtained at the seminar. It gave Robbins a new source of income, and the inexperienced speaker a powerful endorsement and exposure to an audience that was primed to buy. If you expect repeat and long-term business, you can afford to give away a lot.

Sell to Groups First . . .

By selling to groups, you get lots of referrals to individuals. For instance, George Wladis gets individual life insurance sales from his group accounts. If you become the accountant for the contractors local chapter, you're a natural to work for the members. Likewise for computer consultants, as well as many others.

Sell Your Discounts . . .

If a customer is really insistent on a discount or other favorable terms, Mike O'Connor, of Cel-Tec Cellular, negotiates for a referral or testimonial in return. That gives you an excuse to discount, and it helps you collect more testimonials and referrals.

Surgery Cross-Referrals . . .

A plastic surgeon and a dentist specializing in cosmetic dentistry were competitors. For every major job, both gave clients a "total enhancement package" which included a free makeover, hairstyling, wardrobe consultation, nail treatment, and fashion review. These services were all provided by local businesses and were bought at a discount because of the bulk referrals involved. When the two professionals met, they formed an agreement to include a free consultation for the other in their giveaway packages. These referrals were much more successful than average because the patients had already paid for a cosmetic enhancement from one of them. After six months of the arrangement, the plastic surgeon got 18 new cases who had already had dental work done, and the dentist got 30 new cases from the plastic surgeon—very profitable for both of them.

> **Referrals in a Can**
>
> If you want to have referrals at your immediate beck and call, collect written testimonials and carry them with you for when you don't have a personal referral.
>
> REFERRALS

Therapy-Cardiology Referrals . . .

When people have heart attacks they often get depressed, even after they have recovered or had the successful operation. One therapist started specializing in these postattack clients. Once she realized that she had success with them, she began to contact their cardiologists. She eventually used a letter pointing out the importance of overcoming depression and starting treatment early to make the operation more successful, and suggesting a meeting showing how she might be able to help them. She ended up with five referring cardiologists whose patients made up a large part of her practice.

Update Your Customer Files . . .

Bob Brassard works his current files. He calls at least one client a day to keep in touch, update files, and hear about any life changes. Even just leaving a message lets them know you care. This method keeps competitors out, keeps records current, and gets him referrals and

new business. Taking care of your existing customers is 10 times cheaper than
finding a new customer. This works for
laundry services, photographers, detec-
tives—you name it.

Collecting Mini-Testimonials . . .

It's always hard to collect the testimonials that help you sell and get referrals.
Most pros develop form letters their
clients can follow, or they write the
whole thing. Barry Farber says when you
make a sale, get their business card and
ask them to write the main reasons they

Improve Your Mailings

When new competition started
a mailing campaign, one
professional added brief testimonials from his clients to *his*
letters that said how long
they'd been working with him
and invited recipients to call. It
set him apart
from the newer
competition
who didn't
have long-
term clients.

bought from you on the card. You can put these in a
binder and have page after page of mini-testimonials in
the clients' own handwriting. You can also later elaborate
for them based on the brief notes.

References Become Referrals . . .

An insurance application asks for a list of references.
When you deliver the policy to your new client, it's easy
to ask for an introduction to the people listed, or permission to use the client's name when you call them.
Many other services could do the same. Do you collect
credit references? How about other people in the company to contact? Other people who could receive your
newsletter?

Affinity Marketing . . .

If you've ever been offered a charge card with the name
of your college or association on it, you've met affinity
marketing. MBNA bank has been a pioneer. Any arrangement to get your service promoted by an organization
gives you greater credibility through its endorsement,
and many also offer nonprofit mailing possibilities. You
give them a small commission, and it's a painless fund-
raiser for them, while giving you big exposure.

Classic Headline for Testimonials . . .

The headline that reads "They laughed when I sat down at the piano . . . but then I began to play" has been stolen and used successfully so many times that the exact wording of the original is probably lost. For instance, "They laughed when I told them I could make $150,000 a year as a consultant . . . " was used in a successful ad in *Forbes* magazine. "They laughed when I ordered cruising free, but then I showed them my commission checks" was for a cruise sales program for travel agents. This headline appeals to people who are worried about embarrassment. Adapt it as a testimonial from a good client of yours. For instance, "They laughed when I said I could cut my legal costs in half" as a testimonial from a client for a law firm.

Record Testimonials . . .

Remember that your testimonials can be audio or video as well as in writing. Radio station Z100 FM uses advertiser testimonials in radio ads to sell more spots. The ads include a brief bit of interesting trivia and then an endorsement or success story from a current advertiser. This builds relationships with the advertisers by giving them extra free exposure and uses the testimonials for extra sales for the station.

Videotaped Testimonials . . .

Too few people use videotaped testimonials from their customers. A number of large firms have customers give testimonials that each deal with a specific objection. For instance, if the hourly rate of a law firm is the highest in town, the firm includes at least one testimonial that specifically deals with the value that clients get for their money. If inconvenience in dealing with car repair is an objection, the dealer has at least one customer speak about how convenient the service was and how well he or she was treated. After you show the video to prospects, you can ask them, "How would you like to be in my next video?" It's novel, and it works. If your clients are nationwide, do what one firm did: videotape testimonials at the annual trade show or convention. Schedule appointments with clients ahead of time, and then grab a few extra interviews when you see other people.

Using Testimonials . . .

Let's say you've followed the advice here and gathered lots of nice testimonial letters. How do you get people to read them naturally? Tom McNichols carries a folder that says, "Why Work with Tom McNichols?" In it are his testimonial letters. If you put your folder in a reasonably prominent place, people are naturally going to pick it up and glance inside. And, of course, it's filled with glowing testimonials for your services.

· · · ACTION AGENDA · · ·

"An ounce of action is worth a ton of theory."
—Friedrich Engels

Referrals are the ultimate marketing tool. Every service provider wants to rely on them, but few do anything to actively obtain them. Use some of the 63 examples here to accelerate your referrals.

→ Investigate leads/tips clubs in your area. Most will be listed in business calendars. And you can always ask for referrals to them!

→ Who else do your clients use who you respect? Talk with them about cross-referring.

→ What would happen if you asked everyone you met today for a referral? How about asking one person?

→ Collect mini-testimonials on business cards. Then get some of them expanded into letters.

→ Do you have one client who would put his or her name on a general prospecting letter for you?

→ Would audio or video testimonials be useful for you?

→ Who should you butter up with doughnuts or flowers: teachers? secretaries? neighboring businesspeople?

→ What could you send out to clients to pass on to friends? A calendar, planner, discount certificate?

→ Would anyone respond to referral fees?

→ Are any groups likely to be good sources of referrals?

26

Strategy and Tactics in Your Marketing

"To be successful, you must not follow strategies
that your top competitor is pursuing; if you try
to be someone else, the best you can be is
second best."

—Sun Tzu, *The Art of War*

Traditionally, strategy involves broad decisions about who
you want to appeal to, how you will position yourself, and
so on. Tactics are specific ways of implementing strategy. We
talked about your positioning in the beginning of the book;
that is the most important strategic decision you can make
about your marketing.

Jack Trout (*The New Positioning*) has suggested that if you
have a tactical advantage, such as location, you can build a
winning strategy from that. Long discussions of marketing theory and strategy are beyond the scope of this book. This book
is loaded with tactics. Some of them come from strategies such
as relationship building; others suggest strategies, as Trout
describes.

+++

"Negative" Advertising . . .

Sex sells pretty well by itself. But here's a clever news-paper headline for a show. "100s of Beautiful Girls & 3 Ugly Ones." It's good enough to be trademarked. How could you use this in your business? "We have 100 beautiful landscapes to show our work . . . plus 3 ugly ones. But you should have seen the ugly ones before clients messed them up!" Heh, anything can be worked with!

Sell at the Top . . .

MSA Consulting and Computer Services was nearly bankrupt. Two sales strategies helped them turn it around. One was "Sell in the treetops." This means that they work hard to get their foot in the door near the top of the corporate hierarchy. They figure it makes it harder for someone further down the line to overturn a sale. If they can't get to the top, they look for an "angel," an internal advocate in the prospect company who wants to help them sell their services. This new strategy was so successful in turning the company around that they sold it for $333 million and created many spin-offs and millionaires.

Serve Your Best Customers Better . . .

San Antonio Savings followed the advice of Willie Sutton (a famous bank robber). When asked why he robbed banks, he said, "Because that's where the money is!" San Antonio found out that its best customers had only 40 percent of their money in San Antonio Savings. (The nerve of customers!) Knowing there was money to be had, the bank went after it and asked customers what they wanted. They wanted more convenience, and when they got it, they deposited another $80 million and took out loans of $17.5 million in one year!

Better Database, Better Marketing . . .

Selecting the right prospects can make a *big* difference. Before MCI started using database selection to find its targets, each of its 400 telemarketing reps sold 0.4 hookups per hour on average. Now after selecting prospects more precisely, they've raised the rate to 1.0 hookup per hour. And MCI has almost three times as many sales reps, which normally lowers productivity. This is a 250 percent increase in productivity. And results can be even more dramatic from better lists.

DATABASE MARKETING: The gathering of detailed information on customers and prospects and then tracking which variables relate to purchasing.

Target Mail . . .

AT&T decided to promote their 900-number services. They found that advertising in trade magazines didn't pull much, so they switched to targeted postcards personalized to each group, such as banks, government agencies, and fund-raising groups. On one side they pictured the distorted face of an unhappy customer who was being put on hold; on the other side they invited response for further information. Their double-digit response rate is very high for a promotion.

Creative Cards . . .

If you're in a creative business, a creative business card is the least we expect from you. After all, it's a work sample, and you should be your own best client. Creative consultant Jeff Berner has more than one card. A custom black-and-white one features the word "CREATIVE" in a big bar on the front. It's striking, but the kicker is that on the back, the whole card is repeated in mirror image (as if the card were transparent). It gets attention.

Licensed Services . . .

If you want to establish a brand identity for your services, it's possible to license names from product providers. For instance, Dr. Scholl's foot care licenses its name to shoemakers. It could also license to podiatrists. If you'd like a brand identity for expanding nationwide, you could create a franchise overnight. Crayola or Gerber might license child care centers. Brian Tracy and others license their seminars, and so on.

Repetition Works . . .

One ad has run in the classified section of newspapers nationally, with the same headline, for 23 years. They continue to test, but the old headline keeps winning. One reason is that you get bored of your advertising faster than your audience does. The second is that the ad is for job seekers, so a whole new audience reads the ad every week looking for jobs. Once you have a headline that works, don't replace it unless you find a new one that beats it in tests.

> ### Changing Your Image
> The Lake Las Vegas development had an image problem. They finessed past problems by sponsoring exclusive parties for the media, real estate agents, and others. It turned their image around.

Partnering Gets Jobs . . .

The small People law firm has about half minority lawyers. When they approached Chrysler, suggesting that minority representation might help the automaker in urban liability cases, they were turned down as too small. By partnering with Hughes Hubbard, a large, powerful, basically white firm, they got the job. Their joint venture has generated about $2 million a year, and also qualifies for some affirmative action work under government programs. (These programs may have changed, depending on the law this week!) The larger firm says that their relationship with the smaller firm helps them recruit minority lawyers in-house. It also helps the smaller firm recruit lawyers because they're playing in bigger ballparks now.

Targeting Your Audience . . .

Where better for a professional speaker to write articles than in the magazine *Corporate Meetings and Incentives*? Every month, a number of speakers do—such as Dr. Richard Harris, who talks on speaking and listening skills. His article on how to give a presentation was an easy sell because speaking in public is a major fear of most people, including meeting planners.

Communications Analysis . . .

Dr. Vincent Covello has written 30 books on communications. He reviews public relations materials for effectiveness using a comprehensive checklist based on academic research. This procedure makes it easy for him to find flaws and suggest improvements. It also impresses his clients that he has a checklist of dozens of criteria such as conciseness, use of testimonials, clarity of statement, and organization.

Depending on how you structure it, a checklist can be written in such a way that it impresses people with how much you know, but that they can't use it, as is, themselves. You can also use it as a tool for training employees.

> ### Benefits of Checklists
>
> A checklist shows that you know a lot about your subject by the details covered. It can also raise issues for consideration in recipients' minds if they hadn't given thought to some of the items. Plus, it's a good, free offer. It costs you little to print on a couple of pages of paper, yet it has high perceived value. Anyone from a trucker to an investment banker could create a useful list.
>
>

More Checklist Selling . . .

A big security consultant is one of many businesses to use a checklist. In a letter, they said, "I'd like to send you a valuable checklist without obligation by return mail. It could prove priceless. It's a detailed guide to the things to do to protect your family, your home, and your business from burglary, fire, and other problems."

Strategic Giving . . .

Philanthropy can be a basis for marketing if you're strategic but not obviously self-serving. Instead of spreading out their giving, Arbella Mutual Insurance focused on preventing underage drinking and driving. They use trained teens to present seminars at schools in a program called "Krooz Controlled." They offered more than 180 seminars over three years, got lots of good publicity, and probably made driving safer for all— which would cut their costs.

Track Habits for Custom Offers . . .

AmEx uses your spending patterns to customize offers to you. For instance, if you eat out a lot, they may offer a free bottle of wine for trying a new restaurant. They introduced this in Britain where customers get five new offers a month.

Focus More on Customers . . .

A 100-year-old insurance company, Zurich Municipal, had spread their efforts too thin until they focused. To prosper, they created teams responsible for specific markets. This way, someone kept focused on the customers who had been getting lost. Zurich called them champions for the markets. (For products they are called product or brand managers.) They eliminated offices so staff had to spend time with clients! From decline, sales are up three straight years.

Money-Back Guarantees Sell . . .

Many service providers hate the idea of offering a money-back guarantee. But the hardest part about selling services is their intangibility. Peo-

---

Guarantees = Customer Service

One way to think about a guarantee is as a customer service tool for people who aren't yet customers. You make it easier for them to try you so that you can impress them with your service.

---

ple don't know what they are buying, and sometimes they can't judge the quality even after they've received it. This may be true, for instance, in the case of a legal contract or a tax return. That's why yet one more study, this one by professor Sridhar Moorthay at the University of Rochester, found that offering customers a money-back guarantee can be a most effective promotional tool.

What's in a Name? . . .

Why did the tremendously successful Federal Express change their name to FedEx? And they paid Landor, a big-time naming company, a lot of money to recommend it. They were simply following their customers' usage, which had already reduced the name to FedEx, and used FedEx as a verb as well. The original name, Federal, was chosen as a marketing tool to try to get a Federal Reserve contract. They never did, and they didn't end up being a big government carrier. The term *federal* also has negative, big-government, connotations, particularly among South Americans who have never liked the term *federales*.

Performance-Based Billing . . .

Performance-based billing attracts clients by reducing their risks. In areas such as phone bill consulting, it's a standard procedure. If your phone bill is in excess of so much per month, almost all consultants will come in and just take a percentage of what they save you. Many lawyers take court cases on contingency, in which they get paid only if they win the case. From the customers' viewpoint, it's a way of being sure that your lawyer has faith in your case and is not just doing it for the money. Cactus Communications offers to accept pay on the basis of the exposure a story gets if it believes the story is a good one. The majority of companies in most fields hate the idea because they think their competitors who offer it make them look as if they're not confident about their performance.

Can you guarantee your services in some way?

Fax-on-Demand Pays Off . . .

Dan Poynter has gotten to be a guru of small publishing and self-publishing, partly because of his fax-on-demand system. You can order a hundred documents free, such as "Secret List of Book Promotion Contacts," or "Recommended Books for Professional Speakers." He also sells a number of documents over the fax-on-demand system, by simply delivering an invoice with the item. While some of these materials are products, his main living comes from seminars and consulting. The products simply reinforce his image as an expert.

> **Fax-on-Demand Service**
>
> Fax-on-demand positions you as providing 24-hour service, just like a website but accessible to more people at the moment, given the wide usage of fax machines compared with Internet services.

Resell Service "Units" . . .

Why not get paid for your work and then resell the same work to others? That's what happens when many software consultants develop custom applications for clients, and then reuse the code for other clients. Or they subsequently create generic commercial products. Doesn't apply to you? How about the accountant who is paid to research a tax issue for one client, and then can help others faster? Or the lawyer who creates customer "boilerplate" documents? Try it— you'll like it.

Restaurants Sell Products . . .

Have you ever wondered why people pay to wear advertising for the Hard Rock Cafes? Now every other restaurant in town sells T-shirts. (The Homemade Cafe says people want 100 percent cotton, extra large.) Stars Restaurant says they decide on what to sell by what people steal! Now they sell napkins, ashtrays (a dying item!), menus, wine glasses, cookbooks, and so on. Professionals could sell computer disks of relevant articles. Trades such as plumbing could sell joke items. You make a profit and get your name out there more.

Buying Clients . . .

Computer Sciences bought half a billion dollars worth of technology consulting firms in order to get its foot in the door with new accounts. Some services lend themselves to be the entering wedge with a company: for instance, analyzing efficiencies or cutting costs, or determining what computer system is needed. Computer Sciences calculates that every dollar in initial business produces another four dollars in follow-up business.

> **Partnering Position**
>
> When you're able to make your payoff depend on the success of your clients, you're a partner, not a vendor. Sales leaders such as Larry Wilson (*Stop Selling, Start Partnering*) and Neil Rackham (*Getting Partnering Right*) provide lots of examples of why partnering is strong positioning.

Create Your Own Jobs . . .

Aetna Life and Casualty decided that one way to control costs and improve its marketing was to build its own health care clinics. Similarly, an architect could become a partner in designing, constructing, and renting office space. This is much the same model that Perot Systems and EDS use in taking over the data processing capacities of large companies. They run them as partners, thus generating more business.

Credentials Can Help . . .

Credentials are what you make of them. Jeffrey Ranz is an example of someone who made a lot from his work to become a certified financial planner. He explains to clients and prospects what the designation means in terms of education, ethics, and continuing education requirements. His income almost doubled the year following his certification. He's not sure if he should attribute his success to his increased self-confidence, the added knowledge he gained of other products in order to pass the test, or the new credibility he had with prospects.

Dealing with Price . . .

Here are two responses used by sales pros when people ask for a lower price. One is to ask if *they* sell for the lowest price; and when they say, no, ask them, "Why not?" Then after they explain, you say, "Me too." Another is to say, "I'm sure our competitors know the value of their services better than we do!"

> ### More Performance-Based Billing
>
> The huge ad agency DDB Needham Worldwide offers to link its pay to the success of its ads. The agency believes that its performance-based billing system has helped it win several new clients. Of its 12 major clients billed this way, four are new.
>
>

Display Your "Merchandise" Well . . .

Photographers Hing/Norton deliver their final still-lifes beautifully packaged, organized, and labeled. The one they consider best is mounted for display, which draws comments and encourages clients to exhibit it and pass the word. Even contractors can display their tools in a truck in a way that looks professional. As the Jan Carlzon "coffee stain" principle (discussed in Chapter 23) says, people assume that if you're neat, your work will be top-quality too.

Franchising Lawsuits . . .

A number of aggressive law firms have developed successful suits on a local or regional basis against companies with affiliates or branches nationwide. I know of at least one firm that has essentially resold or franchised the lawsuit materials to enable local lawyers all over the country to bring suit against the same company.

It's another way of "productizing" your services when you can sell materials that help other people do the same thing that you do. It might be procedures for a dental office, or an operations manual for a gardening firm. Think about what you have that you could sell in written form, or in seminars to other people like you.

Make It Up in Volume? ...

Few kids love going to the dentist or having braces. Orthodontic Centers has set up a chain of specialists to make braces a "consumer" product. Items such as colored braces attract the kids. Orthodontic Centers spends lots more on advertising than the average orthodontist ($72,000 versus $4,000 a year per doctor) but offers lower prices from economies of scale, centralized management, and more customers.

How can you use this approach? Look for fashion trends if you deal with kids, even if they make no sense to you. For instance, my daughter likes her fluorescent retainer, even though you can't see it glow in her mouth. When you get into mouths, there's no accounting for taste! Also consider joint advertising efforts with competitors in border areas.

More Restaurant Gimmicks ...

Texas is where I first went to an Italian restaurant that featured waiters who sang opera between servings. It turns out there's an informal circuit of these restaurants. They recruit from local music majors. The Ivanhoe in Chicago used to have an elevator to the "dungeon" with scary caves and rattling chains. An L.A. bar has trains running all around, including on the ceiling. A San Francisco establishment had a huge back-projection screen behind the bar with movies of waves rolling in at you. The point is, when people go out, they want entertainment. If you're not novel in any way, why should people remember you, tell others, or come back? At least 90 percent of restaurants and bars don't even try to be unique. And their service, food, and drinks aren't special either!

Name-Change Marketing . . .

Western International Hotels' name was an oxymoron. You can't be both in the West and international. They changed their name to Westin, which tested as more elegant and with an international flair. The right name can be a marketing tool. If you're small, picking one that's descriptive helps people know what you do immediately. If you're large, picking one with the right connotations for your clients can set you apart from the competition. Of course, if you can do both, so much the better.

> ### Are You a Specialist?
>
> If you are a specialist for one or more industries, you should have testimonial and client lists that are customized to those industries. You should also have a selection of articles you've written specifically for them.

Niche Specialist . . .

One professional has 27 different résumés in his computer so that he can customize himself for each prospect industry and issue! One area he developed was municipal finance for cultural projects. One job led to another. He says it's an unusual niche that pays very well.

No Unrelated Behavior . . .

How you behave playing softball may have nothing to do with your skills as an attorney or a consultant, but prospects make their judgments from the information they have. For instance, in the old days, truckers used to be considered the "knights of the road," often stopping to help stranded motorists. More recently, their image has been negative. If you're cut off by a truck, you remember the name of the company, not the driver who did it. Trucking companies actually have the chance to build legends about themselves, as Nordstrom does in department stores. And you don't have to be a trucker to carry battery cables and the like, and to help strangers. You never know when the "little old lady" you help may be the mother of a major prospect or customer—or a prospect or customer herself.

Package Add-Ons . . .

Hertz Car Rental packages what they call their "Number One Club" plan: a group of add-on services for good customers. By putting a name on it with a membership card and so forth, they give it a hard reality ("producitizing"). You can use the same tactic for many other services that people repeat, such as beauty parlors, landscaping, or photography.

Price Sensitivity . . .

In general, it's dangerous to compete on price, but there are exceptions. The Lombard Brokerage firm cut its commissions by half for on-line execution of stock trades, and business boomed. In fact, the half-price cut created more than twice the business, keeping dollar volume steady. When Citibank dropped its fees for home PC banking, it attracted 125,000 new customers, 20 percent of whom were new to the bank.

> **Partnering for Clients**
>
> Simpler Systems Consultants used a partnership with IBM to open the doors to a job for Nike that they couldn't have gotten on their own.

If you can afford to give away something at a noticeably lower price, you can sometimes attract the attention of prospects who wouldn't otherwise try you. The danger is that they will move on to the next bargain.

Realistic Partnering Expectations . . .

According to *Reseller Management* magazine, computer consultants who partner with each other can expect two benefits. Partnering can add 5 to 10 percent to their revenues, plus help increase their technology and marketing skills. However, the article adds, as many as half the partnering efforts by computer consultants and others may fail.

Serious Planning . . .

Sweden-based Skandia Group Insurance Company, with $7 billion in revenues, was worried about getting stuck in a rut. So, they set up multigeneration planning groups to present to their executive council. These groups challenged basic models such as selling their products through broker networks and pushed the company to work toward ignored markets such as women. They also set up on-line brainstorming sessions to demonstrate how many ideas could be produced in short order. It's when you're doing well that you need to push the boundaries in your planning.

> ### Positioning Strategy
>
> "In a mental battle, the odds favor the first person to get into the mind of the prospect. . . . It's better to be a big fish in a small pond (and then increase the size of the pond) than to be a small fish in a big pond."
>
> —Ries and Trout, *Positioning: The Battle for Your Mind*

Services Mass Production . . .

Gensler and Associates is the top interior design firm in the country, with 700 architects and designers. They have become specialists in store "rollouts." By using a similar design and setting up efficiencies of scale, suppliers, and construction, they can help their clients build a chain of stores more cost-effectively than doing it one at a time. They also provide management of projects that they roll out as a value-added service. While you may not approach things on their scale, standardizing certain service modules can save clients money and make you more profitable in any field.

Sharing Your Costs . . .

Leasing companies vary in their rates and terms, just like any other service or product. One way they help bring rates down or extend extraordinary terms is through joint promotions with the vendors of the items for which they are providing lease financing. Think about someone you could work jointly with, who would have an incentive to pick up some of your fees. Perhaps an architect or a contractor could partner with a materials supplier or lumber store? A law firm defending a local dealer for a product liability case could get resources from the manufacturer.

Simple Marketing Plans with a Narrow Focus . . .

Jay Levinson, *Guerrilla Marketing* guru, says you can do a marketing plan in five minutes yourself, or you can pay him $5,000 for it. He uses seven questions to focus you in. I've boiled my "mini-plan" down to three items: (1) Pick a specific, narrow objective such as to get publicity in a particular trade magazine. David Morris Design picked to add three clients of a certain type. (2) Next, gather what you need to carry out your purpose. This might be as simple as looking in the phone book, or going to the library to get a list of publications to contact. (3) Last, budget and schedule your mini-plan. When will you do it specifically, and what will you need to make it happen? For many people, the most important thing is to "budget" the emotional energy to take on a new responsibility, especially if you have a negative image of marketing. Fashion illustrator Sharon Rothman always hated marketing. She found that a plan with clear steps to follow was energizing, not draining.

Target Big Business Customers . . .

It can be as hard to make a small sale as a large one. The majority of the companies on *Inc.* magazine's 500 fastest-growing list serve large business customers. One of the benefits of working with big companies is that often they are more interested in quality than price, as long as you are within reasonable parameters. Are there companies you can target that would bring you lots of business when you got them?

Partnering for Big Game . . .

Infinite Technologies Group wanted to bid on Bank of New York's service contract for its 1,500 PCs and 400 laser printers. Bank of New York is one of the country's 20 largest banks, and Infinite knew they were too small to handle it alone. All the other bidders were major corporations, so Infinite teamed with Digital Equipment Corp., which provided prestige, credibility, and spare parts and logistics support. DEC also gained: ITG brought a personal touch to the contract, and had lower overhead and more flexibility. ITG set up the proj-

> ### Surviving Through Relationships
>
> " . . . as your customers whittle away at their supplier base— and they will—your survival is going to depend on whether you are bringing enough *vision, impact,* and *intimacy* to the relationship to justify selection as one of the chosen few."
>
> —Rackham, Friedman, and Ruff, *Getting Partnering Right*

ect management, and they won the bid. Once in place, they added 5,000 PCs and 450 laser printers, and they expect to add more.

Targeted Mailings, Personal Offers . . .

Citibank mailed postcards to credit card users who quit using their cards. It offered an 800 number to call for a special offer if the customers would say why they'd quit. That gave Citi a chance to recover. For instance, when one user said he'd switched to his Discover Card because of the 1 percent cash rebate, Citibank matched the program for him.

> ### Friendship
>
> "Like life itself, business is a social activity . . . The way to ride the friendship horse is to keep in touch regularly with all your business friends."
>
> —Ries and Trout, *Positioning*

The Right Markets . . .

No matter how good you are, if you're selling to the wrong markets you won't do well. They may be good markets for others but not for you. American General dumped their property and casualty and group life and health insurance businesses which had been the core of the company for 60 years. They felt they didn't have enough control over their agents. They went for areas of the insurance business that they rated more stable and growth oriented. Do you have any big clients that you should move away from?

Working a Niche . . .

What's the biggest car rental company? It's Enterprise by a good margin. Enterprise doesn't fight it out at the airport with Hertz and others. It operates little, inexpensive offices all over the country—more than anyone else. The company has developed its niche in two ways: with target markets and its employees. It gets to know auto dealers and body shops in order to get the referrals when people rent a car for a day or two while theirs is in the shop. Enterprise even sets up offices part-time at some car dealers to help fill out the paperwork and leaves the cars on the lot for customers. And on Wednesdays the company delivers pizza and doughnuts to local garages and other referral sources. Most of Enterprise's employees are college grads (unlike the other companies), but it specializes in hiring people who made the top half of their classes possible because they were so busy partying! Because they finished at the tail end of the class, they appreciate the job, too. With a combination of low overhead and a better workforce, Enterprise has established a niche that is going to be hard to take away, especially now that it is dominant.

You Think You're Generic? . . .

EnergyOne has created a brand for natural gas. Deregulation means competition has come to utilities. Since all gas is the same, big customers buy on price. By adding services such as electronic billing, energy audits, lighting recommendations, and bundled handling, EnergyOne is setting itself apart as "not just another gas service."

If they can "brand" natural gas, you can certainly set yourself apart from competitors.

· · · ACTION AGENDA · · ·

"Yesterday is a canceled check; tomorrow
is a promissory note; today is ready
cash—use it!"

—John D. Rockefeller

Strategy can guide tactics, but tactics can also determine strategy. This chapter provided a potpourri of ideas. Remember that it takes only one of the 45 examples here to be the keystone of your marketing program. Your job is to "cash in" on these ideas by picking one to move on.

→ Should your business card be more creative?

→ Can you create a detailed checklist to analyze your prospects and impress them with your knowledge?

→ Can you offer an aspect of your services on a performance-guaranteed basis?

→ Can you sell some of your successful techniques to others in your field?

→ Can you package some of your services together and sell them at a premium?

→ Can you go after fewer big customers, perhaps by partnering with bigger firms?

27

Strategic Positioning

"What you must do is find a way into the
[prospect's] mind by hooking your service to
what's already there."

—Al Ries and Jack Trout,
Positioning: The Battle for Your Mind

*P*ositioning yourself in a way that will be accepted by your
prospects and customers as unique is key to defining who
you are, as shown in Chapter 1 and in the last chapter. Here
are more examples of how people projected themselves to different markets in ways that positioned them for success.

+++

"Riding" Niche Markets . . .

There are thousands of niches—specialized markets in
which you can have an advantage because you know
more about them. How do you work a niche? You might
have one client in a niche by accident. As you do a great
job for that client, you learn the jargon and special concerns of others in the area. Then you start doing mailings, asking for referrals, and going to specialized groups.
One consultant did it with horse owners! A vet gave him

his first referral. Within months, he had four horse owners as clients and 40 more prospects.

Create Your Niche . . .

You can't sit and wait for business to wander in—too many competitors are stalking your customers. Digital Prepress decided to focus on the select market of real estate agents who wanted professional-looking promotion sheets customized for each house or broker. They used the new short-run, digital color technology to create four-color selling sheets on houses for the agents. By finding and creating niche markets, Digital gets business while other printers sit and wait.

Developing Niches Backward . . .

Every success you have in any industry can lead you to more referrals, more publicity, and more clients. For example, a major law firm successfully defended the first suit against furniture manufacturers after a fire. They used this win as a niche marketing tactic to go after similar furniture companies. They wrote an article for one of the leading furniture trade magazines, and presented a paper at the association convention. This exposure quickly got them on the approved attorneys list of the Society of Plastics Industries. They became a leader in this select area of expertise.

> **Confusing Definitions**
>
> A *niche* is a place you position yourself. It can be defined by where or how you provide services, but it is most likely to be defined by exactly what you do or whom you serve.

Building an Industry Presence . . .

Chris Frederiksen provides yet another example of how specializing helps you get business and referrals. He had one credit union as a client. He asked their trade group for information on niche-specific tax issues. Then he showed them his work. That led to a referral to a second job. He began to speak publicly for the association. (He was the only accountant who'd ever shown that much interest in their problems.) Eventually, he had more credit union clients than any other accountancy firm in California.

Changes Produce Business . . .

When people get married, their lives change. So, one accountant sends newly married people invitation-looking certificates for free consultations to discuss their new tax status. About 80 percent who accept the free appointment stay on as tax clients. Since they come after the tax rush season (mostly in the summer), they help balance the workload. And, of course, some need business advice, and so forth as well. The accountant sends up to three mailings, spaced over time, if prospects don't respond to the first offer.

Newly marrieds would be a perfect group to approach with a free financial seminar, done jointly with an insurance agent, financial consultant, banker, and/or lawyer. You could also follow up with a team newsletter.

You versus Nothing

It's important to remember, and not always noted in discussions of positioning, that prospects are also comparing you with using no one at all. Inertia, or the status quo, is often your biggest competitor.

Partnership Marketing . . .

When you partner, you can appear bigger, serve multi-site clients better, and attract higher-ticket jobs. The Worldwide Electronic Publishing Network is a partnership of 50+ DocuTech printers around the world. Clients can output documents immediately at any site. The collaboration is so successful that they're turning away printers.

Who would make a logical partner for you?

Focused Consulting Ad . . .

Here's an ad that won an award for impact, based on the picture and headline. It shows a picture of a doctor with a tongue depressor and flashlight, looking into the top of a model of a "hospital" that's open like a mouth. The headline says, "When was the last time your hospital had a complete checkup?" For hospital consultants appealing to hospital administrators, it's on target.

Classified Says What They Want . . .

Here's a classified ad in a specialty software newsletter that gets right to the point. It starts, "Law firm seeks software companies" and continues with their marketing pitch. (Of course, they have an Internet address as well.) It's a clean, simple client solicitation. Rather than saying who you are, you're saying who you are trying to serve—which suggests that you have specialty knowledge.

Positioning Attack Ads . . .

Franklin Bank wanted to bring in more small-business checking accounts. It used a series of "attack" radio ads, making fun of big banks and their perceived impersonal service and higher fees. It mentioned its own free ATMs, free courier service, and the available help of a concierge. The ads won awards and also brought in the business. If you're smaller than your competitors, people will tend to believe that you give better service and more personal attention. If you're bigger, they'll believe that you have more resources available to meet their needs. Whatever you have, play it up.

Long-Distance Winners . . .

Dialing an extra five digits to make your long-distance calls may seem like trouble, but so-called dial-arounds have made it a sales benefit. They point out that you don't have to switch long-distance providers, and the calls appear on your regular bill. Star Tech has targeted immigrants by offering stickers for their phones, commercials on cable TV, and booths at ethnic festivals. VarTec Telecom has specialized in mass mailings offering a 10-cents-a-minute rate. They have tripled their market share. And Telco "brands" its long-distance service under many names such as Terrapin Long Distance, for University of Maryland students and alums. All together, these dial-around companies have tripled their market share at the expense of AT&T and the other providers. They are up to almost a billion dollars as of this writing.

Second-Fiddle Winner . . .

If you're competing for customers who are happy with their current service providers, here's a technique. One salesperson asks to be considered as their backup supplier anytime there are rush jobs, overflows, or emergencies, or when their primary service provider is unavailable. Another salesperson tells companies she just wants one small test order to show her value as a secondary supplier. These are logical reasons for the people to get to know you and to test your services. Of course, anytime the primary supplier fouls up, you—like the camel—already have your head in the tent.

"If you first let the camel get his head in the tent, expect to soon sleep with fleas."
—Old Persian saying

Second Opinions Free . . .

Irv Blackman gives a "second opinion free" if he can't lower your tax bill. It's a subtle offer. Blackman sees these clients after the work is already organized and all the "underbrush" has been cut away. In order to look impressive, all he has to do is find one thing that has been overlooked by the previous preparer. Then he gets paid for lowering the client's bill. From the point of view of the client, it's no risk.

Move to Where Customers Are . . .

The Laurelhurst Physical Therapy Clinic is still in Portland, but they've moved, too. They now have on-site clinics in two Pendleton Woolen Mills, at Nautilus gyms, and in several other locations. Arrangements can vary, from renting space to locating nearby with subsidies from companies. By being available, you capture lots more business and help more people.

Virtually Vertically Integrated . . .

One-stop shopping is a positioning statement. The Communications Alliance Network uses virtual vertical integration among five printers and similar vendors to more completely serve customers. Instead of having to own every piece of equipment, you can make money bringing in work for members who have the right equipment already. You become a one-stop "shop" for customers. So-called prepress vendors such as typesetters and printers are a natural for this type of partnership. Similarly bookkeepers and CPAs, lawyers and private investigators, M.D.s and fitness trainers, and so on.

Develop Vertical Markets . . .

Jeff Hayzlett is a consultant who used to own a printing firm. His firm identified key vertical markets—such as architecture, legal, and churches—by examining its best clients. They then specialized more and went after bigger work. You can do this by targeting your sales messages to specialized groups, getting industry-specific referrals, or going all out to thrill key customers who will bring in others like themselves.

Immigrant Niches

One service provider became friends with an immigrant who became his "consultant" in helping the provider appeal to his group. There are specialized social clubs and publications for many groups.

Service Synergy . . .

Many child-care centers—such as Children's Wonderland—are now adding elder care in the same setting. It's beneficial to both generations to spend time together. And both groups like it. Look for synergies in your own services by looking for others with whom you could partner to present a seminar or publish a newsletter. This may also introduce you to other groups you could serve alone.

Half Color, Half Price . . .

Sir Speedy is a national quick printer competing with everybody. They recently used an eye-grabbing postcard mailer. The picture side said, "Color Gets Attention," and they made their point quickly by having a picture half in black-and-white and half in color. This half-color format would get attention for any service. The message side had a price for color copies that was about half the market cost at the time. Price is a sword that cuts both ways, but there is a market for it in something like copies. Price also applies to tax preparation, painting, music lessons, teeth cleaning, and so on: at the right price, demand can expand many times for services that lots of people can use *or* do without.

Bank Sells Students . . .

Barclays Bank targeted new university students. They offered free banking and interest-free overdraft service. Plus each new account was entered in a sweepstakes for free rent (of living quarters) for a year. With the students paying rent for the first time, the promotion made Barclays stand out. Result—student accounts went up 10 percent.

Corny but Targeted . . .

An insurance company mailing to military personnel overseas used a dog-tag graphic as the place where respondents write their names. The telecom company NYNEX used a similar graphic on its billboards with good success. It's trite, but it may work with any specialty target. If you're a swimming pool service aiming at pool owners, why not have them write their names inside a pool graphic? An accountant targeting contractors can use tools—such as a saw—as graphics.

> ### Market Segments
>
> *Segment* is another positioning-type term that can be used as a noun or a verb. You can segment your market by breaking it up into clusters that you can serve or market to in a more focused manner. These target subgroups become definable segments.

A Technological Edge . . .

Spaulding and Slye, a construction management firm, hooked their Lotus Notes to a digital pager system. Now their engineers on-site can get messages *and* retrieve material from the database. Since no one else in their area does it, it impresses clients as well as saves time.

Create Your Own Specialty . . .

When you work for the same types of clients, you gain expertise. A contractor became recognized as an expert on the design and construction of dental office buildings because he built one, wrote articles on the topic for dental publications, and did more work. Simple, but effective.

Working a Niche . . .

An attorney specialized in one type of construction sub-contractor, when there were only about a dozen real players in his market. He now works for half of the companies! It was all because of referrals (which happens when you specialize). Plus you build specialized knowledge, so you're more capable. When he gets all the possible business from this group, he'll gradually add another construction specialty. After all, his clients work with lots of other contractors.

Fight Them in the Niches . . .

Against giants, offering hand-holding is a winning strategy to bring in the smaller, specialized markets. City National Bank is emphasizing personalized service as the giant banks move to less service. City has applied this idea to become the "bank of the stars" because they cater to Hollywood managers of stars. Now they're looking to develop specialties in agricultural lending and foreign exchange.

> ### The Carriage Trade
> The upscale market was originally called the "carriage trade" because the wealthy patrons of restaurants, theaters, and so on were the only ones who could afford to arrive in a carriage.
>
>

Family Driving Ranges . . .

There's always a new way to deliver an old service. Family Golf Centers transforms a passion that takes people *away* from their families to an attraction that *includes* the whole family. They offer upscale driving ranges with other attractions for nongolfers. They also spoil golfers with heated hitting tees in the winter and attractive clubhouses.

How could you transform your firm in your industry?

More Restaurant Gimmicks . . .

Here are some ways restaurants have created gimmicks to make themselves stand out. In Phoenix, one restaurant with a poor basement location installed a slide from the top floor. They also serve "cute" dishes such as rattlesnake meat. Another restaurant in Phoenix used to "warn" you if you wore a tie. Then they'd cut it off, staple it on the wall with your business card, and give you a free drink. Your office can use gimmicks, too. For instance, if your clients bring kids in, have a game room or a box full of toys.

Vendor versus Resource . . .

If you're aggressively marketing your services, people might feel that you're biased, but if you're a general "bureau" that's marketing a variety of people or companies, they're more likely to see you as a friendly resource. "Referral bureaus" include lawyers' 800-referral numbers, contractors' referral numbers, and other similar services. Like inquiry.com on-line (for computer consulting), these resources are usually free to buyers and charge service providers a commission, or for advertising. By changing from an individual vendor to a bureau, you can get more jobs for yourself and make money selling complementary services as well.

> ### Serve Fewer Clients
> The fewer clients you serve, the more time you have to build serious relationships with them. When you become a virtual extension of their business, your competitive position is a strong one.

The Information Center . . .

International Strategies supplies almost 5,000 different free reports on doing business in 80 different countries, using fax-on-demand. Their "support hotline" is covered by advertising revenues from corporate sponsors such as AT&T and *Business Week*. These sponsors promote the service in their own marketing efforts as well. International Strategies also has created an electronic directory of companies that buy and sell internationally. Having more information than anyone else positions them as the experts in the area. They get thousands of requests a day.

Performance-Based Fees, Few Clients . . .

One small law firm became the nation's leader in mortgage fraud resolution, recovering more than $34 million in one recent year. How? They have no typical hourly rate—only fixed fees. Their clients tend to be banks and other large mortgage holders, so it doesn't take a large number to produce lots of business.

Partner with Customers . . .

PSI systems sells software for financial companies. They position themselves as solution providers. PSI says, "We tell our clients that we get paid for our consulting, not for the software we sell." Whether the software comes from them or someone else, their aim is to establish a partnership attitude.

· · · *ACTION AGENDA* · · ·

"For everything you must have a plan."
—Napoléon

There are many ways to find or create a position for yourself. But most people never even try. They just do what everyone else does, describe themselves like everyone else, and get results like everyone else's.

To excel, pick one or two of the 29 ideas in this chapter and plan how you'll apply them to your situation.

➜ Analyze your clients and find an area in which you have one or more strong supporters. Then enlist those clients to introduce you to their industry groups and friends.

➜ Can you set up a referral center, or partnership, to amplify your marketing efforts?

➜ Pick one or more groups with which you like to work and begin to specialize more in their needs. Ask them what else you can do for them.

➜ Become a one-stop center by building a strong referral team of related services and products for your clients.

➜ Who can you become a spokesperson for or against?

28

Research Helps You and Others

"When testing the effects of a variable, start strong.
Vary things that can make a big difference!"
—Kurt Lewin, psychologist

*H*ow can you come up with successful strategies and tactics like those described in the last chapter and throughout this book? The answer is, do research.

Research is simply gathering information. It can be about prospects, customers, competitors, or markets. It can be highly scientific and accurate like modern polls on presidential voting. Or it can be less structured like focus groups. But the "bottom line" is that information gives you ideas. It can save you money. It can develop new services or packages.

You'll find a lot of items in this chapter on how to get input from your customers. The absolute simplest, and most useful research, is to find out what your customers think and want. Whether the president of a hotel chain works as a busboy for a day, or you simply visit your customers, you'll always see new things when you look from your customers' perspectives.

+++

Unusual Customer Research . . .

Your customers may speak more freely to others than to you. Tom Peters uses the example of the car repair place that pays taxi drivers to gather data from customers who leave their cars for repair. A delivery service gets drivers to write down complaints and other comments.

Begging for Negative Feedback . . .

In order to encourage negative feedback, one company sent small bags of gravel to its key customers and asked them to "Throw rocks at us."

Focus Narrowly, Then Cross-Sell . . .

KeyCorp bank needs to sell their own employees on the idea of doing sales work to build earnings. Employees who do well specialize in specific demographic groups, such as elderly people, small business owners, or women. The bank is also mailing very specific pitches to each type of customer with different needs. Cross-selling is possible as well when you know exactly who your customers are (database mining). For instance 11 percent of people who got car loans responded to a charge card offer. The program has resulted in loan volume up 129 percent and investment product sales 173 percent in preliminary testing.

Your Marketing Plan

Even when your marketing plan changes, having one gives you advantages:

- It tells you what information you need.
- It helps you enlist support from others.
- It gives you goals.
- It motivates you to meet your goals.

Gathering Information Ahead of Time . . .

The Ardmore Consulting Group uses databases and directories to gather specific information on prospects before they make a sales call. This way, they don't "have to look at the pictures on the office wall" to understand the prospect's interests.

How to Do Your Homework . . .

Big prospects will judge your professionalism by how much you *already* know about them. You can't expect to go in cold and find out what you need to know from them. Barry Farber gathers the following items about a company before approaching them:

1. History
2. Customers
3. Mission statement
4. Main competitors
5. Positioning within the industry (size and competitive)
6. All their products and services

You can uncover items like this on larger companies from annual reports and SEC filings, as well as from Dun & Bradstreet, Value Line, U.S. Industrial Outlet for Public Companies, and trade directories. The local library may have some of these publications and may have a file on local companies; similarly, the chamber of commerce may be of help. Call the company's trade association, if necessary. If the company is prominent enough, the people who answer the phone should be able to give you a rundown on the business. Other sources of information often overlooked are the company's competitors and its secretary.

Prospecting Homework . . .

One salesperson makes effective cold calls because he's researched every likely prospect in his territory. So, when the chance comes to drop by, he's prepared. He doesn't waste prospects' time with dumb background questions. He is ready to talk business, and prospects are impressed with his professionalism. As the Boy Scout motto says, "Be Prepared." Build your database now. Know who's out there for you.

Still More on Researching Large Customers . . .

"Knowledge is power" is a cliché because it's true. Lazer, Inc., studies large potential customers for months and develops a custom presentation before ever contacting them. Not only does their research create a better presentation, but also prospects know the company did its homework and are flattered. This approach applies widely. A panel of large customers for law firms said that one of the things they dislike during sales presentations is a generic approach where firms haven't done their homework about their specific litigation histories and industry issues.

Sales Research . . .

Hewlett-Packard wanted to expand one market. So, they built a database of 300 key companies and 572 decision makers. When they contacted them, they offered to share information. In return for their providing information, HP would give them the results of the survey. Ninety-four percent agreed, and 30 percent became leads for specific sales!

> **Simple Customer Research**
>
> One restaurant would try new dishes on customers before they put them on the menu. How can you test your services before investing too much?
>
>

Crisscross CD-ROM . . .

It used to be that if you wanted to get a phone number from an address, you had to have an expensive crisscross directory or use one at the library. Today, there are CD-ROMs that purport to have every name, address, and phone number in the United States. While they seldom are as complete as advertised, you can get a lot of information from them. For instance, American Way Real Estate looks up addresses that appear to be overgrown to check if they have been foreclosed, an area in which they specialize. Alumni Systems helps organize high school reunions; they're able to find twice as many people for 20th and 30th reunions since using a CD-ROM directory. Mika Marketing targets particular zip code areas with telemarketing pitches for local lawn care or waste hauling services.

Prove Your Effectiveness . . .

The Center for Nonprofit Management, in Dallas, produced a job listing publication. They conducted a survey of their advertisers and found that the effectiveness of the ads in their publication was rated higher than in any of the other competitive media—and at lower cost. That became a great sales tool for their advertisements.

Any service provider can sponsor a survey rating themselves against others. The results are either a great benchmarking or a sales tool, depending on how well you do! Getting testimonials from satisfied users is the least you can gain from such a survey.

Targeted Mass Mailing . . .

When real estate agent Norman Brown is looking for a home for an executive in his area, he prints out every name and address from streets in desirable neighborhoods using the new CD-ROMs available. Then he sends all of the residents letters asking if they want to sell. It gives him an edge finding houses that aren't yet on the market.

> **RFM**
>
> The most common ways to select customers for special mail offers using a database are based on the *recency, frequency,* and *monetary* size of their purchases. The greater any of these are, the more likely the people are to buy again. It's not a bad starting point. Don't neglect your recent or frequent buyers.

Political Recruiting . . .

The Democratic and Republican parties have the same interest in recruiting "customers" that any company does. Because they are trying to reach everyone in the country who might be sympathetic to them, they have to work with big databases. To decide whom to mail to, they use both positive and negative screens. That is, they select *for* certain zip codes and known behaviors, and *against* certain zip codes and behaviors, such as donations, or response to previous mailings. For instance, one fund-raiser found six criteria to identify Democrats who were most likely to switch parties.

You should be profiling your clients and prospects to see who matches your perfect client profile best.

More Personal Gifts . . .

Giving out pens and calendars imprinted with your name can be useful. But try to find a unique item that people don't get elsewhere. And when you use special-recognition gifts for referrals, they should be even more personalized. One accountant upgraded his gifts. For about 8 percent extra cost, he improved referrals from bankers, lawyers, and clients by 22 percent. But most important, he realized that he didn't know enough about many key clients to give them personalized items.

Do you know your clients' hobbies, children's names, and real passions in life? You should.

Research Publicity . . .

E-Lab is a research firm that likes to use pictures to analyze customer behavior. For instance, customers are sent cameras and asked to take pictures of their stereos. Or they're videotaped in some setting. It's a novel technique borrowed from academic researchers. You could use it to get a fresh perspective, or for publicity in your trade magazine.

Public Relations Survey . . .

Makovsky & Co. specializes in corporate public relations. Until they started seriously surveying their own clients, they missed a lot. Of particular value is knowing how much clients like their account executives. Long-term dislike cost them one big account. And one assistant got promoted to account manager based on the input. The survey now goes out yearly to small clients and twice a year to bigger ones. They make a point to send to everyone involved with them at the client company. They then follow up with phone calls to major clients and get about a 65 percent response. The survey asks pointed questions such as, "Are we giving you your money's worth?" They use a task force to take action on problems they uncover. Client retention is up 20 percent since the program was implemented, and referrals are up too.

Increase Survey Responses . . .

If you really want a good response to your survey of top executives, call them personally to explain that the survey is coming and why. One executive got a 100 percent return rate from peers using this approach.

Focused Marketing Research

A general plan to get publicity should be followed by research on the media you want to approach, specific people you can contact, what types of items they tend to use, and when their deadlines are. That gives you a start *before* you ask them what they want to see.

"Juicy" Niche Research . . .

A large CPA firm specializes in citrus growers. Every year, they do a financial information survey of average operation cost statistics (costs for labor, fertilizer, etc.). They give it to clients to benchmark their operations. And, of course, it's great to attract prospects and use for trade articles.

Scoring Customers . . .

Many people suggest grading each of your customers as A, B, or C. Then you spend more effort and time with the most profitable ones and "fire" or up-sell the low-rated ones. Several fancy statistical programs score customers in much more detailed ways. For instance, the consulting firm Fair, Isaac and

> ### Can You Tell Dollars from Profits?
>
> When deciding which clients you can serve most efficiently and profitably, it's important to be able to separate gross dollar volume from actual profits. What makes a customer profitable for you? Which services are more profitable? It's past time to find out, if you're not sure.
>
> ### GROSS ≠ Net

Acxiom uses a program that predicts customer risk for insurance companies. Then the insurance companies market only to people who aren't likely to have claims. (Naturally! And bankers can offer loans only to people who don't need them.) Buying models developed by others can be expensive. Over time, you can build a good predictive equation yourself if you keep a good database of prospect and customer data.

Ask Customers How to Sell Them and Their Friends . . .

Wolfram Research illustrates the easiest way to research new markets. They'd picked up a few international customers and wanted more. So they asked current overseas buyers for advice; these customers suggested major new markets Wolfram had never even approached. The company found new uses for their software and even licensed custom modifications from customers. Customers also advised them on the best trade shows to attend. This kind of research leads to partnerships and is another good reason to stay in touch, which further builds relationships.

Customer Feedback Pays . . .

It usually takes losing a big customer to wake up most companies. AmeriSuites Hotel lost a big account. That got them out to the customer, who was willing to talk. They upgraded, customized, and won back the account. Why not treat every customer that way from the start?

Ask Prospects What They Want . . .

Many professional societies have seminars for clients to tell them what they want in service providers. I've seen them for lawyers and speakers repeatedly. Your trade publications would welcome an article on the same topic, since everyone wants more business. So why not start researching an article now, or putting together a panel for your group?

> **Personal "Surveys"**
>
> The bigger and more important your clients, the more they are going to want to be treated personally, *not* sent a survey. Always keep in personal touch with your important clients.

Ask Your Clients . . .

Qualitech, a computer consultant (VAR), had to choose which software to support for their clients. Rather than do what was technically best, Qualitech asked their property-manager clients what they wanted. To use Qualitech's words, "If we're going to make a mistake in business planning, we make it in favor of our customers' preferences." They're also going for more profit and less volume with training and other services that don't depend on hardware. Profit growth is now double digit.

Customer Surveys Pay . . .

I recommend you send out a one-page customer questionnaire. Having it *in writing* is easier on you and your clients. However, one CPA firm called its top accounts and asked, "What do you like about our service?" and "What don't you like about our firm or other CPAs?" The company got specific ideas about making its invoices more detailed, and keeping the same account manager with the client over time. Referrals went up, along with client satisfaction. You just can't lose talking to clients.

Early-Warning Survey . . .

Selling can help customers and you. It's another way to get feedback. By the time CitiStorage (which stores records for law firms, etc.) found out that a big client was mad at them, it was too late to do anything. Now they call all customers 18 months before their contracts expire and try to sign them up again. If the customer doesn't bite, they know there's a problem and they have time to do something about it. They found problems they didn't know about and used the feedback to improve their systems.

Surveys versus Talking

Asking customers formal questions gives you different information from what you'd get just talking to them informally. I recommend you always do both. Talk to a few people before designing a survey, then discuss the results with more afterward. You'll see things differently.

Using Mystery Shoppers . . .

Mystery shoppers visit your store or call your office and rate the service received. Experts say be careful to use the feedback as a positive training tool, rather than a club. In one program, reps were trained on what mystery callers would be looking for. Recordings were done of random calls, and feedback was given quickly on each call. (This also reminded reps of the program.) Awards were given for best performances, which made it more of a service contest than an evaluation. And an audiotape of the winning performances became an ongoing training tool.

More Mystery Comparisons . . .

Westin Crown Center Hotel hired a mystery shopper service to compare how different people within the hotel handled calls. They had conflicts because salespeople, catering managers, and reservation agents might all deal with a convention or meeting. AirTouch Cellular used the same mystery shopper service to check on how its reps performed—how many rings before calls were answered, whether they were transferred smoothly, and whether operators could explain services in plain language. Both firms also hire a service to shop *their competitors*! This gives them hard data to benchmark their own performance against.

Asking Your Clients . . .

Ann Olson Girard is the corporate counsel at Hitachi America (she hires outside law firms). She uses the quality of the referrals that firms give her as a measure of their professional judgment. She gets a couple of client satisfaction questionnaires a year to fill out from law firms. But she never sees the results. She prefers to be asked personally. She says don't use an outside consultant to collect information from her. She expects more personal contact.

Shoe-Leather Research . . .

A review of books is a service to readers that looks like a product. Max Rodriguez is a good example of guerrilla research. He wanted to start a publication reviewing books for African Americans. So, he went to his local Barnes & Noble and "accosted every black person who bought a book!" He jokes that it took him about three blocks to interview each one so that by the time he had 500 people, he'd worn out a lot of shoes! Eighty-seven percent said they'd be interested in his review, which probably meant 10 percent would subscribe soon. He now has a Web page (www.qrbculture.com). If he does advertising sales as aggressively as he does research, he'll have it made.

SWOT Analysis . . .

The Mississippi Department of Environmental Education used a traditional SWOT analysis to decide how to best market themselves to the business community. As you might expect, they found out that the small business community considered their regulations a lot of bureaucratic red tape, so they set up a major outreach effort for technical and compliance assistance. Almost any bureaucracy could benefit from that. Could your customers?

> SWOT refers to an analysis of your competitive *Strengths*, *Weaknesses*, *Opportunities*, and *Threats*.

Unhappy Customers Don't Tell You . . .

Professor Dwight Porter found that 24 percent of customers were unhappy with their current supplier. Ninety-six percent of the unhappy customers don't tell you—they just leave. Sixty-eight percent of customers who switch providers do so because of how they are treated, not because of the quality of the product or service.

Day Care Marketing . . .

A chain of 25 day care centers created a special Saturday event in which parents and kids could come and make hand puppets together. It sounded good, but it bombed. When they invited parents to an evening lecture by the author of *When to Say No and How*, 400 people showed up. Many local authors will speak free for you because of the chance to sell their books. And their talk becomes an endorsement of you.

> **Unhappy Customers**
>
> Most unhappy customers don't bother to complain, and most of their complaints never get past employees. The more you can show people that you *really* want criticism, the more you'll gain. Put a dollar value on complaints for yourself or employees. It's easier to "grin and bear" complainers when you know what they're really worth to you.
>
> COMPLAINTS = $

Delivery Guerrilla Research . . .

As Yogi Berra said, "You can see a lot just by looking." One print shop has its delivery people look around when they drop off jobs to clients. They make a note of competitors' labels on delivery pallets. Then the company's salespeople follow up and make proposals. Clients usually respond with, "We didn't know you did that kind of work."

Client Questionnaire Pays Off . . .

Smith Haughey, a Michigan law firm, uses client questionnaires to evolve its services into what clients really want. It includes questions like:

- What do you like about working with us?
- What do you dislike?
- Is our billing easy to understand?
- Are your calls answered in a timely manner?
- Do we have the expertise you need?
- What else could we do to help you?

These questions are simple, but most firms don't ask them. Smith Haughey found, for instance, that higher-level decision makers are interested in a law firm's helping them make better business decisions about their overall workers' compensation strategy, not just defending cases in a cost-effective manner (which was what lower-level managers were concerned about). This changed the firm's marketing strategy to include more education about risk management.

Don't Give a "No-Questions-Asked" Guarantee ...

Arthur Hill, of the International Institute for Management Development, suggests calling your customer service guarantee "no hassle" rather than "no questions asked." You want customer feedback, so you need to ask questions. You just have to do it in a very friendly, nonconfrontational way to meet your no-hassle guarantee.

Guarantee Leads to Real-Time Info ...

Many professionals resist giving guarantees for fear people will abuse them. But the value of finding out about little problems that you can correct can be far greater than the small monetary cost. Kaiser, the big HMO, has been testing a program to offer on-the-spot refunds of copayment fees for anyone who is dissatisfied. Clients may also skip the $5-to-$25 refund and just get a call from the department manager. Kaiser faced a lot of resistance to implementing the program, but very few clients asked for their money back. Key physician Robert Schultz says "This is real-time feedback." Schultz set up the program after hearing about a similar offer at a weight-loss clinic.

Government Bidding Feedback ...

The Government Printing Office accepts the low bid on contracts, but an unusual aspect is that printers can subscribe to find out who's winning the bids. This is good research on your competitors and what it takes to be successful. In analyzing your lost bids for any service, find out what the winner did that you didn't.

Listen to the Market . . .

As an ex-lawyer who developed computer systems to improve efficiency for law firms, the owner of Veritas Technologies thought he'd do well. But even being chair of the local Bar Association technology group and doing seminars didn't help him sell much. The lawyers weren't interested, but they kept referring him to their clients. When he finally produced a generic product, he was able to piggyback on big software companies' marketing budgets, since his service helped sell their systems. He says, "Find people who attack the same market you do and follow in their wake."

Needs Analysis Survey . . .

Mosaic Business Computing uses a needs analysis survey. It focuses on how a prospect company works and what it wants to accomplish. Customers "love it because, right off the bat, it's more of a consultative sale." They often fax the survey before an initial meeting. This means Mosaic goes in more prepared.

How to Pay for Response . . .

You may have gotten a survey from some company with a dollar bill enclosed. Including money does increase the response rate to such questionnaires. One fitness company sent a brief questionnaire that took about 15 seconds to finish. They glued a quarter to the survey and said that they realized that people's time was valuable and since this should take less than 25 seconds, they would be paying them at the rate of $300,000 a year. They got a 67 percent response from top executives, who normally wouldn't bother.

> **"Old Money"**
>
> For a survey, old money gets more attention than new. You can purchase old Indian head pennies or buffalo nickels in worn condition very inexpensively. Respondents will notice and remember them.

Marketing Before They Need You! . . .

Marketing Arsenal's target market is businesses that need to predict customer and prospect behavior. A simple example would be an accountant targeting businesses that had just had a particular kind of financial transaction that they knew would make for a difficult tax situation. Marketing Arsenal uses so-called neural nets, predictive models using multiple variables, to help auto body shops target customers *before* they have an accident. Small auto shops that send mailings before accidents are more likely to be called when the service is needed, even when they are not on insurance lists of preferred providers. This point lets Marketing Arsenal charge a good price for the predictive information. Their next target is chiropractors.

Providers Misunderstand Clients . . .

What do clients want? Usually professionals are wrong in their assessments. For instance, CPAs thought that clients wanted
- Quality work
- Good CPA reputation
- Lots of experience

Clients really wanted
- Speed, timeliness
- Clearer bills and good prices
- Less staff turnover so they didn't keep training new staff

Clients take your quality for granted. And they don't particularly know how to recognize it anyway. Similarly for your reputation and experience: if they're working with you, they already accept those as competent. Your trade association may have data on what your clients want. But it is never a bad idea to ask them yourself.

Pump Receptionists . . .

One Dale Carnegie representative starts his research with company receptionists. He simply tells them which officer he's going to meet and asks them a series of background questions for more effective selling.

> **Compliment Assistants**
>
> Dale Carnegie was big on compliments to "win friends and influence people." Many secretaries and others are relatively unappreciated. You can set yourself apart with sincere compliments.

Really Pushing for Survey Responses . . .

This note was attached to a questionnaire sent out by an editor from the Greater Phoenix Economic Council's News Bureau. "My boss says that if people don't answer this survey, I'm history." The survey got a 50 percent response rate!

Rate Your Customers . . .

With careful cost accounting, any service business can determine which customers are profitable and by how much. Then take better care of the best ones. First United Bank did an analysis of their customers using the TotalMarketer software. They found that, like the national average, only about 40 percent were profitable. Ten percent were break-even, and 50 percent were losing money for them. Once they had identified the most profitable ones, they set up a program to cultivate them. This included contact every three months on a personal level, such as a phone call, birthday card, or gift. Their absolute best customers were tracked on a day-to-day basis. Any unusual activity calls for attention that may be in time to save them. For the unprofitable customers, First United intends to cross-sell in order to improve profitability.

Research Sources

The library is always the best place to start your research. But for overseas companies, the Commerce Department and company embassies are good choices. And customer trade associations are another helpful place to start.

Research Mocks Competitors . . .

AT&T created employee teams to pretend they were competitors for a new marketing campaign. They had been "leaked" the new marketing plan and were to come up with countermeasures to sabotage AT&T's efforts. To AT&T's surprise, within two hours, teams came up with lots of countermoves the company had never considered. It was fun for employees and allowed AT&T to tighten up their plan a lot!

Selling Overseas . . .

Software consultants Hill Art and Entertainment Systems were impressed to learn how different each country in Europe is. For instance, the Germans use last names in addressing each other and prefer garish colors on their computer interfaces. Get advice on each marketplace before you plunge ahead.

Serious Research . . .

When people won't tell you their advertising/marketing budget, you can often surprise them if you're willing to work. Let's say you're selling radio advertising. There are services that monitor TV and radio advertising locally and can tell you what a given advertiser runs. You can then price those media. For newspapers, which would be most common, you can go to the library and scan for their ads. You'll impress them that you've done your homework. You'll also get a better idea of their image and theme for future consistency. And you can often suggest improvements to show that you know what you're doing. (If you overestimate what they're spending, they'll correct you, which also gets you closer to the right figure!)

Surveys with Checks . . .

If you really want a survey answered from a group such as M.D.s who are very busy, consider putting it on the back of a check, as Fairview Medical Research did. Above the endorsement spot they put four questions that required a quick "check off" on whether the respondent had seen a particular rep or used a particular product. Since most of the two-dollar checks were cashed, it shows that most of the envelopes were opened. And, of course, remember that you can use the results of that survey to get further publicity, thank the respondents, and so on.

Testing Inside First . . .

When you're testing a new idea, try it on your existing customers first. If people who already work with you won't buy it, it's not going to fly. Another reason to make offers to your own customers first: your existing customers will be offended if they don't get the same offer that new people do. For instance, Club Med offered $100 discounts to past customers who returned and brought a friend, who also got $100 off.

Time Diaries Surprise You . . .

Frederick Taylor was the originator of time and motion studies (standing over workers with a stopwatch). In a variation, Mid Atlantic Bank distributed computers to employees and set up a program for them to track their own time on different tasks. This helped employees understand the distractions from their new jobs as salespeople of products such as annuities. One thing the bank found was that customer inquiries were a bigger time-taker than it expected. By putting in an 800 phone line to handle them, the bank created more focused time on selling. It also cut down on previously required memos.

> **Measurement and Feedback**
>
> "We have to define results and then see how we stack up in every job, in every operation, in every organization."
> —Peter Drucker

Tracking Competitive Advertising . . .

Getting on the mailing lists of your competitors or tracking their advertising can be of great value in keeping up. *Who's Mailing What* is a subscription service that tries to collect every piece of "junk mail." This means that you can get an index and purchase specific pieces of mail that other insurance companies, and so forth, are sending out. AdTrack is a similar service which maintains a huge database of advertising in various publications. Other similar services now exist on-line.

What Customers Want . . .

Who better to ask what someone wants in a salesperson than the customer? Customer Dave Hoover, who handles computer systems for Hyper Wheels, wants a salesperson to be a business partner as committed to Hyper's success as he is. He needs resource people, for whom the sale is a bonus. They should also provide one-stop shopping and be an expert sounding board for ideas. Of course, great service is a given.

··· *ACTION AGENDA* ···

"Unused talents give you no advantage
over someone who has no talents at all."
—Mark Twain

You now have 52 more examples of "talent" and ideas you didn't have before. But of course the only place "success" comes before "work" is in the dictionary.

With the variety of ideas and examples in this book, your job is to find ways to move ahead. Perhaps some of these will get you started.

➜ List three things you'd like to know from your customers, and then pick a way to ask them.

➜ If you have a lot of customers or prospects, create a better database to track what you know about them.

➜ If there are 10 big customers you'd like to do business with, research them now. Build a file on each, and start your contact program by meeting them at organizations and sending them information (like clippings or a newsletter).

➜ Do research in a customer niche so you become the acknowledged source of expert information on their topics.

➜ Would a mystery shopper service help you? How about shopping your competitors?

➜ If you're in competitive presentation or bid situations, develop a model of how your competitors perform and price.

And for one almost-last quote:
"Nothing will ever be attempted if
all possible objections must be first
overcome."
—Samuel Johnson

Fire at will! Which reminds me:
"What I've dared, I will, and what I will,
I'll do."
—Herman Melville

Afterword

I believe that a long Introduction would have gotten in the way of your reading this book, so I kept mine brief. For those of you who want to hear more from me, here are a few thoughts on marketing your services and this book.

By featuring more than 1,001 real ways that service providers market, this book can cover each case only briefly. However, you'll find that the brief examples cumulate within each chapter to give a broader picture of each approach that makes the material useful for both beginners and advanced marketers. The sidebars give you extra ideas and define some of the technical terms used.

FOR BEGINNERS AND PROS

If you don't know about key marketing ideas such as positioning, niche markets, and consultative selling, you can use this book to get examples as well as ideas you can put to work immediately. But you'll do even better if you have an overall understanding of marketing and a plan.

If you already understand the basic concepts of marketing, you'll find many useful ideas that have produced millions of dollars for some companies. You can open the book anywhere and get a usable idea. You'll be better able to adapt, combine, and apply. I personally guarantee that if you try at least ten of these ideas, you'll see results. If not, send the book to me and I'll refund your money (see page 367).

Some of the 1,001 ideas can be done in minutes (like calling a past customer); some can take months (like a national seminar tour with sponsors). Some cost nothing but time; some cost thousands of dollars. Some fit the one-person, non-professional service; some work better for the largest legal and health care firms.

With few exceptions, each of the 1,001 items includes a real example of a specific person or company. Every idea has actually been put to use and succeeded. Sometimes specific people or companies are credited, sometimes not. You won't have heard of most of them. But you'll recognize a few of the "IBMs."

WHAT IS A SERVICE PROVIDER?

Briefly, service providers sell time and expertise rather than goods. But there's lots of overlap. For instance, restaurants are a service business, but they provide food. Lawyers and accountants are considered "pure" service businesses, but they provide contracts and tax returns.

I won't go into fine distinctions. My purpose is to bring you usable ideas. I even slip in a few from nonservice providers if they can be applied by services. And that's the real point—for you to apply items to your situation.

ALL THE IDEAS HERE WON'T APPLY TO YOU— BUT MANY WILL

You should test a number of ideas to see what works best for your personal style and business. You'll find that hundreds of the ideas *could* apply to you if you want them to. And it takes only one idea to produce big success.

This book includes examples of techniques used by more than 100 different kinds of services. You can look yours up in the index. But don't be too narrow in your reading. Many techniques used by gardeners also apply to contractors—but you'll find that some can also apply to lawyers and doctors! I've given examples in some items of how an approach might be used by other service providers. Your imagination will be the best tool for creating more applications for your situation.

THREE SECRETS OF SUCCESS

The most profitable service businesses get 90 percent of their business from repeat customers and most of the rest from referrals. So, the first secret of success is to take exceptional care of your clients/customers. Good service isn't enough. You have to thrill customers.

The second secret is that marketing is like your health. Short-term "programs" don't work. Marketing takes regular action, continually applied. You need to like the people you serve. You'll be with them a long time if you're successful. You should be able to find ways to build relationships with prospects and customers that you enjoy.

The third secret of success is to *do something*. Building relationships with prospects and customers takes action. Get started. Even your failures will help you do a better job with your next approach. Only with action do you get feedback to take more effective action. (Just keep tests inexpensive so you can keep at it.)

I could go on. But you need to get going. Hopefully, you've made notes as you read through the book. Now start rereading, selecting, applying, and having fun!

PSYCHIC MARKETING—NOT!

Refuse to work at your marketing? A psychic consultant said all she does is sit in her house and meditate, putting out waves which bring customers to her. This eliminates all the fuss and muss of real marketing! Contrary to this "psychic" approach, I believe you have to get "out of the House" to market effectively. So please take action.

Also, please contact me. I'd love to hear about your successes—and failures. I get most of my material for speeches and new books by talking with people like you. If you'll let me know what works for you, I'll probably be able to share some new ideas I'm working with for my next book. I can be reached through my agent, Select Press Bureau, P.O. Box 37, Corte Madera, CA 94976; 415/435-4461.

SOURCES

As I gathered case examples for this book over the course of
more than a year, many people in my seminars, friends, and
publications contributed items. Many sources are cited in the
case examples. Some of the sources for multiple items are
listed here:

American Printer
Art Sobczak's Telephone Selling Report
*The Greatest Direct Mail Sales Letters of All
    Time*, Richard Hodgson
How to Build a Million Dollar Practice,
    Christian Frederiksen
Inc. magazine
Instant & Small Commercial Printer
The Marketing Report
Promo magazine
Reseller Management magazine
Self-Marketing Secrets, Henry DeVries &
    Diane Gage
Self-Promotion, Ilise Benun
Selling magazine
What's Working in Accounting Practice Building

REFERENCES

Many references are cited in the text. Here are a few of them:

Hanan, Mack. *Consultative Selling* (5th ed.). New York: AMA-
    COM, 1995.

Kawasaki, Guy. *Selling the Dream: How to Promote Your Product,
    Company, or Idea, and Make a Difference, Using Everyday
    Evangelism.* New York: HarperCollins, 1991.

McKenna, Regis. *Relationship Marketing.* New York: Addison-
    Wesley, 1991.

Rackham, Neil. *SPIN Selling.* McGraw, 1996.

Rosenbluth, Hal, F. *The Customer Comes Second and Other
    Secrets of Great Service.* New York: Morrow, 1994.

Index